SEX FOR WOMEN

who want to have fun and loving relationships with equals

Sex for Women

WHO WANT TO HAVE FUN AND LOVING RELATIONSHIPS WITH EQUALS

by CARMEN KERR

GROVE PRESS, INC., NEW YORK

First Evergreen Edition 1978
First Printing 1978
ISBN: 0-394-17035-0
Grove Press ISBN: 0-8021-4157-9
Library of Congress Catalog Card Number: 76-14509

LIBRARY OF CONGRESS CATALOGING IN PUBLICATION DATA

Kerr, Carmen.
    Sex for women who want to have fun and loving relationships with equals,

    Bibliography: p.
    1.   Sex instruction for women.   I.   Title.
HQ46.K44   1978   301.4'18'042   77-28038
ISBN 0-394-17035-0

Manufactured in the United States of America

Distributed by Random House, Inc., New York

GROVE PRESS, INC., 196 West Houston Street, New York, N.Y. 10014

TO AUNTIE

who said: take dares.

Contents

ACKNOWLEDGMENTS   Many people helped me over the year I spent writing this book.

First, I want to thank my family for being supportive—after having gotten over the initial shock that their eldest daughter was writing about sex! I am particularly grateful to all those nervous relatives who refrained from asking me, "And what are you doing with yourself these days, my dear?" at all our family get-togethers.

As for providir.g both the ideas and the inspiration, I am most indebted to the many women in all the various groups I participated in and led during the past three years. Sisterhood is indeed powerful. Thank you, all.

To dearest Susan Wolfson goes much thanks, too, for her editing skills and her smart, clear thinking; and, especially, for her ever-loving friendship.

To Claude Steiner, *amigo hermoso,* I say *muchas gracias* for reading draft after draft so patiently, as well as for furnishing such unrelenting encouragement and so many good ideas.

To Patrick ("Motorcycle") Moore, my deep appreciation for being such a good, loving man.

Finally, for their political and personal support, I am indebted to all the members of the Bay Area Radical Therapy Collective—but particularly to Hogie Wyckoff, Beth Roy, and Becky Jenkins.

INTRODUCTION   It has always been my contention that the only "should" about sex is that . . . it *should* be fun.

For over a decade now the sexual revolution has been an accomplished fact. During that time women and men have been discovering that their sexuality is not only a natural and necessary part of their lives, but that it is also a profound expression of their personalities. Our leading social scientists have virtually given us permission to be sexually free. And yet many of us, particularly women, are still not happy sexually. So, the question: Why not?

Sexual problems cannot be solved simply by learning a new technique. They reflect relationship problems—from the simple to the complex—and must, therefore, be examined and solved in that context.

Sometimes these problems result from the simple failure to communicate. Some couples never talk to each other about sex—each doesn't even know if the other masturbates. Other couples, on the other hand, may talk with seemingly great sophistication about sex, only to discover that their problems are more complex: their sexual difficulties reflect the power imbalances in their relationship. These power imbalances are the results of sexist expectations and behavior on both their parts.

We must discover how sexism affects all our relationships in general; and, proceeding from there, we must find out how it controls our sexual involvements in particular. Bereft of this understanding—that sexism lies at the core of most sexual problems—most sex therapy proves in the long run to be mere band-aid therapy, so superficial that it only serves to complicate the problems rather than solve them.

And yet, for all that, sex is not really complicated. Sex is simple.

I have done sexual therapy for three years now. As far as I can tell, there are only two basic ingredients for pleasurable sexual relationships:

1) Feeling good about your own sexuality.
2) Finding a lover who feels good about your sexuality, too.

For women, despite what they have read elsewhere, being unable to have orgasms is *not* the problem. The problem is finding someone you want to share your orgasms with, and having fun doing it. If solving sexual problems with your partner seems more hard work than playful fun, then no technique, doctor, or gadget can change the fact that your sexual difficulties are reflecting non-sexual problems in your relationship.

Most professional sex therapists do not counsel with this understanding. By focusing on techniques doctors, psychiatrists, psychologists, and sex therapists isolate sexual problems from relationship problems as a whole, and make the average woman or man feel that their sexual difficulties are far too complicated to be solved by themselves using common sense.

In illustration of this, a moment ago I was browsing through a glossy brochure advertising "A Weekend Workshop for the Treatment of Sexual Dysfunction." *Dysfunction* . . . the picture it conjures is some broken-down machine waiting to be fixed up with a lube and oil job! Not only that, but the term "dysfunction" also has an ominous medical clang to it, implying that sexual problems are some terrible illness only an expert can "cure." Other terms in the brochure are equally mind-boggling. "Multi-Modal Approach." "Operant-Interpersonal Approach." (I defy anyone to translate them into simple honest English.) And, besides, who wants to "approach" sexual problems? An approach is not a solution.

Even a brief glance over the front page of that brochure is enough to reveal its sexism as well. We are informed that a certain male Ph.D. is "handling the presentation," including such topics as "Masturbation Training (Female)"—how it all sounds like some obedience school for dogs!—and "The Treatment of Female Dysfunction." That a male should consider himself qualified to speak with authority on female sexuality, let alone so-called "dysfunction," strikes me as the height of presumption. And yet I wonder how many confused women sign up for such workshops?

The sad thing is, that brochure is just one instance among many of the superficiality guiding much of the sexual therapy in vogue today. Recently a young woman visited me who had been receiving sex counseling of the Masters-and-Johnson type in a clinic for over six months. Six months—and $2000 later—she was complaining she hadn't had one orgasm in all that time with her lover, and still couldn't figure out why! We talked for over an hour, letting our conversation run in various directions, not all of them specifically sexual. Finally the woman admitted: "I don't really *want* to have sex with him. It's not fun." When she felt safe enough to say that out loud, it became immediately obvious to us both why all the technique therapy in the world had failed to help her.

From my own experience I know that any and all sexual difficulties—unless they are truly physical in nature and thus require medical attention—can be understood and solved by the ordinary person. No ten-dollar words are necessary. Not only that, but you should see practical and encouraging change in less than a month's time—provided the therapist pays attention to the sex-role and communication problems in the relationship.

To put it as succinctly as possible, when sex isn't working out it's because:

1) We aren't asking for what we want because we don't know what we want.

2) Sexism has got us too mixed up about what sex means and how it works.

I realize that not only men but many women still get defensive at the mere mention of "sexism." The word itself seems to threaten them: as if it were the sole moralist at the great orgy of sensual delights supposedly brought about by the sexual revolution. These women still refuse to believe that sex roles and sexism can make major differences in their lives. Well, they can—and they do.

Part of the problem lies, I think, in many people's confusion of the terms "sexism" and "feminism." *Sexism* occurs when one sex has certain privileges of power which the other sex doesn't have. Sexism is favoring one sex over the other. Sexism is seeing the world in terms of sex roles—believing and granting certain privileges according to the notion that men have mutually exclusive abilities and prerogatives and women have others, and consequently the sexes are not equal—and shouldn't be.

Feminism is quite the opposite of sexism. It is the belief that women and men *are* equal—and, therefore, have equal rights to power and privilege. Feminism supports doing away with sex-role privileges and sex-role divisiveness, replacing it, instead, with a feeling between the sexes of unity and wholeness, of brotherhood and sisterhood. That is why both men and women can be, and are, *feminists*.

This book, then, is an exploration of how sexism and sex roles prevent women—and men as well—from enjoying fulfilling and happy relationships.

PART 1

---

sexism and sex roles

Sexuality: A Personal Power

CHAPTER 1.   Our sexual energy is a precious and important part of us. It is our most unique and passionate energy. It expresses our deepest pleasures, our wild, free energy, our true joy. It is our most intimate means of expression. We need to care for it and honor it as we would a dear lover—for it is, as one woman put it, "our sixth sense"; and, as another said, "it involves all our senses—it's a kind of meta-sense." When we understand the true power our sexuality gives us, we can treat it with the care and confidence we, and it, deserve.

The power of our sexuality can best be understood in terms of energy. We are each of us familiar with what our sexual energy feels like. For some of us it is so strong that we feel it controls us; while others feel it so subtly we are concerned that we might not be "normal." But no matter how we feel it, we sense it as a powerful energy that either works for us or against us, depending on how we choose to use it.

Some of us are aware only that this energy is dangerous—a power that gets us in trouble. Our broken hearts, pregnancies, and abortions have left us exhausted emotionally and physically. We've had it with sex. We feel despair and defeat even thinking about it.

Others are full of sexual energy, but don't know what to do with it. It trembles inside, eager to burst out, but for some reason is thwarted. If this is what we feel, our sexual energy may even become physically painful in being so frustrated—since we don't have orgasms, or the ones we do have are so unsatisfying.

Still others remember sexual energy as a thing of the past which faded out, and hasn't made a comeback. We've been swamped with other life-energy demands and perhaps our sexuality is the one thing we don't have time to keep and express. Survival, growing up, making a family—many things can come between us and what we may consider the luxury of enjoying our sexual feelings. As we know from experience, it is possible to go for years without feeling or acknowledging our sexual energy. If we'd had the benefit of sexual energy, those months or years wouldn't have been quite so difficult, though.

Sexual energy is life energy. Sexual energy is the drive for pleasure, reproduction, and intimacy. As a poet friend of mine said, "Our sexual energy is the meeting of matter and spirit." In more everyday language a woman simply remarked, "Sex makes me feel real good and real strong!"

I'm not claiming that sexual awareness is the key to solving all our problems and emerging confident and powerful in the world. But I do believe—and my work with women has supported this—that until we feel comfortable and confident with how our sexuality fits into our lives we will continue to have some unhappy gaps in the understanding and appreciation of our own personal woman-power. Our sexuality is one of our basic levels of personal awareness. Its strong energy should be used for many self-invigorating, self-nurturing purposes. For instance, notice how your body reacts to a creative idea, a happy thought, a strong move. Many women sense it as a rush of energy surging through their bodies—they describe it as "feeling turned on." Some even feel this specifically in their genitals.

Sexual energy is a part of our lives as a whole. But it has been relegated to a secret, dark compartment by social values and Puritan mores. Consequently, our population as a whole has felt sexually restricted for decades and women in particular have lost a sense of the dimension and meaning of their sexuality. Until a few years ago we really didn't have sex—or, if we did, we knew we shouldn't. But recently a new standard has emerged: we are told we *should* be sexy. Tossed between the "don't's" of one extreme and the "should's" of another—and all in one generation—has left a lot of us confused. Just who in the world are we sexually, anyway?

Sexual power, the need for it, the resistance to it, has governed our intimate sexual affairs. Many have learned to use sex as a weapon to force men to give them what they want. We understand its power from that experience. Others have felt the sexual power that men exert over them. And yet our sexual insecurities and needs have kept us in these relationships that are already dead in every other way. As women we are often willing to endure an oppressive relationship solely because of sexual desire. When this desire is coupled with sexism, it keeps women tied to men and men tied to women in unhealthy and unproductive ways.

Sex is energy. Therefore, sex is power. For both men and women. As modern women we are suddenly exploring the question of power. We want it. But like desert dwellers who wish for rain without ever having seen it, we're not sure what we're looking for—or if we'll recognize it when it appears. By starting with ourselves and learning about our own personal power, we begin to understand power as a world force. Woman sexual power and woman power as a whole are inseparable and complementary. When we learn to take care of ourselves sexually, we become independent in a part of our lives that has always been traditionally dependent upon men. And once we become sexually independent and happy, we can apply what we've learned to other areas of our lives as well.

Recently a young psychology student, very much a feminist, whom I was training to lead women's sexual problem-solving groups suddenly decided she could not continue. She was dropping out, she said, for political reasons. As she explained it, the sexual approach didn't cover enough. Also, she was appalled by "the low level of consciousness and utter unawareness of their oppression" the women in our groups exhibited. "I can't focus on orgasms or love-making when I see how much other work needs to be done first," she explained. "I'm concerned with women gaining power. I don't see how this narrow focus on sexual work helps."

It's too bad she didn't stick around until the end. She would have understood that working on sexual problems together in groups is the first step many women must take toward an understanding of their own self-power. Our sexual problems originate from sexist attitudes, imposed on us by our upbringing and reinforced by our culture; and these attitudes affect how we think about sex and about relationships. Because these sexist attitudes are cultural, the origin of most of our sexual questions and problems is social, not medical. Hence, they are not individual difficulties, but are common to all women and to all men. That is why talking about them in groups is so important: we see then that we're not isolated "neurotics" but rather, to our immense relief, just one more normal, if highly uninformed or misinformed, member of the masses.

The most important result of the group experience is a woman falling in love with herself. Women have been accustomed to getting their approval and feelings of O.K.-ness from lovers, be they other women or men. Our love comes to us from outside sources, and it is difficult to conceive of ourselves as loving ourselves. When I introduce women to the group format at the first meeting, I explain that this work will first and foremost be a love affair with their best lover—themselves. I encourage women to use their loving creativity on themselves in the same lavish, careful, all-encompassing manner they do upon their other lovers. When women discover the beauty of their own bodies, the sweetness of their genital fragrance, the sensuality of their own touch, and the rightness of their sexual feelings, then they can't help but fall in love with themselves. Reclaiming our sexual power is as important as gaining economic or social power. It is a personal strength that we need in order to know we are *whole* women.

Very often sexual problem-solving offers women a first step in the process of feeling good about themselves as women. Because lack of orgasms, either alone or with lovers, cuts across all class and economic lines, and all ages and races, women who join groups are not necessarily "hip" or politically sophisticated. Often they have heard about feminism, but still haven't felt its effect on their lives, nor do they understand its importance. When they realize the greater social issues surrounding sexual problems, all at once feminism becomes personal. It suddenly makes intimate sense. Sexism as an oppressive force becomes practical reality for the first time.

The group situation also provides women with help in becoming more assertive. In order to become orgasmic (i.e., capable of experiencing orgasms), we women must learn to ask for what we want from ourselves and from our lovers. The group gives women homework assignments which are structured in such a way that women learn to take control of their sexuality. To be successful in these assignments women must arrange time and space as well as decide what to do with lovers, and give themselves permission to explore and appreciate their sexual desires and needs.

Incorporating what they have learned about their needs in order to become orgasmic with a partner, women must also ask for what they want. It isn't enough to think very intensely, "Oh, touch me there, touch me *there!*" Lovers cannot be expected to read minds. Both partners, to get what they want, must ask and show. When a woman rechannels her energies away from trying to figure out what her lover wants into asking for what she wants, the results of her assertiveness will affect other parts of her life as well.

This assertiveness enables women to begin to feel equal with their lovers, particularly if the latter are men. Most women who are having difficulty achieving orgasm express the feeling that they have never been able to choose their own love life; that, rather, it was imposed upon them by the assertiveness of more aggressive men or women. Consequently, many women feel one-down in sex. Their partners seem to be sexu-

7

ally O.K., while they themselves aren't. This is a powerless position. As a result, many women discover that they can control sexual situations only by withdrawing from them. (Withholding sex is an historical way women have always employed to exert power and influence. In Aristophanes' *Lysistrata* the women of Athens unite in a "no-sex" strike to force the men to end a war.) When the only power a woman has is to say "no," she is not in a peer situation.

Sexual problem-solving provides many women with their first experience of the beauty of sisterhood. Women have been socialized to be competitive, especially over male lovers and, hence, sex. Many women arrive at a group fearful of revealing their sexual feelings and dubious whether other women, lacking degrees and the authority maleness seems to exude, can truly help them and support them. "Women are boring." "Women are catty." "Women can't be trusted." "Women don't know anything." That's what one often hears in the confessions of new members. But by the end of the groups, women have changed their opinions and come to love and appreciate one another. After all, having shared your most intimate secrets and finding that the women around you offer support and concern and honest feedback and praise certainly changes negative feelings to positive ones. Womanhood, then, becomes a quality to be valued, not only as a woman learns to love herself, but, gradually, to love other women also.

Learning to be responsible for our sexuality also helps us become aware and responsible for our health. I encourage group members to take self-help health courses at local feminist clinics, to read about women's health, and to question their doctors intelligently. When a woman begins to value her body and her feelings, her health becomes important, too. It is not unusual for women who have long felt themselves uncomfortably overweight to begin to lose pounds as they get turned on to themselves; or for other women who eat poorly, smoke too much, or drink too heavily suddenly begin to become concerned enough over feeling good and physically strong that they start taking better care of themselves.

At the final meeting I always ask women to comment on their growth throughout the group. The one thing women who are now orgasmic always say is, "Now I know I'm O.K." That's a wonderful and novel way for most women to feel about their sexuality. We realize that they will have ups and downs, for sexuality is not a steady feeling, but as variable as good moods and bad ones. But the group experience provides women with a solid base of good feelings about their sexuality. They may not be orgasmic all the time, they may question again, and they may go through periods of difficulty; but, underneath it all, they have now had an experience that has taught them that they are really normal, resourceful, creative—and, above all, splendidly unique—women. And they know how to solve the sexual problems that they will, in all probability, confront in the future.

"My sexuality is very precious to me now," many comment. "I choose my lovers for quality now, since I don't need them just to satisfy me sexually." More self-esteem and confidence are felt after these groups. Women often rearrange their love-lives quite drastically, breaking off unhappy love affairs, choosing to be celibate and remain alone with themselves for a while, or else deciding to be bisexual or gay. In any case, they have equalized their relationship with their partners in not only a sexual sense but also as a whole.

Women who entered group with what they felt were insurmountable obstacles to finding enough time to enjoy their sexuality, because of the demands placed on them by jobs and children and homes, plus the cultural belief that ageing diminishes sexuality, are happily surprised. For instance, child care must be arranged so that each woman can spend at least an hour a day (the required homework time) alone. Women with families are often under the impression that children deserve one hundred percent of Mom's time. In this way, a woman learns two valuable lessons from arranging child care. She learns that it can be done; and, what's more, that her children get along just fine—if not better—without her constant supervision.

9

Women with heavy work schedules learn to plan ahead to arrange time alone or with their lovers simply to enjoy sex. An evening previously spent with someone else, just for the sake of company, can now be spent enjoying sex with one's self, for example. Or a woman can pace her day so that she has enough energy and time left at the end to spend it with a lover she enjoys.

As for age: an "older" woman, which in our youth-happy culture means anyone over thirty, when she reclaims her sexuality, is overturning sexism at one of its bottom lines. The support of other women her own age is the only support many older women have to reclaim or continue to feel and express their sexuality.

The group effects are strong and often dramatic, causing great changes in a short amount of time. For this reason we acknowledge at the final group session that women might find themselves feeling depressed in a few days, missing the group, wanting the support of nurturing, strong women. We advise those who feel this way to join a woman's group so that they can continue to get support for changing their lives.

The Politics of Orgasms

CHAPTER 2. For all the information about women's sexuality, many women in our society still don't have orgasms—while most men do. And many more women don't enjoy the orgasms they do have. Physiologically, orgasms are simple: they are the body's response to pleasurable stimulation. So why, then, are so many women not enjoying? The standard answers women have been getting when they ask this question are: "frigidity," "low sex drive," "dysfunctionality due to neurosis." We've also been counseled to be patient and re-devote ourselves to our partners' needs. At least that's how doctors, psychiatrists, psychologists, and ministers—and, until recently, women themselves—have explained the problem. Non-orgasmic women, or women otherwise unhappy with their sex lives, were treated as individual women having idiosyncratic sexual troubles.

Fortunately, this view is changing. As the women's movement has made women realize that so many of their problems are socially induced, women are also understanding that their sexuality hasn't escaped the demands of a sexist society. The Hite Report has verified with statistics what many of us already knew: namely, that women's sexual problems are a result of societal attitudes and injunctions concerning women and what they ought to know and do about sex. Hence, the problems are more often social rather than individual. Women don't experience orgasms, or don't enjoy them, because they have not been *expected* to—it's been part of their general "femininity" training that they shouldn't. Women have received either no information, or else distorted, negative information about their sexuality. For instance, how many of us were told it was only whores, or "loose women," who had strong sexual desires?

This sort of sex instruction causes women today, of all ages and races, to question their worth as women and as healthy human beings. Fortunately, they are forming and joining groups to discuss this great concern, deciding to turn on to themselves by turning off to this cultural indoctrination.

What does sexism in sex look like? In our culture, sex is power. It has become a commodity, like anything else that is important to people and is in short supply. Good sex is hard to find, we all know that. Thus, when we get together with someone who makes us feel good and healthy sexually, we don't want to let him or her go. In this way, the person has a certain power over us because she or he can supply us with this most wanted, most intimate pleasure. Because of social patterns in our culture which keep women isolated from women, and men isolated from men, it is traditional that women will learn about sex from men, and that certain men will bestow sexual pleasure that will make a woman know she's all right. For example, it is only through a man that many women even learn they have a clitoris. This means that a man has it in his power to make a woman feel she's sexy and, therefore, healthy. Because of this sex-role pattern, love-making, too, reflects sex roles; and it follows that sex serves as the most convenient scapegoat for all kinds of power struggles within relationships.

Sexual mystification, which keeps women dependent on others for sexual satisfaction and knowledge, also oppresses women by preventing them from valuing their own feelings as highly as they do those of their men. A good sexual relationship is a lot more than the right technique, position, gadget, or "getting it on three times a day." *Good sex is when both people get what they want and enjoy it.*

When a woman takes her sexuality seriously, she takes herself, her emotions, and her pleasures seriously, often for the first time. By reclaiming her bodily pleasures from deadening, numbing sexist socialization, she learns to be assertive in figuring out and then getting what she wants, not only sexually, but in a general sense as well.

Not only that, but when she discovers and defines her own sexuality, her view of the world also changes. Now that she knows she's all right, she has a base from which to question critically a world that conditioned her to think otherwise. Her new awareness profoundly affects her intimate sexual relationships, particularly with men. (I should note here that in gay relationships power struggles can be just as oppressive and sexist as in heterosexual couplings. Intimacy based on stereotyped roles remains oppressive, regardless of the sex of the individual partners.)

Sex roles in sex are oppressive to men, too. Most men of good conscience are not any happier with such a situation than are women. It's a tremendous burden to have to be responsible for the success of every sexual encounter, to be always in control, to bluff expertise, and, on occasion, an erection and orgasm as well. In my experience, men are eager to learn all they can about enjoyable sex and how to please their partners. But they need to be told, to be taught, what is pleasing. Because, for all their apparent knowledge, men are as woefully ignorant of the technical, emotional, and personal intricacies of sexuality as are their partners.

You don't believe it? Just ask a man to tell you his sexual history. Where did he learn about sex? The locker room. Rumor. Gossip. A book his father left on the bureau. "Oh, uh, the bar mitzvah group took a bus to the local whorehouse. You know, as part of the *rite de passage* or whatever into manhood." "Well, some guys in the dorm set me up with the town whore—we did it under a car in the school parking lot." "I was married for years to somebody as dumb about sex as me. We never even spoke about it." With such backgrounds, it's no wonder men are no more knowledgeable about sex than are women. They are as oppressed by their sexual sex roles as are women by theirs.

That's why there's a lot in it for men to adopt a feminist perspective with regard to sexuality. Relieved of sex-role expectations, men are released from total responsibility for sex as they give a woman back her share of power in sexual situations. Such men are freed to have feelings, rather than just perform; to take as well as give; to be inconsistent and unsure; to say no as well as yes; to be playful and sensual; to consider their whole body, and not just their genitals, as erogenous zones.

For years now women have been working at trying to untangle themselves from the male ideologies and standards that dominate every facet of our society—economics, politics, and, naturally, sex. Regardless of all other struggles, we cannot deny that sex is a foremost concern for a great majority of us, and particularly for women who are unhappy with their own sexuality. For, even in the area of sexual pleasure, women tend to compare and define themselves—their bodies, their feelings, their expressiveness—in terms of what pleases men. For example, many women want their bodies to respond as quickly as a male's to sexual stimulation; they believe their orgasms should occur exactly like men's. Trying to match men in timing and style, they wonder why nothing works, and conclude, "It's all my fault."

The sexual revolution liberated women to enjoy sex. Unfortunately, the only model available was the male model, which is based on performance and conquest. This need "to be good in bed" made women sexually competitive with each other. Pitted as rivals, we didn't feel safe discussing our sexual problems or preferences with other women. "If I told her I can't come then she'd know she's sexier than me," we worried. Even multiple orgasms became status symbols, causing many women to feel inadequate. We valued quantity or quality in lovers, we tried to come in five minutes, as we attempted to isolate our genitals from our hearts. Like men, we tried to turn our bodies into high performance machines—and soon had no idea what we ourselves were, sexually. All the sex revolution seemed to do was release us from women's sex-role oppression and "liberate" us into men's oppression.

Sadly enough, the sexual revolution has created a whole new set of "should's" and "don't's." When it became scientifically clear that women are sexually healthy and whole, and when their capabilities were set forth in studies for all the world to read, these new discoveries only served to impose upon us a whole new set of standards to be followed. Rather than liberating women and men from past oppression, the new standards found most of us stretching and straining to be as "hip" as we imagined the rest of the population to be.

The sexual revolution has, of course, given us some benefits:

—Sex is now a legitimate topic of conversation.

—Satisfactory and satisfying orgasms are considered everyone's right.

—Masturbation is seen as a fulfilling sexual experience in itself and one that often improves partner sex.

—Homosexuality and bisexuality are no longer merely tolerated as forms of deviant sexual expression; they are seen to be as normal, and as natural, as heterosexuality.

—Women have become as sexually assertive as men, and sometimes more so.

—Anything goes, so long as it doesn't hurt anyone else. Porn, props, fetishes—whatever anyone enjoys is, at the very least, interesting.

—Oral sex is extremely popular; cunnilingus and fellatio are as acceptable as any other kind of intercourse. In keeping with this has come the feeling that intercourse isn't all it's cracked up to be, anyway, and is a complementary of, and not necessarily the central activity in, love-making.

—Non-monogamy is seen as a viable alternative to

monogamy; and some couples find they can survive, even thrive, by expanding their sexual horizons.

All of the above aspects of the sexual revolution are fine. They are all true, but only within certain boundaries and under specific conditions. The danger exists in making them "should's," in adopting them as absolutes. Like, "I should masturbate or I'm not sexually liberated." Or, "I should be non-monogamous or I'm too uptight." Or, "I should enjoy anything in sex or I'm not groovy." Women in particular are susceptible to falling into this trap because we feel more unsure of ourselves sexually and thus are more susceptible to pressure from partners to be as "sexually free" and "together" as possible. (A gay friend of mine points out that gay men are also particularly vulnerable in this respect.) Women often feel they *should* be orgasmic under all circumstances, *should* enjoy any and every thing, *should* be assertive, and *should* be bisexual or gay. Already there are more "should's" about sexuality than there is freedom to discover and enjoy what genuinely pleases us.

Women's Sexual Scripts

CHAPTER 3.   A simple way to see what we're up against in determining what it is we *want* to be sexually, rather than *should* be, is to look at our sexuality in terms of having a script.

A script is a transactional analysis term indicating "the blueprint for a life course."[1] Each of us, according to this theory, has a life course laid out before us which we are following according to parental and social predestination. We put together this script in our childhood, combining parental injunctions ("With her imagination wouldn't she make a fine artist?"), social messages ("Little girls should be seen and not heard"), and personal decisions ("I'll never trust men like my father"). In this highly simplified example, the little girl in question grew up to become a beautiful woman and an artist—but one who lived alone and rarely spoke to others. Her script made her continually depressed except for brief periods now and then when she suddenly felt quite optimistic and happy. During these times she found a lover, her art work went well, and she shared her thoughts easily with friends. But these happy periods never lasted; inevitably she'd return to her

---

[1]Claude M. Steiner, *Scripts People Live* (New York: Grove Press, 1974), p. 51.

former depression and moody silence. In transactional analysis, these times of optimism formed what is known as the "counterscript"—for it was then that the original script was, for at least a brief period, completely reversed.

Not only does each of us have a life script, but we also have a sex life script. We have all received injunctions and instructions and undergone experiences which formed a blueprint for our sexuality. Scripts, of course, are not *us*. They are not intended to label people. Their purpose is merely to point out certain types of behavior that keep us from getting what we need in order to be sexually happy.

In working with women in sexual problem-solving groups, I have noted three specific sexual scripts that prevent orgasms. They are all romantic in conception and unworkable in reality. Because too many women have been taught to believe that most sexual experiences are wonderful fairy tales with gloriously happy endings, these three scripts manifest themselves in storybook plots with momentarily thrilling and temporarily rewarding counterscripts that, in the end, leave women both emotionally empty and physically miserable. The scripts are: "Sleeping Beauty," "Daddy's Darling," and "The Temptress." In each of them a woman has been scripted to use her sexuality to get and control her partner. Such scripts define a woman's sexuality only in terms of what pleases her partner (usually male), and thus never allow any women to enjoy the uniqueness of their separate selves.

SLEEPING BEAUTY

Sex Life Course: Sleeping Beauty is young, innocent, cursed, and comatose. She gets out of this predicament only through being rescued by a Prince Charming. Romantically, it's wonderful; realistically, it's defeating. Most of us were dished out a daily dose of this fairy tale along with our morning cereal—and thus this is a very common script.

Sleeping Beauty has made waiting for her Prince her life action. She is a passive Princess, even willing to wait one hundred years for her man. In real life, she bypasses all other sensual and sexual adventures, concentrating on saving her love for the Prince. She knows he will want her pure and fresh, so she makes sure she stays that way.

This all began at puberty when Sleeping Beauty pricked her finger (read: started her period). Her parents warned her about the responsibility of her sexuality with: "Nice girls don't do it" and "You'll ruin your life if you get pregnant." She becomes fearful of sex and its consequences; and, cooped up in the cold castle of social myths, she protects herself by turning off her sexual feelings. She has fantasies, though, and dreams of the prince whom she knows she'll recognize by his magical kiss (read: penis) that will turn her on and finally set her free to have orgasms (a mysterious phenomenon associated only with True Love).

And sure enough. After a few years of waiting, Sleeping Beauty is embraced by the Prince who sweeps her up in his arms and carries her off on a honeymoon to Hawaii where his Magic Awakener keeps her up day and night.

Yet for all his fervor and all her desire, after the first year of happily-ever-after Sleeping Beauty still hasn't had an orgasm, although she has had some very exciting sensations which she's fooled herself—and him—into believing are orgasms. She finds sex excites the Prince more than her. She appreciates his lust for her and continues to act sexy with him, happy that he's so happy. As a matter of fact, her favorite sexual time is just after he's ejaculated . . . because she's so happy she's made him happy.

But after a while this becomes boring, and perhaps even painful. Sleeping Beauty feels concerned about her "problem" of "frigidity," as she self-diagnoses it. She tries to solve it by having a baby: she's heard women who have babies also have orgasms. It doesn't work for her, of course; and now with a baby, no orgasms, and the fear of disclosing her "inadequacies" to her husband, she's at her wit's end. "I'm sick," she concludes; and begins visiting doctors, ministers, and therapists to cure her "dysfunction." She spends a lot of money trying to get cured by someone else—usually a man, since men fill most of these counseling positions. They give her lots of advice, prescribe drugs—even hypnosis and Sodium Pentothal—and suggest she read Masters and Johnson and go to porno films. She tries it all. To no avail.

Sleeping Beauty concludes she'd best continue pretending to have orgasms. She contrives ways to avoid or shorten sex, and ends by deciding that orgasms aren't all that important, anyway. Of course, she doesn't talk about this situation with anyone, not even her closest women friends. After all, she's sure she's the only Princess unhappy with her Prince.

Counterscript: Sleeping Beauty and the Prince occasionally have sex under very special circumstances and she experiences an orgasm or two. But because she's intoxicated at the time, or away from home, or has spent hours being teased by the Prince, she feels these orgasms are Magical since she cannot re-create them at will.

However, they occur so rarely that the Prince soon gets bored with Sleeping Beauty's increasing avoidance of sex and, as he puts it, her "wooden" response. He ceases to have any sex at all with her, and may even find another woman who is more responsive to him.

This is the apex of the crisis. At this junction the relationship either breaks up, or both partners adapt to their miserable situation. The intelligent solution would be each partner realizing the part he or she plays in the fairy tale and the woman working to become free of her script.

Sexual Decision: At puberty Sleeping Beauty decides to await Prince Charming who will take care of her forever. She dreams this romance will be sexually exciting, but accepts the possibility that the Prince may not be a good lover. She is willing to adjust her expectations accordingly, security being more important to her than sexual fulfillment.

Therapist's Role in Script: It is difficult to find a sexual therapist who is neither sexist nor sexually competitive. When Sleeping Beauty tells her therapist about her orgasm problems he discounts her by advising her to keep on waiting. "Look how he takes care of you. Be grateful for what you have," he admonishes, advising her not to rock the boat. He assures her, "When your head is together, your sexuality will naturally fall into place." He also prescribes years of therapy with him in addition to tranquilizers, sex manuals, and purchase of a vibrator. Sleeping Beauty agrees with him that the problems are basically hers due to "psychological hang-ups." Privately, the man believes she's just another frigid woman; he also feels a little angry and scared working with her because his own sex life matches hers, and he's unwilling to admit he has no practical idea what to do.

If the therapist is sexually confident, he may consider seducing Sleeping Beauty and "curing" her himself, a solution which only complicates the issue and certainly creates more problems than it solves. (See *Women and Madness* by Phyllis Chesler.) After all, the therapist is no Prince Charming.

Script Cure: Sleeping Beauty needs a problem-solving situation where the focus is on education, not pathology. She needs an opportunity to discover for herself her sexual needs and desires, independent of any Prince. In such a way she can find out she is not "frigid," merely unaware and unaroused. Because no male can understand a woman's sexuality as well as can other women, the strongest validations for her sexual health come from working with a group of women interested in the same problem. Sleeping Beauty can wake up with her sisters, find out Princes are people, discover she is her own best lover, and begin to decide for herself how to live happily ever after.

DADDY'S DARLING

Sex Life Course: Daddy's Darling has been taught that her sexuality gets her where she wants to go in life and that the person who will take her there is a powerful, successful man known as The Catch, or Daddy.

At puberty Daddy's Darling learned from her parents and schoolmates that she is very sexy. She also learned how to use such sexiness to her advantage in obtaining economic and social favors which she knows only men dispense. She always appears eager for sex and works hard convincing her lovers they are virile. Going to extremes, she flatters each new Daddy by telling him, "Wow! I never had a mind-blowing orgasm like that before!" She believes faking orgasms is a justifiable means to an end.

Daddy's Darling has been told to "marry for money first, then for love" and "get all you can from men—use your wiles." Always on top of it sexually, she is highly competitive with other women and has few female friends. Secretly, she is pleased with her ability to beat out the competition and therefore doesn't see much value in having other women as friends unless they are enamoured with her or less sexy than herself. She believes her sexuality is her strongest weapon in this war for survival.

On the prowl for Daddy, Daddy's Darling looks for a fat wallet, an influential position, good looks, and reputation. When she meets a man with all these qualifications she seduces him, turns him on like he never has been before, and basks in his worship of her as a sex goddess. She and Daddy pair up in adoration of each other's power, planning to live happily ever after.

However, as in all fairy tales, reality intrudes. Daddy's Darling keeps waiting to fall in love and figures she'll know about it when she has orgasms. But she's so busy performing she doesn't ever have any. Increasingly frustrated, she concludes the reason she's not orgasmic is Daddy's fault: he's not as powerful as he appeared to be. Unwilling to lose him as a secure asset, she secretly takes a lover. In the final play of this game Daddy's Darling shocks Daddy by revealing her lover to him, thus insulting Daddy's sexuality. The relationship ends here, or continues under the rules of Frigid Couple.

Counterscript: At the beginning of their exciting union Daddy's Darling is very turned on by her role as the delightful goddess whom Daddy is so generously taking care of. Happy and secure, she spends hours pleasing her partner sexually— and, in so doing, is occasionally surprised by having an orgasm herself. But because her sexuality is so performance-regulated, these orgasms occur rarely; although they temporarily do convince her she is in love with Daddy.

After a time, with security assured, Daddy's Darling tires of the Daddy who may be too sedate by now to be much fun, and so she avoids sex. If she leaves him, it will not be until she finds another Daddy to take care of her. And so the script continues.

Sexual Decision: At puberty Daddy's Darling decides the way to succeed in life is with the material help and love of the most powerful male in the arena. Since she knows men are very susceptible to being controlled by sex, she begins a career of pursuing men by using her sexuality to seduce gurus, intellectuals, wealthy sons, etc., placing social power and security over her own sexual and emotional contentment.

Therapist's Role in Script: Due to her competitive feelings about women, Daddy's Darling usually chooses a male therapist, or a woman she can outsmart. With the male she confides all the trials and tribulations of her sexual exploits. He is fascinated and either turned on or Parentally judgmental. If she finally decides he qualifies as a Daddy, being a successful professional and in a Daddy's advisory role, the script may repeat itself with a therapist–patient seduction. This does not cure her script problems, obviously. And if he is a judgmental Daddy, she will not stay with him for long nor learn how to stop this crazy merry-go-round of affairs. He may privately conclude she is a "nymphomaniac" and advise her to quit being sexually aggressive. In all likelihood, he'll direct her to assume a Sleeping Beauty script. In either case, her orgasm problems will not be solved.

With a female therapist, Daddy's Darling may have trouble admitting to orgasmic difficulties, fearing a Parental attitude from a rival about her so-called promiscuity and "star-fucking."

Unless a therapist is aware of how sexism and the need for power affect sexuality and can confront Daddy's Darling with a lucid explanation of the bind this has put her in, sexual therapy will be virtually useless; or, worse, it will contribute to her script by making her even more devious and "sexually sophisticated."

Script Cure: Daddy's Darling needs some straight facts about female sexual physiology in order to clarify the orgasm phenomenon. After clearing up this problem, a feminist perspective on sexual problems would alert her as to how she keeps herself from being sexually fulfilled. Her sexual problem-solving can be a first step in her consciousness-raising as a woman.

In a problem-solving group with other women Daddy's Darling will recognize that women are sisters, and not necessarily competitors. She will discover they have much valuable information and support concerning not only sexuality but about men, women, and life in general. When she learns to masturbate to give herself her own orgasms the group will be there to give her protection in this break from her script that up to now has dictated complete sexual and emotional dependence upon men. By the conclusion of group she will not only know she determines her own sexuality, but she will also find out she likes women and has new friends, thus putting Daddy's role into a new perspective.

THE TEMPTRESS

Sex Life Course: The temptress fears surrendering to men, and the ultimate surrender for her is having an orgasm with a man. She equates orgasms with power and believes that letting a man give her an orgasm would render her totally in his control. Thus she enjoys the tease and temptation part of sex, but rarely yields to actual sexual contact. She is waiting for Mr. Wonderful, the Man with the Golden Apple (read: penis) powerful enough to force her to yield to him. She believes she will have orgasms with him because his compelling power will force her to be orgasmic.

Unfortunately, the hitch in this plan is that Mr. Wonderful is always a fantasy. He is hopelessly unobtainable; he's in love with someone else, he's chaste, he's a superstar—always beyond The Temptress's reach. He attains God-like proportions and no human being can replace him.

The reason The Temptress has developed this fantasy lover is because her script includes messages that powerful men are not to be trusted, and are most dangerous sexually. The only way she can maintain her independence and safety is to remain aloof from them—out of their sexual grasp. However, she has also been told that there is a good, perfect, strong man somewhere out there who belies all these stories of danger. So she continues to look for him and dreams of him, planning for his arrival.

The Temptress is proud and passionate, a raving romantic underneath her cool exterior. When she finds Mr. Wonderful, however, she's like a starved cat who suddenly discovers a fish: she goes crazy with gluttony. She overwhelms him with all her pent-up love, spends a passionate night with him, and then watches him slink away the next morning, terrified of her need. The encounter with him was so brief and so charged with expectation that she probably didn't have an orgasm; but she came very close.

In between such encounters The Temptress has sex with "friends" (as she calls them)—men who are nice, but not per-

25

fect. She doesn't have orgasms with them because they aren't powerful enough to induce any such emotional response.

Frequently The Temptress is very angry at men. She's angry because she is afraid of them. She's angry because they have power. She's angry because not one of them loves her the way she wants to be loved. She's angry because she knows what she wants—and yet, for all her efforts, can't find it. She will often be heard disparaging men with insulting remarks, recounting with glee situations in which she took advantage of them by using her flirtatious ways. Underneath her anger she feels hurt; but pride and power fears won't ever let her admit that.

Sometimes women with Temptress scripts are concerned with what they call their "rape fantasies." Fantasies of being overpowered, brutalized, and then forced to enjoy sex make sense: for when a woman is expecting to be overwhelmed by love, after a while the only thing that seems capable of penetrating her fears and living up to her expectations would have to be an act of passion as violent as rape. (It is important to note that it is not the actual event The Temptress usually wants, but rather the emotional force behind it.)

Counterscript: A man overwhelms The Temptress as she is teasing him. She cannot do anything but surrender; and, being totally out of control, she has an orgasm. If he doesn't leave the next morning in a *macho* exit, she discovers as she gets to know him better that he is only human. The romance ends.

The Temptress may settle down for a time with someone imperfect whom she cares for as a friend. Deeply in love with her, he may devote much time to pleasing her sexually. She may occasionally have an orgasm which she either discounts or doesn't recognize because she is still waiting for "the real thing" with Mr. Wonderful.

Sexual Decision: At puberty The Temptress realizes sex is powerful and can be dangerous; she fears if she's not careful she may become a slave of her passions to some man. So she decides to control her feelings and give them only to Mr. Wonderful who will match her passion by giving her orgasms almost against her will. Holding out for the best is worth all sacrifice; but, in the meantime, she keeps herself from being too lonely by occasionally being sexy with some mediocre partner.

Therapist's Role in Script: Temptress's interactions with a male therapist are like those involving any other man. She fears surrender, so refuses to "submit" to therapy. If she does, she may fall in love with her therapist as Mr. Wonderful. She decides to give herself entirely to him, believing her sexual health depends on his response. When he doesn't return her attentions she grows hurt and angry, and her script messages about men are proven. If she seduces him, it will prove brief and leave her non-orgasmic and as frustrated as after all her other encounters.

A woman therapist could understand The Temptress's dilemma and tell her to quit playing sexual games. However, unless the therapist is aware of how sexism affects sexuality, she will not comprehend her patient's rage, much less be able to advise her how to extricate herself from this unhappy script. Sympathy gets a Temptress nowhere.

In either case, it is unlikely that most therapists would recognize the real problem: the question of power; and the concomitant sexism that leads to female sexual adaptation and unhappiness.

Script Cure: The Temptress needs to de-romanticize the idea of orgasms by learning to give herself orgasms. Once the physiology is clarified and her orgasms are in her own control, she can recognize the true basis of her anger and fear regarding men: namely, their use and abuse of power. A feminist women's group can validate the fact that men do have powers women don't, that many males use such powers to oppress women in sexist ways, and that one means of oppressing women is by sexual manipulation. With the support of other women The Temptress can learn to see these power abuses for what they are and stop them on the home-front with lovers. Using personal relationships as a basis, she can begin to counter sexist power-plays not only in her work but in her social life as well.

It should be stressed that no woman absolutely fits any of these scripts. The purpose of such scripts is not to label women—enough has been done of that already—but, rather, to make women aware that orgasmic and other sexual difficulties are *social*, not medical, problems. The scripts I have defined above (and there are many more) demonstrate how women are frequently scripted to sacrifice their sexual pleasure in order to gain the security and social power that men hold.

Male Sexism in Sex Roles

CHAPTER 4. Men's sexism in sex justifies and complements women's perfectly. Two examples familiar to us all are "Mr. Dysfunctional" and "Mr. Technique."

MR. DYSFUNCTIONAL,
or, Help My Penis Is Out of Control!

"Congratulations! You're impotent!"
I am not being sarcastic when I congratulate men on experiencing sexual problems. A perfectly natural and quite common reaction to the sex roles men are expected to fulfill in sexist relationships is to be unable to fulfill them. This has been called "dysfunction." It applies to a man whose penis can't perform correctly.

A man is considered dysfunctional if he is impotent; a premature ejaculator; is unable to ejaculate (or only with great difficulty); or can't feel his orgasms when he does have them.

In my experience from talking with men with such difficulties, the primary reason for their problems stems from the sexist performance demands on them. A dysfunctional man is one whose body is trying to tell him something. It's on strike, registering a perfectly valid protest. "How can you do this to me?" a man asks his uncooperative penis. And it replies, "I don't like what I'm supposed to do and I want some changes made. Therefore: On strike!" For many men, the first indication they have of not feeling content with the sexist status quo is impotency or premature ejaculation.

In almost every respect the dysfunctional male is the counterpart of the non-orgasmic woman. He is out of touch with his sexual feelings, as ignorant of his sexual possibilities, as caught up in myths and fears, as the so-called "frigid" woman. And the traditional ways of dealing with his problems are as sexist as the standard methods employed to "cure" women.

Take the word "dysfunctional." "Dys" is a prefix meaning "diseased, difficult, faulty, or bad" according to the *American Heritage Dictionary*. Who wants to acquire such a label? It sounds like some broken machine. Dysfunctional. We only use that word in our vocabulary to apply to machines—or men.

The lexicon of the sex-therapy business is a mixture of medical and mechanical terms. "Premature ejaculation"—very technical, very medical, quite impressive—enough syllables to choke a horse. It really supports the myth that sexual problem-solving can only be done by someone who has earned enough degrees to be able to mouth that label and still keep a straight face. "Premature"—premature is a relative word. Premature compared to what? Premature compared to her orgasms. What if she doesn't have orgasms? Where does that leave him?

"Ejaculatory incompetence." That's the guy who can't come fast enough. Again, it's a relative term. Fast enough for whom? Competent enough for whom?

So here we have two dysfunction terms: one for the man who's too fast, another for the man who's too slow. If I were a man I'd feel caught between Scylla and Charybdis trying to figure out just what constitutes a suitable performance. If one doesn't do it right, and do it well, there's always a medical technical term available to brand you.

Not only is there a technical label, there's also a technique to "cure" you. Male sexual problems are often viewed with the same attitude engineers use to build a bridge or make sure a skyscraper is earthquake-proof: How to get it up and make sure it stays that way is the only problem. There has to be a gimmick that'll work. Memorize the Yankee line-up backwards. Count from one million sideways. Use the Squeeze Technique forever. Hire a surrogate. Buy a gadget. Find a prop. The only solution overlooked is a man's feelings.

So what's a man to do? Begin by rejecting labels. Understand that no matter what the physical manifestations are, the fundamental problem is men being expected to get it up and keep it there under all circumstances, whether they be hurt, angry, alienated, exhausted, unhappy, laid low by swine flu, preoccupied with the bar exams, drunk, or—guilt of guilts!— just *not* turned on.

Consider the problem in light of the applicable situation. Under what circumstances *do* you come too quickly? Discuss the problem with the person who feels you are coming too fast. How come it happens? What are you both willing to do about it? The most valuable problem-solving method is communication, talking, rapping.

A couple of years ago a close friend and lover of mine had a premature ejaculation problem as far as I was concerned. On the "ask-for-what-you-want" principle, I gathered up my courage and wondered aloud why he came so quickly. "I didn't know I did," he said, rather astounded. We talked about it. I told him how frustrating it was for me, and asked him to learn how to hold on a little longer. This was not an easy discussion to have. I felt I was destroying his ego. He felt guilty and embarrassed—a lousy lover, a poor performer. The only thing that saved us from running away from each other and giving up this crazy project was our friendship. We wanted it to continue. So talk we did.

He figured the reason he came so quickly was a combination of anger and habit. He was angry at me for a number of old, unspoken reasons. We cleared that up, too. His ability to come quickly, he explained, had been developed when he was married to a woman who did not enjoy intercourse and made it clear she wanted his penis in and out as fast as possible. Years of bathroom onanism had reinforced this speediness.

We agreed to give the Squeeze Technique a try. As I recall we did it once—talking and laughing the whole time. The talking was what worked. To take the pressure off intercourse, we found new ways to give each other orgasms. I don't recall when he stopped coming too quickly—it occurred quite naturally as part of our sexual exploring.

Many years later we are still lovers. In the rare instances when he comes too quickly I know he's angry or tired. We always talk about what's going on and proceed from our feelings.

Looking back, I realize I never thought of him as "dysfunctional"—just quick. I assumed we had a communication problem and he had a bad habit, and we approached it that way. It turned out to be a good plan, although it was unplanned. I didn't think he was dysfunctional, since I thought I was doing something wrong to cause him trouble. I wanted to know how to "perform" better and I needed him to tell me. Our talking, in turn, brought my own performance anxieties to my attention and enabled me to relax.

Men need to figure out what they want in sex and ask for it. A bit of advice to men: This is where it becomes important to find a group of supportive, brotherly non-competitive men with whom to share your thoughts. Even one solid male friend who doesn't believe the same myths you do is a gem. Find out who else is having, or has had, the same difficulties. Just as pre-orgasmic women think they're all alone, so do men with erection problems. You're not. Every man around you has had a sexual problem at one time or another. It is a tremendous relief to discover that, and to find out he took care of it.

The group, or a close male friend, can back you up to make the changes you want. With the exception of a few cases of real physical illness (diabetes or high blood pressure, for example), the cure for sexual problems is to quit adapting. You don't have to say yes every time; you don't have to end each evening, each flirtation, with intercourse; you aren't responsible for her orgasms. You *are* free to enjoy, to ask for what you want, and to declare your independence from sex roles.

It is vitally important for men to support each other in freeing themselves of sexist stereotypes. It is as sexist for women to provide the total support and incentive for men as it has been for men to provide sex therapy and advice for women all these years. Solomon "Sam" Julty, writing about the causes and cures for his impotency in *Ms.*, states something every man should take to heart: "The way out of the maze [of male performance expectations] is to tear up the sex roles. Feelings of defeat toward this problem are not individual but social. The solution is political: Roles which offer dubious rewards in exchange for heavy responsibilities should be put aside. The true measure of a man is neither the number of his war wounds nor the times he's bombed out in bed. His true measure is how he feels about himself and the human beings around him."

MR. TECHNIQUE
or, The "Liberated" Macho

"I'll give her orgasms."

Mr. Technique can often be recognized by this statement: "Didja cum?" He displays the over-achiever's never-say-die response to the sexism of the sexual revolution. He's certainly an improvement over the classic *macho* who doesn't need a woman except as a repository for his orgasms. But he still has some of the trappings of *macho* behavior.

Mr. Technique considers himself liberated, un-*macho,* and maybe even a feminist. He has read all the right books and participated, perhaps, in a men's consciousness-raising group. He's a good guy at heart. Good because he likes women and he's doing his damnedest to be the kind of man women like and desire.

However, for all his good intentions, he's having some

problems understanding what equality between the sexes means. Used to being successful, to excelling and controlling, he's aspiring now to become the expert liberated man. He appreciates women's long years of oppression and feels some guilt about his own sexism. He bends over backward now to help women, to atone for his years of sexist attitudes and privilege. He wants to help.

And that's precisely where the difficulties lie: he wants to help by creating her orgasms. Basically, this is a good impulse. But when he incorporates paternalism and his feelings of expertise into his desire to be helpful, sexism is perpetuated. "I'll help her with her problems," he vows, and to this end he is nurturing, infinitely understanding, and sympathetic. Yet, underneath, he believes he must do this because, as a man, he is strong and O.K. and capable—but she, due to her long years of oppression, is not as strong, not as O.K., not as capable. (See the Rescue Game.)

When he applies this combination of guilt and helpfulness to sex, there's some good news and some bad. The good news is that he's a considerate, willing, conscientious lover. He knows more than the average guy about female sexuality and he's willing to hear suggestions about how he can do better.

But that's where the bad news begins: Doing it better usually means polishing up his own performance. It's still a performance—even if a more liberated one. He's still in charge because his attitude includes that need to help her, and he often chooses women who need help. Once again, a good sexual experience is still his responsibility because he's an expert on women and on sex. And because he's the expert in these areas he feels qualified to help any woman find sexual satisfaction. All too often she agrees, and waits for him to do it.

This good/bad conflict shows up most clearly once again around orgasms. Specifically, the phrase that cues it, "Didja cum?" asked after a roll in the hay. When this is asked sincerely by a man to determine if his lover feels satisfied, it is a good and thoughtful question. After all, many women have felt afraid of asking their lovers for what they want and a man who is eager to give must make his willingness clear. Asking her if she has had an orgasm communicates his desire to please.

However, when this question is asked as a performance critique, it is offensive and sexist. A man who has read the latest sex literature and hopes to continue as a good performer wants a woman to come a lot. (He wants his work to pay off in her orgasms.) And if she doesn't come or come enough, then he will suppose she's not really liberated or sexy. A high premium is placed on orgasms—the more the better. A *macho* lover feels this and uses the number of orgasms a woman has to measure his own sexual potency. He believes he gave her these orgasms; so he has a right to take stock of his skills by asking her how well he did. The reason that some so-called liberated sex feels uncomfortable is because it is still actually a question of power: of his over her.

Women often express anger at being asked about their orgasms because they sense this power situation. They feel that, by being asked, their orgasms are somehow taken away. They become his, not theirs. In addition, they feel great performance anxiety for the future because they know they'll be asked again. Having to give a report every time at the end squelches sexual enjoyment.

This question can signal competition, too. Men do not have the orgasmic potential of women. At least, they haven't been able to develop it so far—though many are trying. Men will frankly admit their jealousy over this inequality. Some concede it scares them. Some women have come to group reporting that their partners have tried to squelch their orgasms because they were frightened by their powerful feelings. "Just as I'm about to come he says, 'You're too tense. Relax!' Then he stops touching me and so I don't come, and I get angry."

Other men display their envy and sexual-power needs by wanting to have sex with women who are multiply orgasmic. Her orgasms are notches in his gun, so to speak. When a woman is coming she is out of control and very vulnerable. A man on a sexual power trip knows how to exert his force best—for by controlling her orgasms he controls her. This can be quite sadistic when taken to extremes.

When a woman's orgasms are admired and appreciated, that's good. But when they are envied and co-opted for male gratification, that's not good. Once again, it's male domination and control of the sexual situation.

Such expectations don't lead to a cooperative sexual situation. Once again, the man is doing sex to a woman, rather than with, which isn't liberated at all.

GOOD SEX = (M + J) + K + P + TH + V = O.

Mr. Technique relies on formulas to make each sexual encounter a success. Because he's been educated to make sure that each woman he has sex with has a happy experience, he has discovered that he can best achieve this by condensing into one formula all his techniques that have worked best with the greatest number of women—so far as he can tell.

My best friend and I have an in-joke about this kind of lover. Whenever we spot one we giggle and ask one another, "Where's the vestibular bulb?" That phrase, which we've made infamous in our group, was uttered by a man who saw a slide show of female genitals and was struck by his lack of knowledge concerning the vestibular bulb, which lies in the tissue beneath the labia. He concluded that the reason his lover wasn't having orgasms was because he had failed to pay attention to this minuscule part of her anatomy. It was with great relief he now spotted this last—and certainly correct—button to push to finally make her come.

Still, it's not all his fault he thought of women as motorcycles rather than people. Men are taught the importance of thinking linearly in step-by-step systems. Mathematics, mechanics, science—the sex-role dictated fields of study and occupations for men—all require this sort of mental discipline. The ability to be rational, to reduce everything to simple systems, to be in charge, to take care of business, these all demand a mind that can add up the options and spew out an answer that is operable and successful.

Thus it is common for men to impose the same style on a sexual performance. Sex becomes a linear equation, a formula, with specific facts that ask a reasonable question: "How do I solve the sex problem and make it successful?" The answer is reached by deductive reasoning; and soon a series of steps emerges which seem to be most successful, having been tested with a number of women repeatedly in the same situation. The equation that follows is an example of the formula many linear-thinking men may use:

Good Sex = (Masters and Johnson) plus Kissing plus Penis plus Thrusting plus Vagina Leads to Orgasms;

i.e., $(M + J) + K + P + Th + V = O.$

A man can repeat his formula with woman after woman and be a successful lover—at least in terms of supplying her with orgasms. Routine, but successful. After a while he and his partners may notice that sex is always the same: the only thing that changes is the woman. This gets boring, needless to say. A man can cope with this boredom in two ways: He can change his technique and quit performing; or he can keep his performance and change his partners.

Linear thinking like this may win Nobel prizes, tune a car, or get a man to the top of Mt. Everest; but it does not make for very spontaneous, creative sex. As more than one outraged woman has put it, "I'm not a car and I do not have orgasms when I'm treated like Chapter 3 in the Fix-It Manual!"

It's intriguing to have a man explain his system. Here, for example, is my friend José's routine, proven successful by more than twenty-five years of no erection difficulties, a numberless stream of lovers, and never a change in the act. José solves his boredom by changing lovers, rather than by altering his style. He's been summed up by numerous women lovers as "a good stick man," since his routine is totally penis- and intercourse-oriented. I think José's approach is quite typical.

"The point," José begins, "is to fuck, and I want both of us to come."

His goal is stated already: intercourse and orgasm.

"I start by kissing and then I touch her breasts to turn her on. I'm always worried I won't get inside her, that I'll get hard but she won't want to fuck. So I'm always working to get in her. I know that if I can get my finger into her vagina I'm home free. It means that I'll get my penis in there next.

"I admit I feel a little frantic until I get my finger in her vagina. After that, I can relax a little, but I want to get my cock in as soon as possible. As soon as I'm in, I know she's committed to fucking. Then I can move slower.

"I really like her to come. The more orgasms she has the better. I don't like to fuck women who don't come—it feels like an energy rip-off—very unequal. I give new lovers a chance. But my rule is 'three strikes and you're out!'

"Yes, I'm very focused on my cock. I know I should be more into the rest of my body. Last year I got into my nipples. But I really don't notice touches on the rest of my body, so foreplay isn't that important to me. I do it to her if she wants it, of course.

"I like intercourse. If a woman wants something else, I'll do it. But I don't like to fool around very long. I get bored unless I can fuck, so that's what I try to do.

"I don't like to talk about sex too much, either. I mean, it should be spontaneous, just a fast, relaxing fun thing. Talking about it ruins it. The best sex is sex that just happens."

Having a sexual routine is often a defense against having feelings. And coupling it with the romantic notion that talking about it takes the fun out enables men to perform without benefit of feelings. When a man has a performance system, he doesn't need to question whether or not he's enjoying what he's doing. He just does it. Like working at a job. In order to tolerate the routine he can't ask questions or pay much attention to his own desires. If he did, he might discover he doesn't want to be doing what he's doing, that he wants to do it differently, or that someone else wishes he'd do it a little differently. At work, this could jeopardize his job; in sex, his manhood.

Many men don't ask any more questions in sex than they

do concerning the rest of their emotional lives. They do sex because it's expected of them, and because they know no other way, or fail to appreciate any other way, of getting physical, loving stokes.

Mr. Technique may have some moments of panic when a lover, asking for what she wants, requests a change in performance, an alteration of the formula. He may find himself having temporary problems controlling his penis. It may come too quick, not get hard on command, or feel totally removed from his body and out of his control. It's important to remember that this is temporary, and does not mean he's become— gasp!—dysfunctional forever. As in any new situation, it takes time to adjust and accept changes. When Mr. Technique makes changes, he gives up some power in a situation he's accustomed to controlling. He'll need assurances he's O.K., patience and humor to weather him through this trauma, and also a reasonable amount of time to get his mind and body coordinated to this new, equal situation.

When a woman begins to discover how to give herself orgasms, many men become upset because their role in the sexual situation has been usurped. "If you can have your own orgasms, what's the point of my being here?" they ask. And that's a good question. Is a man still sexy when he's receptive and not in charge?

Ask a woman.

What's in It for Men to Change?

CHAPTER 5. So what in the world could dissuade a man to give up his old comfortable "I get enough" habits? Is there any reason for a crude sexist, a dysfunctional male, or a Mr. Technique to take a look at the situation in terms of sexism—and make changes accordingly? What's in it for men to give up their sex roles in sex?

It's pretty obvious what's in it for women. They gain power in a situation where they are classically powerless. But, at first glance, it seems that expecting a man to cease sexist sexual behavior is expecting him to give up power—all power. One man defended his sexism to me by saying, "If I give it up I feel like I'll be neutered, somehow. I'll be giving up my past, my roots—and I like all that about me." You'd think he'd been asked to give up his penis (a common paranoia men have about the expectations of women who identify themselves as feminists). Becoming equal in sexual situations is not becoming neuter, it is not giving up one's penis. It is important that feminism never be misconstrued as a more sophisticated, intellectualized form of castration. In truth, parting with sexist attitudes and expectations, coming to understand the mutual benefits to both sexes of feminism, actually means acquiring power—although it may not feel like that at first.

According to men who have struggled through all this, the benefits are many and obvious:

"Women like men who aren't sexist. So men get more sex because they're desirable to more women." (Now, that's a real opportunist talking! He's got some foresight.)

"Being with a woman who asks for what she wants is a real relief. I don't have to do all the asking or mind-reading and I'm free to relax and enjoy."

"Men who think they aren't good lovers discover they are because they don't have to perform."

"Women are really getting it together. If men don't, when we're old and gray we won't have women to talk to—much less have sex with. Consider the future!"

"It's more fun to be real open and frank about sex. It turns me on to talk about it. It really does!"

The power acquired by giving up sex-role stereotypes is unfamiliar to men locked into, or devoted, to stereotypical male roles. Male power in sex has been felt and recognized as dominance. Many men believe that no one can deny them sexually. ("Show her your penis and she's all yours.") They enjoy being the creators and controllers of fantasies, orgasms, and sexual encounters. And they insist on proving their sexiness by boasting of quantity of conquests (I know of one man in group who actually announced, "I've fucked 6000 women"), rather than quality of relationships. Men who don't get excited about these standards risk being labeled as effeminate, "wimps," or "schmucks."

It is clear that eliminating sex-role stereotypes comes down to being an issue of power. Consequently, only those men who are interested in and committed to being equals with women—in every respect—will be confident enough to be successful in becoming equals in sexual relationships. As women are understanding and appreciating the benefits in giving up the power of passivity, so men must understand and appreciate the benefits in giving up the power of dominance. And that's hard to do, at first.

In being so scripted to dominate in sex, men have sacrificed understanding the power of surrender. It is considered the stereotypical feminine role to be receptive rather than initiating. Passive, it's been labeled; and that's not manly, heaven knows.

What's powerful about surrender? Not having to perform, that's what. Then a man can open himself to the moment, experience fully that particular time as a unique occasion with a unique person. Surrender is getting, as well as giving. It involves asking for needs and desires, as well as anticipating those of his partner's. Not performing enables feelings to be top priority, rather than the routine. A man who rides close to his emotions and is able to talk and deal with them comfortably is a sight for sore eyes to women who have been looking long and hard for men with emotional power. A man who is in touch with his feelings is as refreshing and moving to women as a woman who can think clearly and support herself economically is to sex role-weary men. As men who wish to be equals with women find it stimulating to think with a woman, so women find it stimulating to share feelings and playfulness with men.

Giving up performance power opens the way for playfulness. Sex as a performance is a very serious, intense business: there's work to be done, goals to be achieved, success to be realized. Women complain about this, expressing longing for "a man who can play. I want to be silly and giggle and flirt and make out and take lots of time to be sensual." Men who enjoy doing this are highly regarded. Being able to play, a very significant role reversal, does not deny the meaning and importance of sexual intimacy. It complements it. Unless sex is fun, why bother?

Giving up "me active, you passive" Tarzan and Jane roles eliminates the necessity for both partners faking it. There is nothing more humiliating for a man than to discover the woman—or women—he has performed so well for have been faking their orgasms. And nothing is more humiliating to a woman than being subjected to a performance, being treated as an object, another notch on some man's cock. Don't kid yourself: To someone really tuned into his or her feelings, faking can be detected, no matter how clever the performance.

With the elimination of sex roles, out goes required performances. Honesty and forthrightness become natural expectations, not shocking truths. As a woman in group put it, "I'd much prefer a guy to tell me he's not turned on than to have sex with me because he feels he should."

Because of the time lag between women's liberation and men's, women are in the demanding position of having to re-educate males about sex. It's fine for men to learn what they can from the women who care enough to share. But the weakness of this is that it is comparable to men telling women about female sexuality. No matter if it comes from the goodness of the heart, women don't know as much about men's sexual feelings as do men.

I strongly advocate the formation of men's groups similar in structure to women's groups. If the men were as open with one another as women are, the experience couldn't help but be of significance to each man. However, it is hard for me to imagine a man bursting into tears and admitting he feels hopeless about his premature ejaculation problem. And it's equally difficult not to believe that some guy wouldn't endanger the confidence of the group by insisting he has no problems, merely advice to offer all those less fortunate than himself. A men's group not only has to deal with sexual issues, but also the power plays that accompany them. I wish these groups would happen and give men the warmth, support, humor, and practical advice that women give each other in groups.

There's a lot in it for men to toss out dominance and performance approaches, and replace them with spontaneity and open sharing. Good times, good women, good men, good lovin'—these are worth all the sacrifice entailed in giving up those old, deceptively comfortable sex roles.

PART 2

equal sexual relationships

The Revolution of the Spirit

CHAPTER 6. If we look at our problems as being merely personal without seeing what's happening in the rest of society, our myopia can make us miserable. Big changes are occurring; and by employing broader vision, we can be more optimistic about their results.

We are in the midst of a revolution in this country. It is a revolution of the human spirit. And when the human spirit changes, so do all human systems. In this basic way, the personal is also political. Whatever we do in our personal lives can't help but affect our politics, our attitudes toward our fellow human beings, and how we see the world as a whole.

This revolution of the spirit is unique in history. For it is a revolution for life, for people being good to each other, for people learning to share their skills and become equals in order to survive. It is a revolution celebrating humanity, out of which we are creating a good-for-people, good-for-nature world.

We have much freedom. Many new opportunities are open to help us change our lives. There is a growing concern that humanistic values be injected into the bureaucracies of our lives, those systems heretofore controlled by "experts"—by politicians, doctors, lawyers, psychologists, teachers, priests. We are tired of the cold and the isolation. We want to exercise control in our lives, to exert power over the powers that control us. We want to be able to live in a way that enables us to express our emotions, from loving warmth to righteous anger.

Prompted by the women's movement, and given a vocabulary by the new psychology, men and women are looking at each other with heightened awareness. We know we cannot afford to isolate ourselves, to proceed alone in ignorance and disinterest. As we discover more about ourselves, so we do about other people. We understand more, care more; and out of this is emerging a humanistic desire for cooperation, as opposed to competitiveness, and for equality as opposed to inequality.

We have more freedom than ever to feel and express our personal power. And as we feel more personally powerful, we must look around us and try using some of that power to make the world around us better, too. By merging and sharing our abilities with others we find ways of effecting action in the world.

As we become more aware of what's beyond our small selves, our ways of relating to the world change. And, closer to home, our relationships do also. Our new concern for humanity and our awareness of the oppressiveness of sex roles makes such change inevitable. It may be painful, and we may blunder along at times unable to see the light at the end of the cave—but we *are* changing.

Sex is intimacy of varying degrees for different people; nevertheless, it is intimacy. So, as we change, these changes are represented in our sexual relationships. In other words, we can talk a good line about being "liberated" and "free" and "humanistic" and so forth; but if we don't put some action where our mouth is, the contradictions will be quite evident whenever we are intimate with people.

We cannot say, for instance, "I'm a liberated woman, I earn my own income," and in the next breath add, "But I still like a strong man, at least an inch taller than me, who earns more money than me, and really takes charge in bed." Nor can a man say he's liberated if he continues to expect a woman to take sole responsibility for providing him with her pleasurable orgasms or if he considers women who are uninterested in doing sex his way as "frigid." In learning to enjoy our sexuality as equals we must be prepared to confront such contradictions within ourselves. We may say, "I want to be equal," but do we really? Doing so entails taking on the responsibility of being able to undergo changes. It means learning to tell the difference between use and abuse of power. Sexually, it means both sexes discovering and then figuring out how to get what they really want. It means learning to compromise and accept disappointment. It means changing our minds about who does what. It means taking dares.

Our sexual relationships are microcosms of our relationships as a whole. They cannot be ignored in this revolution of the spirit. The changes in our sexual relationships free both women and men from the burden of performing as sex-role stereotypes would have them do. This freedom enables us to create and enjoy new types of sexual relationships. I call these ideal new relationships "the New Romanticism."

About romance. Some people believe that talking straight—that is, asking for what we want and saying how we feel—takes the romance out of sexual relationships. Thanks to this ridiculous belief, thousands of people attempt to have intimate, happy relationships solely by reading each other's minds. More people conduct relationships built on mind-reading and various private paranoias than they do through expressing true feelings and responses.

A woman currently in group with me has been untangling herself ever so slowly from this romantic pitfall. She is typical of all us romantics who conduct our relationships via paranoias rather than realities. She and her equally romantic lover have been reading each other's minds now for five years. It has recently become clear that neither of them knows what the other is thinking or feeling. They exist day to day in a state of acute paranoia and have become increasingly suspicious of each others's motives. He looks grumpy in the morning, she panics, assumes he's angry at her, and spends the rest of the day trying to figure out what her "sin" was. By the time she comes to group she's guilty and terrified and announces wildly, "Our relationship is over!" Cooler heads then persuade her to ask, quite simply, "Why the long face, Jack?" She asks. She finds out he had had a bad dream and didn't want to go to work. The look had nothing whatsoever to do with her.

Jack is just as prone to this kind of craziness. One particularly rough week he didn't talk to her at all, except for a few words that sounded angry to her. He refused to discuss what was going on and had her reduced to tears before he finally coughed up an explanation. It seems she'd had an affair six months earlier when their relationship had been on the rocks. Jack still held the resentment, and every time she asked him to please her sexually he recalled his feelings of being cuckolded and grew critical of her sexuality, rather than appreciative. But rather than asking for anything from her that would help him overcome these old feelings, he preferred to punish her by holding on to them. Not only was this a power play on Jack's part, but it also made him fear relating to her; and he, too, would cry at a moment's notice, "Our relationship is over!" It never occurred to him that sharing his feelings and fears would eliminate the problem.

This pattern carried over into sex. As she learned to ask for what she wanted it became clear that the two of them had different pleasures in sex. Sexism crept in. "Do we have to talk about everything?" he argued. "Let's just do it!" She became intimidated by his wish for silence, gave in to what he wanted, and then felt bad about her sexuality all over again.

So much for mind reading. So much for traditional romance. The latter is sexist in tradition and thus discriminates against sexual pleasures, particularly for women. Actually, when you add up what romance requires, it precludes having intimate relationships with equals. If you want to relate to peers, old romantic notions must be sacrificed.

Romance traditionally means men being strong and women being fragile; it means trusting fantasy more than reality; it means total and continual harmony which can only be achieved by ignoring differences and playing down inequities. In sex this means the woman not being explicit while the male always leads the activities. It insists upon perfectly ethereal sex from the first embrace and the only utterances a woman can make are sounds of orgasmic satisfaction.

What's good about romance, however, is that it's fun. The reason we are so willing to hang on to its negative aspects (other than because we know nothing different) is because the fun side is so wonderful. Romance is being in love, and having wonderfully ecstatic feelings. It's being sexually excited, to the point you were back in high school—so hot you can hardly stand! It's doing things together, blissfully, in total communion; it's writing poems and sending flowers; it's being silly and indulging fantasies; it's letting passion go unbridled; it's feeling beautiful and strong and secure. Heady, euphoric stuff, that old romance!

The price paid for such wild flights shows up in the unhappiness of many women who come to sexual problem-solving groups. We've noted that the women who adhere most strictly to old romantic practices are the ones least likely to be orgasmic. We've found, too, that women who are orgasmic alone, but not with their partners, have many more romantic notions to toss out before being able to enjoy sex with their lovers.

Rules of romance are sex role-stereotyped. They keep us in roles that prevent us from being creative or from expressing our feelings honestly. The emotions of romance, however, are full and fanciful—and fun. The trick is, though, how to get the romantic emotions without having to follow the sex-role rules.

THE NEW ROMANTICISM

The basic ingredient for the New Romanticism is: straight talk. Add to that, being honest and taking equal responsibility, plus an understanding of sexism; if you have all these you can also enjoy the poetry and euphoria of old-fashioned romance. In that way you get the best of both worlds.

Even the most innovative non-monogamous people need things like commitment and sincerity and roses and sweet talk. But what they don't need are the stereotypes that made old-time relationships unequal and restrictive.

It seems that the only thing that falls apart faster than relationships these days are international peace treaties. People come together and separate quickly and regularly. Divorce rates are up; but then again so are marriages. Counselors who advise friendly divorces are a new, and well-fed, breed. As a matter of fact, we know more about how and why to end our relationships than about how and why to make them continue.

I believe much of this breaking apart is absolutely necessary to the two sexes for asserting their own identities. Old-style relationships were ill-equipped to provide both women and men with equality and freedom. As our consciousness got raised, our relationships grew unsatisfactory and outdated. We left them, or else became involved in painful, seemingly endless struggles to make them better.

So here we are, so many of us, separated from our partners; others among us are hanging on, hoping we can improve our current relationships; and those of us desiring to start new relationships are wondering how to do so without making the same mistakes.

I believe in primary relationships: those in which both partners regard their particular relationship as the most important in either of their lives. It is not being a silly romantic to believe that two people can fit together, love each other, and help each other to grow more interesting and live more happily. But I'm also practical and very much a feminist. Good primary relationships—"good" meaning "equal"—are hard to create due to sexism and, consequently, power struggles between people.

Equality can only be had by couples who have no investment in being one-up on each other. And yet it must be understood that it is not possible for *all* relationships to be equal. Those built on false assumptions, on classical sex roles, and vast differences in people's expectations, don't usually succeed for long; and unless both partners are willing to make changes, they cannot be transformed from inequality to equality. Women need to be aware of when their relationships are no longer viable; and also know they can survive and flourish without them.

Often when a woman and her lover decide to seek sexual counseling, they are surprised to discover that their sexual problems reflect their relationship's difficulties in every other area. There is a tendency for us to divorce sex from our relationships, to put the two in separate compartments and not see how greatly they influence each other. Sex is intimate communication—and communication is what makes or breaks relationships.

(I notice as I read this that I tend to speak of the behavior of men and women in what could be misunderstood as absolute terms. Readers, be aware that I speak generally, and in terms of the most banal sex-role stereotypes.)

The chapters that immediately follow will furnish some useful guidelines for making good equal sexual relationships.

Mechanics of Equal Sexual Relationships

CHAPTER 7. Equal sexual relationships require balance in three categories, which can be conveniently summarized as "The Three C's:
1) Chemistry
2) Compatibility
3) Cooperation

We've been led to believe through romantic novels, television, and adolescent fantasy that good relationships just happen: they either work or they don't. For that reason, we have little understanding of the components and workings of relationships. We're as "romantical," as one young schoolgirl put it, in relationships as we are in sex. Blind faith and mind-reading lead us in never-ending, unrewarding circles of confusion. We take stock of our love-lives and realize, to our despair, that we have been repeating the same pattern in all our relationships. The only thing that changes are the lovers. "Where's the magic all gone to? And where's that Certain Someone?" we cry, looking about (but pretending not to be looking), hoping he or she will suddenly appear.

This waiting is tiresome. And the repetition of old mistakes is depressing. It is important to realize that doing relationships is like learning any skill or any art. Like diving. You can either repeat belly flop after belly flop, or you can analyze your mistakes, get advice from people with more experience, and learn to make beautiful swan dives. You can learn to do equal relationships just as you can learn to do anything you want.

Relationships have parts. In good ones, all these parts coordinate and work well together. In unhappy, unworkable relationships, these parts don't complement. There is some portion missing. (Usually what's missing is a balance of power, which we will discuss later on.)

What's encouraging about understanding the components of relationships is that relationships don't just happen. They can be worked on, improved, kept alive, or even discontinued sensibly. Doing good relationships is a learnable and teachable skill.

As you have a right to pleasurable sex, you also have rights to pleasurable love relationships. Too often women believe that pain and unhappiness are unavoidable in relationships with men. We used to have no other choice but to tolerate misery. But now we do. We have many more social, political, economic, and personal options.

If you're concerned that your relationships are more pain than pleasure, analyze them on a percentage basis. Rate your relationship according to what's important to you. For example, let's say you want fun (that includes good sex), no boredom, and no hassles with your lover. Ideally, it should be 80% fun, 10% boredom, and 10% hassles. All the same, you may be happy with 50% fun, 40% hassles, and 10% boredom. If fun dips below 50%, then seriously consider why you are continuing to remain in such a relationship. If it's for security, or out of fear of loneliness, ask yourself if the price you're paying is a fair one—and don't let yourself be afraid to make major changes.

CHEMISTRY

Chemistry is the one bit of magic in sex. It's the dreamy, hot, can't-sleep-at-night part. It's being inexplicably sexually turned on to someone. You can search for reasons to explain why, but they never seem to be adequate. There's just "something" about the person, a certain blend of ingredients, that excites you. Smell, vitality, appearance, movement, fantasy—all these combine to create chemistry.

Some of us sat down once and decided to make lists of our chemical matches. Louise added up all the things her lovers had in common. Her list included: curly black hair, olive skin, intensity, gat teeth, intellectual adventuresomeness, good smell, nice hands, lean build, wild sense of humor. Shortly after compiling her list she fell madly in love with someone she described as "incredibly chemical" who in no way matched this list, and as a matter of fact was quite the opposite, being blond and pudgy and easy-going. "He's got a wild sense of humor, though!" she noted.

So what is chemistry, anyway? No one knows. It's too whimsical, too primitive to capture in words. Maybe it's the response of the primeval soul within each of us, that animal that still lies deep inside us. Current phrases like "good vibes" and "a real turn on" refer to this warmth-seeking animal, while earlier generations understood it as "love at first sight."

In our women's groups we've noticed that we feel chemistry toward more people as we each feel more freedom to be turned on. When we've been adapting sexually, doing it with partners not exactly of our choice, we have little sense of what truly excites us. As we begin to get an understanding of what we like, we begin to notice this chemistry. It is especially enjoyable when we don't feel pressured to do anything in particular about it—but just enjoy feeling it, indulging our fantasies. Women, frequently, decide to just watch and sensually enjoy people on the street and all around them, feeling safe with their permission to be sexually turned on because now they are in control of those strong feelings.

Chemistry, alone, cannot make a good sexual relationship, however; and some people unfortunately get confused, believing it can. "This is IT!" they announce—then wonder why it's over in two weeks. But chemistry *can* make for an enjoyable, even passionate—though brief or infrequent—affair. Or it can provide the cement which bonds people together when a relationship is undergoing profound changes. Chemistry has its good points and its bad ones. Even if the bulk of a relationship is terrible, when such chemistry exists the bond won't break. Many women endure restrictive and dead-end relationships purely out of chemistry. For, without it, a sexual relationship may be fun and enjoyable and pleasant—but it will lack the thrill of passion.

Chemistry can be lost, too. It can go flat, like bubbles leave champagne. When a relationship becomes unhappy and overwhelmingly inequal as to compatibility and cooperation, the magic may dissolve. This is usually a gradual process, with women waking up one morning weeks or years later and realizing, "but . . . it's gone!"

Even if you have sexual chemistry with someone, then, don't count on it to carry you through everything. It's important; but it cannot take indefinite stress. Chemistry alone is not enough for a good, equal sexual relationship.

COMPATIBILITY

Contrary to the adage, "Opposites attract," various psychology studies have shown that people with many interests in common have happier and longer lasting relationships. The belief in the attraction of opposites is often a justification for many sexist relationships. The traditional opposites, for example, are her feelings vs. his mind, his money vs. her sexiness, her beauty vs. his brilliance, his dominance vs. her compliance. In such a way, the two halves of a whole model is perpetuated. This presumes that each person in the couple is incomplete and made whole only with the complement of the other. They may not be compatible—but they sure do need each other!

Compatibility is the friendship of two essentially whole human beings who have interests, viewpoints, ambitions, and sexual appetite in common. Such people enjoy each other more than they don't enjoy each other. They like similar things.

A couple's degree of compatibility can run the gamut from "we have a nice time together" to "we inspire one another." Compatibility differs from chemistry in that it's rational and practical. You can look at the situation and say, "This is why we like each other," and be able to list the reasons.

Ideally, compatibility and equality go hand-in-hand. People who are compatible feel equal in power to each other. Yet, in conventional relationships, compatibility often means she admires his power and he admires it, too. The role reversal of that is equally unsatisfactory, featuring the "henpecked" husband and the dominant "bitchy" female. Truly compatible people may not be equals in all aspects of their lives or talents, but in the long run their power balances out and they respect each other as equals.

For example, take this couple. The woman is a psychoanalyst while the man manages a motorcycle shop. Despite their career differences, they have much in common that has made them good friends. (They even have chemistry, which has also made them good lovers.) However, secretly, he feels one-down to her intellectual abilities and she feels one-up to his life as a lowly mechanic. Imbalance exists here: they both agree she's more successful. They may be compatible but they're not equals in their careers, which is an important source of power. Now, to reverse this, let's suppose she secretly wishes she could handle a bike and run a business as well as he does, and he views her skills as useless, thinking, "Therapy is a waste of time." In this situation, he's one-up and she's one-down and, again, they're not equals. Ideally, they would both admire, and even envy a bit, each other's talents. He would like to know more about therapy, while she wished she knew something about motorcycles and running a business. Compatibility equals make for good friendships.

After studying such phenomena, one can begin to predict who will get along as equals and who won't. I've gotten so good at it now that I can predict with amazing accuracy whether or not a relationship will be a lasting one between two people who have recently met.

First of all, I note if sexual chemistry is there—for both of them. If one feels it more than the other, that is a crucial imbalance and will cause future problems.

Then I ask questions to determine how much these two people have in common. Also, how do their jobs match? If he's a successful professional who makes lots of money, and she has not yet decided on her career and makes barely enough money to get by on, they are unequal right off the bat—and I predict jealousy and competitiveness in their futures.

I also look for life-style compatibility. Do they have the same number of friends? Do they have economic class differences—and are these differences complementary or competitive? Have they both lived with people before, or have they lived alone? Are they equally gregarious, or equally reclusive? Do they respond to their differences competitively or do they enjoy their disparateness?

You can do this for yourself. Next time you fall in love, check out how compatible you are. Are you equals, or halves of a whole? Do you have as much to give as you have to get? Is it beauty and the beast—or two beauties who bring out the sweet beasties in each other?

Compatibility and chemistry can come together or separately. Just because I have chemistry for someone doesn't mean we're necessarily compatible. It's certainly wonderful when both occur, but it is rare.

However, chemistry and compatibility are still not enough to make a good, equal relationship. One also needs cooperation, that part of a relationship where power equalities and inequalities are most apparent.

Sexual Compatibility Exercise

An easy exercise to find out if you are sexually compatible: Each of you, separately and privately, writes down everything you want sexually. Do not allow fear or any other such considerations to inhibit you. Make it 100% what you want—no holds barred, all fantasies on go. Write down your fantasy of the most wonderful love-making you can imagine. Say what you want as to time, atmosphere, seduction, touches, orgasm. Leave nothing out.

After you've both done this, sit down together and compare lists. Most couples are surprised to see how much they have in common.

Strokes

Before proceeding to the third "C"—cooperation—I should explain here two terms that are prerequisites for making cooperation work: Strokes and the Rescue Game.

As for strokes, everybody needs them. Strokes are signs of recognition; they are stimulus from one person to another. Strokes are compliments, warm touches, verbal acknowledgement, attention. As Eric Berne, who coined this term, noted, without strokes, babies' spines shrivel—and they die. Adults without strokes may not suffer from shriveled spines, but they suffer from shriveled spirits.

Strokes are why people pursue and want good sex. It is the most intimate means of communication, and at its best provides warm touches, attention, compliments—the good strokes we all need and deserve. It feels good. It satisfies. It makes us warm and full and happy when it is sincere.

When sex doesn't go right and feels bad instead of good, people feel unhappy and lonely, even angry. We need strokes so desperately we often tolerate unhappy sexual relationships because having a few strokes is better than none at all. But sexual relationships without rewarding, positive strokes cannot continue to be satisfying for long.

That's why knowing how to masturbate, to be our own lovers, is such a freeing skill. It enables us to give ourselves sexy strokes. Being able to make ourselves sexually happy is a way to love and enjoy ourselves and come to expect the same care from others. To help women realize this, I ask them to list, as part of their homework hour, all the reasons why they love themselves. I suggest they hang that list in their room as a love letter to themselves, to be read when needed for strokes. Suzanne did this by writing a poem to herself:

I like the way I clean house—it feels whole and Zen
I like the clown in me
I like the way I relate with friends
I like my left hand—it is soft and fluid
I like how goddam hard I try
I like the newness I feel
I like the way I touch people
I like myself
I like my eyes
I like the roundness of my stomach and my breasts
I like the way my body shakes—it is alive
I like my hair and the way my face flushes
I like the way my body opens and relaxes when I'm turned on
I like the way I write—it is adolescent and blunt.

Strokes are as much a prey to sexism as every other aspect of our relationships. Men and women are expected to want different kinds of strokes. For example, men desire and get strokes for being number one, for achievement, for assertiveness, for winning, competing, succeeding, being tough, for being good daddies. Women desire and get strokes for being supportive, generous, willing to sacrifice and give, for softness, patience, adaptibility and sweetness, for being good mommies. When we cross over sex-role lines into opposite territory we are liable to slander. For example, when he's aggressive, he's stroked for taking care of business; but when she's aggressive she's labeled a bitch, sometimes even a castrating one. When she is hurt or scared people feel sorry for her and care for her; but when he is hurt or scared he's called a wimp and advised to keep a stiff upper lip.

In sex, too, men and women get strokes which reflect basic social sexism. Physically, she is given strokes for her visual appeal, her hair, her legs, her breasts, her ass, her lips, her eyes, the way she dresses. He may be stroked for his appearance; but the standards for what comprises a good-looking man aren't nearly as stringent as those for women. A man who fails to meet media standards of beauty is given the stroke of "having character." As for sex itself, women get strokes for happily accepting and having orgasms owing to whatever routine a man performs. Her strokes are for being seductive, receptive, and amiable. His strokes are for aggressiveness, thrusting, size of cock, and hard-on endurance.

As for actual verbal, demonstrated strokes expressed in relationships, sexism takes its toll there, too. Men, in accordance with their "feelings-are-a-weakness" cultural conditioning, fail to recognize the importance of giving strokes other than sexual ones. So women in group complain their partners don't give them the kinds of strokes they want. "The only time he touches me is if he wants to have sex," they say. Or, "How can he expect me to be turned on when he ignores me except for sex?" Women want more strokes than genital sex offers. They want verbal attention, spoken compliments; they want to hear they are valued and appreciated and loved, not just sexually, but for their intelligence, ingenuity, and strengths. As for sexual strokes, they'd like them to be specific and personal. They want to hear a partner say "You're beautiful" and "I love how you smell" and "Your cunt is divine."

But in the competitive world in which most men work, who can afford the luxury of a compliment or a soft word? Being complimentary to someone means one of two things: You feel one-down to them and are, therefore, weak; or you are trying to hustle them for a favor, and your strokes, therefore, are manipulative.

The Nixon administration demonstrated this attitude by turning the term "stroking" into one that meant to praise someone falsely. "Stroking" was used to get people to solicit votes, to flatter wealthy campaign contributors, to commit crimes. It was easy for men to understand this, accustomed as most sexist men are to giving strokes purely for ulterior motives. ("I love you. Give me your food stamps," I heard a bearded man cooing to a young woman in Levi's.)

No wonder a stroke can't be trusted. Men are taught to survive without compliments, to "tough it out." At its worst, *macho* precludes real giving strokes. Giving strokes scares such a man. It makes him feel out of control, as if needing warmth and affection and compliments is a weakness and not as necessary to a human being as food. There is the myth, too, that men who enjoy "softness" are homosexuals, which terrifies many men. Consequently, real strokes (i.e., those without ulterior motives) are, traditionally, women's work. Little wonder this sort of social conditioning can make getting genuine strokes from a man like trying to squeeze water from a rock.

Women, on the other hand, give strokes with ease and, quite often, all too readily. Women—who are thought to be weak anyway—are supposed to handle the weaker aspects of living. Strokes are for sissies, so let women do them. They have been taught that stroking accompanies all sorts of nurturing, like cooking meals and raising babies and catering to men's emotions. Women complement the male role by reading the male mind, intuiting what strokes are needed and then supplying them in a most nurturing manner. Stereotypically, women are the nurturers in our society; thus strokes are, supposedly, their responsibility.

For this reason, men become dependent on women for most strokes. (It's "good old Mom" all over again.) Many women exploit this dependence and use their stroking ability to manipulate men. Stroking ability is a powerful skill. Men count on a woman's stroke ability being as bottomless as Grandma's cookie jar. Hence, in the most conventional relationships, couples trade their survival skills: she supplies the emotional stroke security and he provides the money stroke security.

Which brings us to the concept of the stroke economy. As Claude Steiner pointed out in "The Stroke Economy"[1] people handle their strokes like they do their money. We fear there aren't enough strokes to go around so we hoard them. We become stingy and give them out only when we're guaranteed return on our investment. We never give strokes for free if we can help it. We treasure like misers the ones we get, jealously guarding them. In our everyday life, we juggle strokes, ponder over them, manipulating them like a banker does his money. But the less we spend, the less we get. And the fewer we get, the fewer we have to spend. Economically, the stroking situation becomes tight and with tightness comes stroke envy, stroke competition, and stroke starvation.

But we were tricked. In actuality, there is an abundance of strokes—as we soon discover when we start recognizing and giving the ones we feel. If we acted on every impulse to hug someone, to say a friendly hello, or send a warm note, our stroke economy would be humming happily. Stroking would become as accepted as any of our creature comforts. And strokes would then replace the objects in our economic structure we've been conditioned to buy to take the place of human strokes—such as television, junk food, cigarettes, and pet rocks.

Perhaps the most obvious sexist situation of saving strokes for a big cash-in is the woman who holds on to her virginity until she meets Mr. Right. She's been saving up all her sexual and loving feelings for years, waiting for this occasion. After the deflowering, she gushes with love and passion—she has

---

[1] Claude M. Steiner, *Scripts People Live* (New York: Grove Press, 1974), pp. 110–117.

been finally freed. But often she finds, to her pain, that Mr. Right only meant to dally, not set up housekeeping. He has more strokes available and hasn't made the same sort of emotional investment as she. If she'd had a better stroke balance in her life, she could have approached the situation more realistically from the start.

Stroke starvation of this sort exists in many women's lives. Weary of stiff-lipped men, they hunger for warm words and friendly touching. (They know they can get it from other women and they do—if sexism on their own part doesn't prevent it.) This hunger for nurturing men creates a stroke economy problem. Men who know how to give warm strokes run into stroke-hungry women. Women, aware that strokes from men are as rare as emeralds, assume a lot when they receive such men's strokes. They assume this means love, a serious relationship, and they overwhelm the man with attention and expectations. This is not surprising. A man who is capable of stroking has an immense amount of power and appeal.

A lack of strokes in sexuality usually indicates a lack of strokes in the relationship as a whole. Most of us fail to understand how important it is we tell our lovers what we appreciate about them. Too often we assume they know. We think that, since *we're* thinking it, *they* must be hearing it. Or because we earlier told someone else how wonderful they are, we also said it to them. So pay attention to the strokes in your relationships. Are you getting the ones you want? Are you giving the ones you have? What strokes do you wish your partner would give you? What strokes do you have for them that you've never explicitly expressed?

If strokes are a problem for you, then talk with your partner about it. Such a conversation could go something like this:

SHE: I feel like you're taking me for granted. I want some strokes so I'll know you're not.

HE: You know how hard it is for me to give strokes. It's like a blank spot in my brain or something. I mean to do it, but I can't seem to do it right or often enough. But I'll sure try.

SHE: I know it's difficult, but I need them. I'm not turned on to you when you don't give me strokes. So I'll ask you; and you give them to me when you figure out if you have them and how you want to give them to me. I want strokes for what you've learned from me. And I want strokes for what's sexy about me and why you like me.

HE: (*a few hours later*) I've been thinking of all the strokes I have for you, and I want you to know there are a lot. I've learned so much from you. Why, I never realized how much! Like the ideas we figured out at work, and you taught me how to fix my bicycle, and you taught me the importance of letting my sense of humor out. You are my main advisor, my best friend, and my lover. I love you for all these reasons. As for sexiness, I love your body and your passion and I hope we're sexy forever.

The improvement in loving is dramatic when two people start exchanging strokes.

Rescue Game

After strokes, the second fundamental necessity to having good sexual relationships is an understanding of the dynamics of the Rescue Game. This game is illustrated by the Rescue Triangle. As Claude Steiner explains it,[2] there are three positions: the Rescuer, the Victim, and the Persecutor. They are arranged in a triangle to show that people can move quite easily from one position to any of the other two. This series of moves is called the Rescue Game—meaning people utilize it, rather than more direct methods, as a scheme to get what they want in their lives. A game is a specific set of complementary ulterior

---

[2]Claude M. Steiner, *Scripts People Live,* pp. 146–54.

transactions which result in a predictable outcome. The outcome of the Rescue Game played in sexual relationships is unhappy sex that often can end the relationship. Let's see how it works:

The Rescuer believes: You need me. Consequently, he or she only feels strong when obligated to help out those who are weaker. For example, a woman may Rescue a man sexually by not telling him that she doesn't enjoy sex with him because she wants to protect his ego. Or a man may Rescue a woman sexually by always taking responsibility for whether she has an orgasm or not.

Rescues can be done from a position of one-up or one-down. That is, a person may be a Rescuer because she feels (and may indeed be) more powerful than the other person, and hence obligated to do more than she really wants to take care of him. Or a person may Rescue because he feels less powerful than the other person and consequently that all he has of value to contribute to the relationship is Rescues. Often these Rescue positions are sex role-determined. Because women often feel less powerful in relationships with men, they will resort to one-down Rescues coming from a position of "I'm not O.K. so I have to do more than 50% here to prove my worth. My 60% is worth the 40% return." Because men often have more power, they will tend to do one-up Rescues. They feel, "I'm O.K., she's not. She needs me. I'd feel guilty if I let her down."

The Victim position neatly complements that of the Rescuer. The Victim believes, "I'm not O.K.—I need you," and relies on others to take care of him/her. For instance, in sex the man falls into despair whenever the woman asks for a change in their love-making; or the woman acts helpless about achieving her own orgasms.

The Persecutor is a Victim or Rescuer fed up with the role. The Persecutor feels, "I'm O.K. You're not—and it's all your fault." For example, a woman finally blows up at her lover because she hasn't been enjoying sex; or he blows up at her when he finds out she's been faking pleasure. In another case, he blows up at her for expecting him to run the show; or she makes him feel guilty when she doesn't have an orgasm. (Yes, guilt-tripping is persecutory.)

The feelings accompanying these game positions are predictable. You can easily tell where you are on the triangle. A Rescuer? Depending on your power position, you're feeling over-extended, ripped off, or guilty. A Victim? You're feeling helpless; everything is a crisis; you're desperate and out of control, hoping to get a Rescuer to save you, because you fear being Persecuted. A Persecutor? You're angry and resentful. You may attack with outright insults and accusations, or you may merely sulk and withdraw. Most people have a favorite position on the triangle, but once the Rescue Game gets underway people often switch from one position to the other. The Rescue Game can become a crazy, vicious merry-go-round if it's not stopped.

As an example, let's examine the game dynamics of two classical Rescues observed in sexual relationships: the Rescue of Her Orgasms and the Rescue of His Penis.

THE RESCUE OF HER ORGASMS

This Rescue features a nurturing man with a woman who is not able to have orgasms. (See Figure 1.) Because he is easily orgasmic but also feels responsible for making sure she comes, too, he takes it upon himself to make her orgasmic. He Rescues by assuming responsibility for both their orgasms. To this end he works hard, to the point of pain or exhaustion. His penis hurts, but he keeps on going. Sex becomes work rather than pleasure.

His lover is the Victim. She feels "frigid" and sexually helpless. She relies on him to discover what makes her orgasmic. When he gets weary and bored, though, then he becomes the Victim, having sacrificed his sexual pleasure for hers. She can Rescue him at this point by saying, with a sigh, "Oh, that's O.K.—I don't really mind not coming." Or she can Persecute him for not taking care of her: "You're lazy" or "This is a hopeless situation."

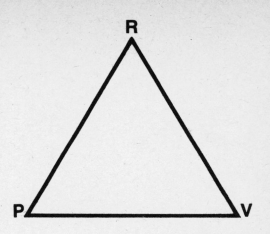

1. He R: I'm sexually O.K. She's not. So I'll help her.
   She V: I'm not sexually O.K. You are. Turn me on, I need help.

2. He V: My penis hurts. This is work. I'm tired.
   She R: Oh, that's O.K. I don't really mind not coming.
   or
   She P: You're a lazy lover, you come too quick. This will never work. I hate sex.

3. He P: Get your sexuality together or I'll have to find another lover.
   She R: (Fakes orgasms, pretends to enjoy sex, goes into therapy agreeing it's all her problem.)

Sexual Rescue of Her Orgasms
Figure 1.

He feels angry because she is so helpless and accusatory. Now it's his turn to become a Persecutor. "Get your sexuality together," he instructs, blaming the problem on her. He may also threaten to end the relationship and find another lover. She gets scared, fearing his threats and believing the problem is, indeed, all hers. She doesn't want to lose him or the relationship. So she Rescues him by adapting to sex with him. She may even fake orgasms to convince him all is well.

Their behavior has thus not solved the problem but only set into motion a whole new Rescue Game. When her Rescues are confronted—because she can't fake forever—he'll be hurt and angry, and around they'll go again. Ultimately, they will quit having sex or end the relationship if these Rescues aren't stopped.

THE RESCUE OF HIS PENIS

Another classical sexual Rescue is that performed by a nurturing woman whose lover is a premature ejaculator. (See Figure 2.) She Rescues by appearing to enjoy sex, or at least agreeing to have sex under such conditions, telling herself and him, "Orgasms aren't that important. I enjoy sex anyway." She does this Rescue for a number of reasons. She may not know that he can learn to maintain longer erections and assumes, as many women do, that she should learn to come faster. She believes his ego is too fragile to handle any criticism of sexual performance. She feels so hopeless about the sexual situation she thinks she should be content with whatever she gets.

He's the unwitting Victim, believing all is well since he's satisfied and having his orgasms. He doesn't know a storm is brewing.

As time passes, she becomes the Victim. She dreads sex, afraid of getting turned on and then being left frustrated. She begins to find excuses to avoid sex; she complains she can't have orgasms with him and does all she can to avoid the confrontation. As her minimum duty she gives him perfunctory orgasms—still it's obvious she's not enjoying sex.

He moves into Persecutor. He doesn't understand what the problem is; so, of course, blames her. "What's wrong with you? You used to be turned on." He tells her to get her sexuality together or he doesn't see how their relationship can continue.

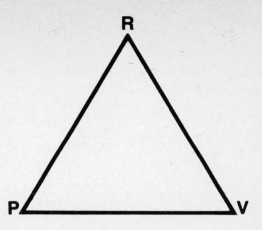

1. She R: It's O.K. you come fast. I enjoy sex anyway. Be-
            sides, my orgasms aren't as important as yours.
   He V: I really had a good time. Sex with you is good.
            You're so giving and sexy.

2. She V: I have a headache. This hurts. I take too long.
   He P: What's wrong with you? You used to be turned
            on.

3. She P: You're not a good lover. You don't turn me on.
            What's wrong with you?
   He R: (Stops asking for sex; half-heartedly does Squeeze
            Technique therapy.)

Sexual Rescue of His Penis
Figure 2.

She retaliates as a Persecutor. "You get your orgasms. I
don't get mine," she accuses. "What's wrong with *you*?" Or
she refuses to have sex with him, particularly after discovering
that he has gone and had an affair. She, too, may then find
another lover.

He may now become the Rescuer. He ceases pressuring
her for sex and/or half-heartedly agrees to sex therapy.

The Rescue Game can go on and on, accelerating as it gets

more complex and Rescue builds upon Rescue. Around and around the triangle the players go.

Individuals in these game positions have two choices. They can continue on the triangle and watch their relationship disintegrate; or they can each take responsibility for stopping the Rescues and learn how to make themselves sexually happy. In the first example, she can do so by learning to have orgasms and he by learning to pay equal attention to his own pleasure. In the second example, she can ask for what she needs and he can discover how to match her pacing. When sexual Rescues stop, the relationship becomes clear. A couple can then see just what they truly have for each other, and determine honestly if they have the making of a good sexual relationship or not. For good sex to begin, Rescues must stop.

When sexual Rescues are stopped, the Rescues in the whole relationship become obvious. This can cause some real shake-ups. As you realize your Rescue patterns, be gentle and careful with each other. Don't Rescue and you won't Persecute. And if you Rescue, don't blame your Victim.

In stopping Rescues, keep patience and nurturing in mind. The stance of anti-Rescue is a Persecutory one. In anti-Rescue the former Rescuer says, "I did that for a year! I've had it! No more!" Don't become hostile and blaming. Remember, it took two to play. You did your share, no matter where you were on the triangle.

COOPERATION

Once you have an understanding of strokes and the Rescue Triangle in your relationship, you need a viable framework in which to integrate these new ways of relating. The new framework is the third "C": cooperation.

Traditionally, sexual relationships have not been mutually cooperative. The standard style has been for one person, usually she, to cooperate by obeying the wishes of the other. (This is not cooperation. This is coercion.)

The alternative to this is competition. In competitive relationships the partners vie with each other for power, each asserting their rights over the other. In this set-up there's always a winner and a loser. The winner has better and more lovers, better and more orgasms, better and more fantasies. In the end, nobody wins because a relationship built on competition exhausts itself.

A new, alternative relationship style is cooperation. It is recommended for those people who want their sexual relationships to be enjoyable, easy, and constructive, with more fun and less fighting. Radical psychiatrists counsel rules for cooperative relationships,[3] and these are extremely valuable in making sexual relationships successful.

Rules for Cooperative Sexual Relationships

1. *Equal sexual rights and responsibilities.* This means that each person in a sexual relationship has equal rights to being sexually happy and getting what they want. That includes everything—from orgasms to fantasies to caresses, to not having sex when you don't want it, to having as much sex as you do want. Where inequalities exist, partners must recognize them and make compromises. This means the aggressor must agree to give up a little, and the less aggressive person, usually the woman, must learn to stick up for herself and make her wants known.

Until recently, sexual conventions have dictated that men have more sexual rights than women. Men have felt sure of their rights to sex, viewing it as important to their health as fine food, proper exercise, and friends. A woman has a much harder time believing she has a right to a good sexual situation.

[3]*Ibid.,* pp. 295–302.

Because she has often traded sexual favors for security she may feel she has no rights. Also, her sex-role conditioning has taught her that sex is primarily something men initiate and control and so now she has a difficult time switching roles. Women talk of years of agreeing to unhappy sex because they were unable to justify their reluctance well enough or withstand the pressure their partners exerted.

And men can be very pushy about their needs. Perhaps the ultimate example of this is a statistic quoted by Marta Segovia Ashly, who runs a center for battered women in San Francisco. She reports that fifty percent of the men who beat their wives do so when they are drunk, demand sex, and are refused. Mrs. Ashly emphasizes this sort of violence is not restricted to the poor or minority groups, but cuts through all income brackets and all classes of people—from Ph.D.'s to truck drivers. At a recent conference in San Francisco on "Sexual Violence and Women," many women expressed aloud for the first time the sexual battering they had received from men. Men who bruised women's vaginas with their penises, strangled them at orgasm, bit their genitals during cunnilingus, tore at their breasts, locked them in bedrooms and, of course, raped them. Many men get sex and violence confused, and women do too when they assume that sex is supposed to be painful—either emotionally or physically.

Women have a hard time becoming equals because often we don't know what we want sexually, how to ask for it, or how to refuse what we don't want. Too often we think we have to be nice, too often we also have a male sex role in our minds that we expect men to live up to. Even though liberated in all other respects, we still may expect our partners to initiate and control sex. When a man steps out of role, when he asks instead of gives, thus exposing his insecurities, we may get scared. Women in group have panicked because suddenly their lover is showing "weaknesses" they never expected. "He's not able to have an erection all the time," said one, "and that never used to happen." Or: "He gets a little weepy now when he talks about his feelings. I've never seen a man cry and I don't know what to do."

Fortunately, equality in sexual pleasure helps create equality in emotional expression. And that is a major step towards men and women becoming equals.

Equal responsibility means taking equal responsibility for sexual problem-solving. It is not fair to say, "I'm O.K.—The Sexual Problems Are All Hers/His."

Because men generally don't have orgasm difficulties, feeling satisfied rather than frustrated after sex, they fail to take seriously the fact that sex problems in a relationship are in any way their responsibility. If a woman fails to achieve orgasm, it is *her* problem. Or if the man is a premature ejaculator, it is *his* problem. Often women agree. But men tend to be reluctant to participate in sexual problem-solving when their partners request they do so. The man may refuse to believe he has a problem, or he may think that dealing with sex demeans his manhood, or he may feel too competitive about the situation to be able to approach it reasonably.

This difficulty with men refusing to see a counselor is so common that until recently we had to lead groups of women with partners which only the women attended. This created a very sexist situation: even if the manifestation of the problem was *his,* the woman still did all the problem-solving and took it home to her partner, where he reaped the benefits with a minimum of effort. She found the group, joined, paid, bared her heart, shared her deepest doubts, scheduled her week to accommodate the homework, and then conveyed all the information to him. The situation was extremely lopsided.

There is only one situation in which it is valid to say that orgasm difficulties might be primarily hers: and that's when she is not able to have orgasms by herself through masturbation. The same holds true for men. Unless a man cannot masturbate to a satisfactory, enjoyable orgasm, the relationship orgasm difficulties are mutual, not individual. It can be said that, as a rule, sexual problems are mutual; and that these mutual problems are often due to the communication difficulties and relationship problems.

2. *No sexual power plays.* Power plays are psychological ways of convincing people to do something they don't want to do. They are indirect ways to get what we want, used when we believe that asking outright will not be successful. In sex, power plays enable people to control the sexual situation, and get what they want, but often at the expense of their partner's pleasure. Power plays keep people unequal. If a partner feels a power play must be used to get what is wanted, rather than talking straight, the relationship is not a cooperative one.

There are two types of power plays. One-up power plays and one-down power plays (just like Rescues). One-up power plays are performed by the person in the relationship who has the most leverage, the most power (typically, the man). One-down power plays are executed by the person in the relationship who has the least leverage (just as typically, the woman).

The most traditional one-up power play is done by a man when he power plays a woman into having sex with him against her will. He can use any number of psychological ploys: "You're uptight." "You're my wife." "You don't love me." "You're frigid." "I'll leave you." All these are designed to make her feel un-O.K. if she isn't interested in sex. Or he can rape her. A significant number of rapes are committed by men on their wives, and there's not a legal step a woman can take. After all, he's her husband and he has his "conjugal rights."

The most traditional one-down power play is used by women: withholding sex. Women withhold sex to express anger they feel towards their partner, to starve their partner into agreeing to do something they want, or to convince their partners to take their feelings seriously. Or they will withhold their own orgasms to keep themselves from falling in love, to refrain from being under the control of their partners, or to deny their partners the ego-rush that goes with "bringing a woman off."

What follows are some typical sex power plays, from crude to subtle, one-up to one-down.

STANDARD MALE POWER PLAYS ON WOMEN

Rape. Procuring sex by sheer physical force is a power play available to men because men are generally stronger than women physically. Actually, sex is secondary to many rapes. Rape is a crime of violence and a display of power over women through the sexual act.

"I'm your husband. I have my rights." If sex is down to this level, as my Aunt Agnes, a veteran wife of four husbands, always said, "Get a divorce, honey!"

"If you don't have sex with me, you don't love me." This can convince a partner that she is not a loving human being. Some women hear this and fear not being loving—a horrible fate for a woman—plus being tossed out of the relationship. (I remember a horrible night in the Sierras, curled up tight and alone in my sleeping bag, with my male camping partner yelling at me, "You don't want sex because you're a cold, heartless person!"—and, at moments, I actually believed it.) It must be understood that having sex and making love can be two entirely separate activities, and are not necessarily related.

"You're frigid." This is the crude form. "I'm really sorry you have so many psychological hangups about sex" is the Liberated Macho form.

In this era of the sexual revolution and the liberated woman, nothing could be worse than being uptight and not groovy, right? This power play dares you prove you're sexually O.K. You may not enjoy the sex, but god knows you're healthy. I usually counter this one by just saying, "I'm a prude and I like it." This gives them something to think about.

"So, why not? I mean, why not? Why? I don't understand why you don't want to have sex with me. Why? . . . ad infinitum." Repeated twenty times, this power play asks for endless justifications. You'll either be up all night explaining, or you can give in and get a good night's sleep. The point is to wear you down until you do consent. You actually have no obligation to explain why you don't want to have sex with someone. "I'm not turned on," is enough. If you want to explain, just say it once.

The way to circumvent endless explaining is to make a demand. It's hard to argue with a demand. Follow "I'm not turned on" with "and I do not want to have sex with you."

"But look at all I've done for you . . ." So he bought you dinner and talked nice to you and told you what an understanding and beautiful woman you are and then he said he'd love you forever and that he was your true friend forever—and at the end of all this wonderful stuff he wants to fuck. If you feel like it, fine. If you don't, don't. Sex is not a reward for services rendered. Unless there's something enjoyable in it for you, don't feel obligated. Equal rights, remember.

"You weren't into sex so I got it on with your friend (or another woman)." It's so messy when this happens. This is a very competitive and hostile power play. You have a lot of talking to do to figure out the source of this one.

"Like it or lump it. I am what I am and I don't change for nobody." Some competitive egomaniacs refuse to compromise about anything for anybody. If a man is so insecure about his sexuality that he can't risk changes, then you must decide if the struggle is worth it. If not, call off your sex-life with this person. If so, prepare for a hard battle.

"I know you're refusing me just to turn me on—you're playing hard-to-get." This constitutes a total discount of the woman's feelings. Even if you tell him how you feel, he is sure you don't mean it. The more you resist, the more turned on he gets. When he finds out you really do mean no, he may even have the audacity to be angry. Don't be ambiguous. Make yourself clear, and stick up for yourself.

STANDARD FEMALE POWER PLAYS ON MEN

"You're the best. I can only have orgasms with you." This makes a man feel very potent and exceptional. This gives the woman a lot of leeway with him. I've seen orgasm monogamy used most effectively by non-monogamous women who want secure relationships with monogamous men. She power plays

her love into not minding her many other lovers because she assures him that she has orgasms only with him, Numero Uno.

"That is the most wonderful orgasm I have EVER had with ANYBODY!" Women who are looking for a powerful man to take care of them often use this power play to win them. Not only does it stroke the man for being potent, but it also strokes the woman for being so receptively sexy. If a woman uses this one often, she better hope her lovers never compare notes.

"Fuck?! You!? After what you did?!" Many couples fight as a passion substitute for sex. Often it is the woman who picks the fight. The fight enables her to avoid dealing with her sexual confusion and it exercises the power of denial over a partner to whom she may otherwise feel one-down.

"How come you don't want to fuck. You gay, or somethin'?" Since men can't say no, and they greatly fear the label of "homosexual," this power play can dare a guy to get an erection and prove he's a man.

"Yes, I do. No, I don't. Yes, no, yes, no . . ." Teasing is a traditional woman's way of controlling a man's sexuality. Often women truly don't know if they mean yes or no. Sometimes, however, they really are teasing. A general rule to keep away from the dangers of this one is: Say it straight. If you mean no, say no and mean it. And if you're ambiguous, explain the ambiguity. If a man thinks he's being teased, he should ask the woman if that's her intention. If it is, he should ask her to stop it and be direct.

"I have a: headache, yeast infection, test tomorrow, etc." When a woman feels guilty or scared about saying no to sex, any number of excuses can be utilized to put off her partner, especially if he's really pushy and insistent. If you find yourself saying no to sex with excuses like these, stop. Figure out what's going on. What are the real reasons you don't want sex?

"I'm pregnant. Marry me and/or give me money." When all else fails, this is the age-old way to nab a man.

"Help me make it through the night. I'm so lonely." How can a man leave a damsel in distress? She knows it would take a

particularly tough guy to say no to her plea for sexual company. Many a man who'd rather be alone or with someone else has Rescued a woman who wanted a partner for the night.

"You don't really love me. There's someone else." The point of this ploy is guilt. Women find they can get a lot out of men by playing on male guilt. What's a man to do with this one? Have sex with her to prove he loves her and there isn't anyone else? This doesn't sound like a real good reason for having sex. Often this power play is accompanied by a variation on the theme called:

Monogamy. In the monogamy power play, a woman insists that her lover, who has no desire to do so, become monogamous to prove he loves her. Despite all his strokes and reassurances that his other lovers don't take anything away from his feelings about her, she feels so insecure that only total sexual fidelity would convince her of his devotion. This doubly binds him. If he stays with his lovers, he feels guilty. If he gives them up for her, he's unhappy and resentful and will Persecute her, because it's a Rescue.

"But I made a wonderful dinner and it took all day and I spent my whole pay-check on this outfit!" This is the female version of sex is a reward. She may be beautiful, she may be a great cook; but if a man feels the lack of chemistry or compatibility—or he's just plain not turned on—there's no reason to get power-played into sex he doesn't desire.

"Sex roles in our current society make sex oppressive. I won't come until the Revolution!" I mention this power play because it tickles me so. I've heard a couple of women who consider themselves political radicals use this political justification for not wanting to have sex. Certainly society is oppressive and sex roles are, too. But who comes first—you or the Revolution? Using a more-political-than-thou argument to avoid sexual problem-solving is inventive, but not honest.

Sexual power plays destroy a relationship rapidly. If you believe your relationships use them, stop the process with some honest questioning and frank explaining. Otherwise, you'll soon be walking away hurt and angry and embittered, believing you've flunked sex and have no appeal, or that there are no good men in the world.

3. *No discounts: listen to each other.* Although discounting is a form of power play, it deserves to be singled out and highlighted as a necessity for equal relationships. Discounting is when one person fails to hear, or arbitrarily choses not to hear, what the other person is saying. A discounter assumes he or she knows better, or that what the other person says is of no consequence. If people get discounted enough, they can go quite crazy.

For instance, a woman may tell her lover "I want my clitoris stimulated" and he may discount her request and continue focusing on her vagina. He does this because he doesn't believe she really knows what she's talking about; and, besides, he wants to do things his own way.

Most commonly this happens when women tell men that they do not want to be sexual with them. The men discount the women by assuming that when they say no they really mean yes. The results of this sort of discounting are very unhappy.

Usually discounts are not overtly sexual. They occur in the relationship in general, and result in people being angry at each other and, consequently, sexually turned off. It may happen like this: A man shows up, uninvited. He's an old lover and he stopped by to say hello and get a little. He assumes that the woman will want to be sexy with him, too, and so he presumes a degree of intimacy immediately. She is annoyed and tells him so. "You're not annoyed," he replies. "You're hurt. Because I didn't call you before I came over." In one sentence he discounts her feelings by reinterpreting them. He presumes to know her emotions better than she. Also, it's more flattering to hurt someone than to merely annoy them.

This discount angers the woman. "Now I'm angry!" she says. "Sorry I hurt you," he continues. There is no resolution to this conversation because the man insists he is right and she wrong about her own feelings. Naturally, this discounting not only turns her off to him sexually, but in many other ways.

In sex, discounting causes communication problems. If a

woman says she likes a certain position and her partner happens to enjoy another so much he doesn't want to stop doing it, he may ignore her preferences. She, feeling pressured to do what she doesn't enjoy, may adapt to please him but resent it. Later on, since she has now Rescued him, she will Persecute him, and they will fight.

One of the most blatant signs of sexism is men failing to listen to women—to really hear what they are saying. In order to be equals, women and men must listen to each other. Sometimes it seems to me we are two different cultures trying to communicate. That's why we must pay close attention, and not resort to power plays like discounting to get what we want. 4. *No sexual secrets.* The rule of cooperative sexual relations is: no secrets. One of the major ways we Rescue in our sexual relationships is by keeping secrets. The biggest secrets we keep are not asking for what we want and not admitting to what we don't like.

We assume we should enjoy anything our partner does. We worry that what we want is weird, or wouldn't be enjoyed by our partner. We fear our lovers will leave us if they know the truth. And we worry that we will hurt his/her feelings if we ask for a change.

People have a right to sexual secrecy. But not at the expense of being unable to enjoy one's sexuality. When keeping secrets begins to interfere with pleasure, a decision must be made: Take a chance and divulge the secrets? Or not share them and continue not enjoying sex? Of course, this is an area of personal choice. No one can advise another about which secrets to keep and which to divulge. Still, the sharing of secrets usually has a favorable outcome for most couples.

Most secrets seem terrifying when we keep them bottled up inside us. Bringing them to light makes them less frightening. Often, just talking about sexuality with a group of women helps. We discuss things we swore we could never mention to anyone else in a million years. We talk about how we masturbate, about what turns us on, what our fantasies are—in great detail. After this sharing, we notice how warm and cleansed we feel. Our secrets turn out to be quite natural.

In relationships, it is important to express our needs openly. If a woman keeps it a secret that she likes to have her breasts kissed during intercourse, she will be dissatisfied and frustrated all those times her partner refrains from doing so. If her partner keeps it a secret that he'd like to have his penis kissed, he is going to feel equally unhappy whenever this doesn't happen. They will both feel they are missing something, and thus never fully enjoy sex together because of the anxiety caused by their secret needs. Obviously, they could both relax and enjoy it much more if they said what they wanted.

Basically, there are two types of sexual secrets. First, there are the turn-ons. These include fantasies and yearnings and may range from wanting a *ménage-à-trois* to craving curly hair, from using certain phrases to employing certain positions. They are infinite and can change from moment to moment. That's why it's important to communicate these needs. One day you may be into rubber alligators; and, the next day, just when your lover has brought you a dozen rubber alligators, you suddenly find you'd really prefer an entire day of petting and flirting. If you desire flirting and your lover is plying you with alligators, you will have trouble enjoying sex.

Secondly, there are the turn-offs. These are more difficult to admit. It will help to express them as a positive wish. Rather than saying, "I don't like your sweaty smell," say, "It would turn me on if you took a shower."

A turn-off to one person may be a turn-on to someone else. To use a personal example, cigarette-smoking is an absolutely non-negotiable turn-off to me. But I know a woman who finds both the taste and odor of cigarettes erotic and she prefers her lovers to be smokers. If something about a person revolts you—and it's something they could do something about to help turn you on—don't keep your suggestions to yourself. Ask for the change, and take a chance you'll get it.

However, if what turns you off about a person cannot be changed, explain to them how you feel rather than leaving them confused and unhappy. It's perfectly all right to tell a blond man that you're just not into blonds, but prefer your lovers to be dark-haired. Of course, he might go out and buy a wig—but deal with that one when it happens. The point is: You do not have to be turned on to everybody.

The more intimate and long-term the relationship, the more complex becomes the problem of secrets. Do you tell each other about affairs with other lovers? Do you say when you feel turned on to someone else even though you've both agreed to be monogamous? Does intimacy require each fantasy to be divulged? These are agreements you must make between yourselves.

Some secrets are yours and yours alone. (Like the ones you keep when you masturbate.) Others serve only to create paranoia and bad feelings between you and your lover. The distinguishing factor is whether or not a secret affects your sexual relationship in a negative manner. Sex is for fun, for pleasure, for sustenance. When considering secrets, think: first things first. Total psychological nudity between a couple need occur only when a commitment has been made to relate, to build, to endure. You can judge what needs to be shared and what doesn't by the extent of your intimacy.

SEXISM: NON-MONOGAMY VS. MONOGAMY

The biggest secrets between couples seem to revolve around two words: monogamy and non-monogamy. How much freedom do we really want? How much can we take? What do we do about jealousy? What is fair to our partner? and to us?

Many couples have decided they don't want to be monogamous, even though they are devoted to each other in a primary way. Yet, in the interest of opening up their relationship and enhancing their lives by allowing in more strokes, they consider the possibilities of being non-monogamous (or "non-monotonous," as one couple terms it). Any agreements made must be done so with this in mind: very often non-monogamy is discriminatory to women.

Non-monogamy favors men because sexism gives men more sexual freedom than women. Men's higher emotional capacity to participate in recreational sex—plus the comparative lack of sexual discrimination against them as they age—offers men more choices and opportunities for finding other lovers. If a couple in their forties decides that monogamy is too confining, chances are the man will find a lover long before the woman does. A fortyish man is still considered virile and will attract women of all ages. A woman in her forties is considered old and past her sexual prime. If the man works while she remains at home, he'll have the entire secretarial pool to consider, while she'll have to hope that the mailman or washer-repair man are cuties. A man's cultural scripting enables him to have affairs without becoming emotionally involved. A woman's scripting is the opposite; she finds she can't have enjoyable sex with a new man unless she truly likes him.

Unless a woman leads a life with as much availability for strokes as a man's, non-monogamy will be very difficult for a couple to handle.

Nor can non-monogamy ever be considered a cure for relationships that are faltering. Some couples use non-monogamy to avoid intimacy and to gloss over problems. A man may desire it because he's bored with his wife but wants to avoid confronting the problems between them. Some women use it to find another man so they can exit from one relationship into another without ever having to be alone in between. Because of the power-play potential of non-monogamy, don't consider this innovation if your relationship is having difficulties. Solve your problems first; and then see if non-monogamy still interests you.

As for what to do when one person wants monogamy and the other doesn't: Unless you are living together, you are both free to have the sex lives you want. If a man doesn't share his territory with a woman, he has no right to demand she be monogamous, or vice versa.

If you live on the same turf, then negotiation and compromise are needed. If he's having other lovers and she watches him come home from a night out, unless she's very secure or his affairs secretly excite her, she can't help but feel jealous. (And it works the other way, too.) This is a difficult problem and requires a strong relationship where both partners feel confident in themselves and each other.

So let's say you both decide you want your relationship to be non-monogamous and you both feel good and equal about the agreement between you. Now the next thing to consider is who to be non-monogamous with. This is another area where equality is just as important.

If you are in a couple relationship, it is not fair to expect a person not in a couple relationship to get deeply involved with you. If a man is emotionally committed to a primary relationship, it is expecting an unequal situation to succeed if he asks a woman without an equally strong and important relationship to have an affair with him.

It may work once or twice, but not much more than that, without her getting hurt. Women usually like to have sex with friends, people they can count on. If a man is committed emotionally to someone else, he cannot be the true friend she may want.

You have two choices when you decide how to have non-monogamous relationships:

— You can choose to have them with equals; or
— You can talk straight about your situation to someone who isn't equal to you and see if they remain interested.

If you chose to have other lovers, you must do some honest-talking. Be they male or female, you must find out if their hearts are as involved with others as yours is—and if their expectations concerning this affair are the same as yours.

Jealousy

Your lover and you have made a non-monogamy agreement. He says it is O.K. for you to have other lovers and you give him the go-ahead as well. Now, what about the jealousies and fears you both can't help but feel?

To begin with, decide how much you want to know about your lover's other lovers. You want to know all, you say. Why? Are your motives honest—or do you want to hear so that you can act hurt, and thus hope to make your partner feel so guilty he'll decide to give it all up and stay solely with you? You don't want to hear anything, you say. But won't that make you paranoid? Won't you wonder every time you make love with him if he's thinking of you or comparing you with someone else? Just how much truth can you tolerate in such circumstances? Too much can hurt—and too little can drive you up the wall.

If you are of the rare breed that is actually titillated by accounts of your lover's affairs, then you'll truly want to hear all. But if you belong to the majority, you'll be jealous. And thus you'll need to compromise. Here are a few suggestions.

If you don't live together, you have no right to exercise control over another's sex-life. So if you inquire about their activities, you are responsible for taking care of yourself when you hear the truth. If it upsets you, it's not fair to expect your lover to glue you back together, or for you to fall apart and make him feel guilty. Call a friend and talk with her until you become more reasonable. Or figure out why you're feeling so bad and ask for what you need to feel better. "Do you still love me?" you can ask, for example.

You can also ask your lover to not make comparisons. Often people get a rush of power comparing one lover to another. This can turn quite vindictive. For example, if your sex-life hasn't been so hot lately, and your lover has until now been exhibiting nothing but patience, he can express his secret resentment by suddenly raving, "That one should be in the

Guinness World Book of Records—she has so many orgasms!"
While you seethe with put-down hurt and anger, he can pretend innocence. As a rule, comparisons are power plays.

Understand that jealousy is a perfectly natural feeling whenever you feel you're not getting something you need and you see someone else is. Jealousy is quite appropriate in such a situation, so when the ugly green monster raises its head, decide if your jealousy is valid. Then ask for what you need to dispel it. "I need to know I'm special" or "I need a contract for at least a year-long primary commitment" are common requests women make.

Whatever agreements you make regarding monogamy/ non-monogamy, keep in mind you're being innovative and that is not always smooth sailing. Ask friends to help you out—don't get trapped behind secrets while trying to appear cool and "groovy."

Time and Place for Telling Secrets

At a workshop a few weeks ago, a woman raised her hand and said, "I asked for what I wanted and he wouldn't do it."

"How did you ask?" I inquired.

"Well," she began, "it was about three o'clock in the morning and we had just gotten into sex and—"

I told her to go no further. "Your timing is off! That's one reason you got 'no' for an answer."

Which brings us to another subtlety of the no-secrets rule. If you have a secret you want to share, how do you do it? Do you deliver it at the breakfast table, very casually, like: "Pass the granola and, oh, by the way, your friend George is great in the sack"? Or do you spring it in bed, just as you're both getting turned on, by murmuring, "Let's stop for a minute. I want to discuss our lousy sex-life."

In order to be heard, you need to speak when the circumstances are most auspicious. To discuss sexual secrets that are inherently difficult to divulge, first create the atmosphere most conducive to getting the results you want. Early morning hours, when one is stoned or drunk, or just getting turned on, or in the middle of a crowd of people—all these do not furnish an atmosphere for open minds and attitudes.

If you are trying to share a difficult secret, don't do it in the bed. It's a good idea to not discuss sexual differences in bed, period. Rather, make arrangements to talk to each other over a drink or dinner, so you are both at your best. Some people even prefer exchanging letters rather than talking.

If you have fun secrets to share, don't be shy. Be impetuous. Shy about saying it right out loud? Then send a note, or a little poem. One man in a group gave a woman lover a bracelet that reminded him of her vagina. She felt very flattered.

If the secrets you are keeping are big ones and appear to be non-negotiable, even possibly destructive to your relationship, phone a friend. You may find it helpful to ask a third person you both trust to sit in on the conversation and support you both while you talk your secrets out.

Cooperation is the most difficult part of relationships because people have not been taught to do it. Men have been taught to compete with other men, women with other women. Women have been socialized to "cooperate" with men by doing what they say. But most men have never even considered cooperating with women. To them cooperation means being "pussy-whipped."

Consequently, learning to be equals in cooperation is the most challenging part of making good relationships. It is where inequalities, competitive feelings, needs for power, and jealousies are revealed at their ugliest. Yet it is also the area where the regard and care you have for each other can be proven. By listening closely to each other, women and men will learn new ways of relating that will give them not only the magic of romance but also the security of reality.

Asking for What You Want

CHAPTER 8.   Many women complain, "It's not romantic to talk during sex. It spoils it." They're right on one count—it's not old-fashioned romantic; and wrong on another—it doesn't spoil it. One of the biggest myths passed on to us is: The Golden Silence of Magical Sex. This has us believing that True Love and Romance is embodied in one classic love-making bout where we and our lover meet, unite perfectly, and have a simultaneous orgasm—all in five minutes flat. So how many times has that happened to you lately?

According to most women I've spoken with, the first time is often the most uncomfortable. Styles are different, likes and dislikes aren't obvious, and neither person is a mind reader. A lot of cues and "radar-beamed" desires are missed. Like first conversations between two people, it is often an anxious, tentative affair. Many women admit, "I never can come the first time I make love with someone. Too much else is going on."

The idea of perfect love being silent has made more women miserable—and men, too—than I would care to count. Due to this myth, women have faked orgasms and continued for years to have sex they didn't enjoy, feeling guilty because they weren't "really sexy" and taking all the blame for not enjoying it. Silent sex means: "Don't ask for what you want."

Women often refrain from asking because they're afraid their assertiveness will have disastrous effects on their lovers.

"He'll go limp." "He'll think I'm pushy." So, shrugging their shoulders, they "adapt."

In order to enjoy sex together, both partners must feel free to abandon themselves. You know that elsewhere in your life, whenever you let yourself go, you've first made sure the situation was safe enough to allow you to do so. The same holds for sex. You must first establish an atmosphere conducive to your abandonment to sexual pleasures. If you can't count on your lover to come through for you, the situation isn't safe—and you won't be able to relax. Therefore, you must construct your environment for sexual pleasure carefully. Only by talking as you proceed, telling what it is you want and need, can you make it safe.

HOW TO ASK

"Ask for what you want" is easier said than done. After being told for so many years not to ask, it takes a little while to get our asking abilities in working order. Even now, after doing this work for three years and trying my damnedest to practice what I preach, I still find myself thinking I'm being specific in asking for my needs, and then discovering I'm being obtuse.

Determining Where Sex Goes Wrong

It is helpful in learning to ask to first determine at what moment sex starts going wrong and feeling bad to you. When I was first asked to do this I replied, "What do you mean? Why, the whole thing feels bad!" When forced to clarify, I realized that there was, indeed, a point where I turned off, where everything started going wrong—and, as a result, the whole sexual experience felt bad.

Because I'm such a romantic fool—and I love it for the most part—love-making for me was one great amorphous experience, beginning with kissing and ending with intercourse—and, hopefully, orgasm (at least for him)—with a lot of huffing and puffing in between. Reviewing this whirlwind of activity to locate the point where it began to feel bad was like trying to distinguish the one rotten apple in a jar of applesauce. To help myself out, I finally broke down the act of sex into five points. (I must emphasize that these are not to be turned into a rigid system that wipes out any spontaneity you've got going for you. These are merely guideposts to help you decide where it is you want your own love-making to start feeling better.)

1. *Anticipation.* This is the fantasy stage, the part before you even touch, when your mind is full of plots and schemes and hot feelings. That is, you feel this way if you are anticipating *pleasurable* sex. However, if sex worries you, this Anticipation phase may be the first point when you begin to turn off. Instead of pleasure, you grow fearful, disinterested, skittish.

One woman confided that, as soon as sex got going, it felt great. But the anticipation scared her. "I'm afraid I'll have to perform, do something I can't." Another said, "I worry so much I can't ever get excited. I worry I won't come. I worry I'll get pregnant. In the end, all I do is . . . worry!"

By determining what would turn you on rather than off in anticipation, you can devise ways to relieve yourself of such concerns. One method is deciding long in advance with your partner when you want to have sex; thus, you can be prepared and not at all surprised by his sexual expectations. You can also discuss birth control, body smell, and orgasm expectations ahead of time so your worries are resolved and you're free to happily anticipate a sexy time.

2. *Commitment.* At a certain point in your anticipations, you must decide 'yes' or 'no'. When you decide yes, I like it, I'll do it, you make the commitment to plunge into sex.

Many women never have a chance to make a clear commitment. It is done for them by their partners, usually men, who assume that sex is part of every encounter. We go along, uncertain: Do I want this? Maybe I do. But I'm not turned on. Well, maybe I'll feel better after he sticks it in. No, I don't like this. But I have to now—I'm committed!

Understand that your lack of active commitment is still a commitment. Being silent or passive is making a decision. When you go along because you can't say no, then you're committing yourself to sex on his terms. This can be a pretty mediocre experience; so what you've committed yourself to is more unhappy sex.

A way to avoid being wishy-washy is making a deal with yourself beforehand. Before getting into it, hear yourself say "Yes, I want this" or "No, I don't." Don't throw your mind away and get carried along passively.

You can also tell your partner that, for the next week, or until you talk again, *you* want to be the one who initiates sex. If it is going to happen, you will be the person who asks. By making such an arrangement you both get a chance to relax. He is relieved from having to do all the initiating, and you're relieved from having to constantly say "No, not now" or "Well, I suppose." With this cooperative arrangement you will both be sure that when sex is proposed, it is truly wanted.

3. *Abandonment.* After you've made the commitment to jump into sex, you must let yourself go. This means truly abandoning yourself to the good feelings of sexuality, to the pleasures of allowing your mind to float away and your body to become vitally alive.

But stop for a moment. If you aren't enjoying what happens this far, how can you truly abandon yourself? Maybe this is the point where things go wrong for you. Any number of complications can keep you from letting go. Perhaps, just as you get turned on, he wants intercourse. This throws you. You need more love-play—but you don't know how to say 'no' to intercourse yet. Maybe the problem is not being able to tell your lover what you like.

Some women report their parents' scowling faces loom before them whenever they become sexually aroused. Others hear certain nuns haunting them. "There's Sister Mary, scolding me for being a bad girl!" they think, regressing to childhood terrors. The voices and faces of people who gave us negative associations toward sex as children can prevent us from feeling pleasure as adults. Certainly the voices of sexism prevent many women from enjoying sex. "Nice girls don't" and "I'll look ugly if I let go" are sexist injunctions that dampen the passions of many women.

In order to abandon yourself, you must create an atmosphere in which you feel safe. That's why choosing your environment, talking honestly to your partner, knowing what you like to give you orgasm, and having support to express your sexual feelings are so important. When you have these securities, then you're finally free to let go—and enjoy.

4. *The Orgasm.* If you feel safe and you know what you need in order to come, you can usually have an orgasm. "Selfishness" is a prerequisite to coming. That means you focus solely on your own needs during that part of sex in which you want your orgasm. Usually women have trouble being orgasmic because they give most of their attention to their partners. We worry about whether or not he's enjoying, and if he's going to come too soon, or not at all. If we put as much focus on ourselves we'd have more orgasms. "Self-centeredness" is necessary to achieve your orgasm and let it come sweeping over you.

One woman told the group that there were times when she'd had splendid orgasms. That only happened, though, when she was so completely absorbed into herself and her excitement that she lost touch with her partner. "After I quit coming I opened my eyes and was surprised—'Oh! You're still here,' I'd say to him. He'd laugh. He knows he's been there because he's been the one turning me on." You must feel safe to get as lost as this woman in order to enjoy your orgasms to the fullest.

If you're having trouble coming, don't be critical of yourself. Read the chapter on Masturbation (Chapter 10) and do the specific exercises given to help you share orgasms with a lover.

To clear your head, air all your feelings. Then keep in mind how it is you achieve orgasms when you masturbate and re-create that situation with your lover.

Don't be left frustrated. Masturbate with your partner, or by yourself later, to give yourself an orgasm. Needless to say, constant frustration establishes a negative pattern, to such an extent that you may become afraid to get turned on. I remember a woman who had been on the excited edge of orgasms for years and yet had never once "gone over the top." She said her knees hurt so much now she couldn't sleep; so she refused any sort of sexual contact with her fiancé to avoid this pain. As soon as she gave herself orgasms by masturbating, the knee pains vanished. "Now I only feel weak in the knees!" she said, for she no longer feared having sex with her lover.

5. *Afterglow*. After an orgasm, women feel relieved, stimulated, refreshed, exhausted, happy, sad; a whole gamut of emotions. This is the time when women say they want to cuddle, and men get up, take a shower, go to work, or else they roll over and start snoring. You're left alone.

If you don't like sex because you anticipate this lonely ending, take care of yourself. Complain. Explain how it feels. Tell your partner what you want. Most partners discover it's nice to stay in bed a little longer, snuggling up, giving each other strokes.

If your lover is the type who exits to work shortly after love-making and has all sorts of elaborate reasons to explain it, don't feel you have to accept the situation. Trust your intuitions. Is he merely using you for some good old alienated sex? Is he more into "getting his rocks off" than into mutual fun? Is he a "workoholic," more in love with the office than you?

If this is his style, get another lover. Or else agree to have sex with him only when he has enough time and interest to do it the way you want. In any case, make sure you discuss it and say what you want—no holds barred. You have a right to know what is going on with him, and you have a right to ask for, and get, what you desire.

The Art of Asking

Because we all get tongue-tied and nervous when it comes to asking for what we want in sex, here are some basic techniques women in groups have found useful.

1. *Rehearse ahead of time.* In asking for what you want, begin by rehearsing it ahead of time. Do this either with your women's group, or alone at home in front of a mirror, or both. Rehearsing enables you to smooth out all the kinks ahead of time. You can get as excited, melodramatic, shy, scared, or angry as you'd like before your mirror or group and thus refine this inchoate mass of emotions into the most sensible approach before confronting your partner.

For example: Joan said she was so scared when she told her lover how to touch her that her voice hardened and she sounded, and felt, like a traffic cop. "To the left. Stop. Go. Up. Down. Etc." By rehearsing with her in group we were able to help Joan relax, letting her go over it until she felt confident and comfortable saying it.

Margie said she once spent an entire day pacing her apartment, delivering a dramatic monologue to the walls in preparation to telling her lover what she wanted. "I tried a million different approaches and techniques. I yelled, I cried, I cajoled, I whispered—the works. When I finally did it in reality all my work boiled down to one or two good sentences. But it paid off—I got what I wanted."

It's difficult to overcome both female "passivity" and the social injunction not to ask for needs. Practice makes perfect.

To take another example, Kay didn't enjoy "sixty-nineing" with her lover, Sam. At first, she didn't even bother to bring it up in group. She assumed that "sixty-nine" was something everyone who was sexually healthy enjoyed, and that her revulsion was just another of her personal hang-ups. But after various women began voicing other dislikes, Kay realized she didn't have to like every sexual possibility.

Kay now had the courage to speak up. "I don't know if this is true of anyone else, but I don't enjoy 'sixty-nine.' " She paused for breath, and Libby immediately jumped in. "Oh—that's true for me, too." With Libby's support, Kay felt more confident and went on: "Doing 'sixty-nine' confuses me. I can't get into feeling what he's doing to me because I'm so busy doing to him. But I'm afraid to tell my lover. He'll think I don't like him." The group then suggested Kay role-play asking her lover for what she wanted. (You can do this by yourself by saying out loud, before talking to your lover, everything you want to say. Remember, this is only a rehearsal. Do it in front of a mirror to watch how you come across. By the time you talk to your lover, you'll know exactly what to say and how to put it across.)

Kay began, "Honey, I know this may sound weird to you, but, uh, there's this problem I'm having with sex. Uh. (Cough.) I don't . . . enjoy doing . . . uh, 'sixty-nine.' Anything else—I love it—but not 'sixty-nine.' "

The group then suggested Kay switch roles and reply as she believed her lover would. Kay continued:

"But, sweetheart, I love to do that with you. I love to turn you on that way."

"I know that," Kay herself replied, "but I don't. I mean, it's not my favorite thing. I don't want to hurt your feelings, but 'sixty-nine' confuses me so much I can't concentrate on enjoying what you're doing to me."

The role-play conversation continued along this line for a few more minutes. Kay would justify her displeasure with "sixty-nine" and her lover would come back with how much he enjoyed it. Round and round they went, trying to convince each other. Finally Libby got so impatient, she stopped Kay. "You still haven't said what *you* want! You've explained and explained—but you have not made a single demand. You haven't actually made a request."

This illustrates a common problem in asking: We think we've made it clear because we've explained it. Yet all we've made clear is our dislike, not our like. Women are often afraid to make demands about sexual needs. We worry that our decisiveness will turn lovers off. But if we don't make demands, we don't get what we want. We suggest what we'd like without stating it clearly. Such ambiguity defeats us because it's a Rescue and we'll ultimately Persecute. Also, when you make a demand, you don't have to keep justifying. A demand can't be argued away—it must be dealt with.

Finally, Kay said, "Sam, I don't want to do 'sixty-nine.' "

"Why not?"

"I don't enjoy it. It doesn't feel good. But I love to eat you and have you do cunnilingus on me—separately. O.K.?"

"You mean all these months you haven't been turned on to me?"

"That's not true. The only thing that doesn't turn me on is 'sixty-nine.' Everything else about you does."

"O.K. Let's do it your way now."

When Kay went home and did this for real, her role-play turned out to be quite accurate. Initially, Sam was disappointed and had difficulty getting an erection because he felt insecure. Finally he admitted he was worried she didn't enjoy sex with him at all.

"I kissed his penis and tickled him until he got turned on again. I told him how sexy he was. After that we did just fine. What a relief, too! I didn't have to worry the whole time about *that* part. I felt free to enjoy myself for a change. This asking-for-what-you-want stuff isn't easy, but it sure pays off!"

2. *Don't ask in bed.* The first time you ask for what you want, try not to do it in bed in order to avoid this kind of situation:

It's two in the morning. You and your lover have had a fine evening and you want to top it off with some good sex. You get into bed. You go through all your regular preparations. But just as he decides he'd like intercourse, the same way he has always done for months now, you stop him. "I don't like intercourse," you say. "Let's massage instead." He's exhausted, he's already on the edge of an orgasm, and his patience is wearing thin. Rather than responding to your suggestion, he rolls over and falls asleep. You're furious. "So much for asking for what *I* want!" you fume, muttering to yourself phrases like "chauvinist creep."

Women have discovered that it is better to discuss major changes they'd like in love-making *before* getting involved in the sexual situation. Talk about such things when you're not sexually excited. When you're turned on, who has the patience for a complicated conversation?

Many women like to initiate telling their partners what they like by talking over the phone. If you're shy and face-to-face contact causes lockjaw, the telephone can provide the right amount of anonymity to protect you.

One of my favorite ploys—because it's such a great tease—is to spend dinner discussing what you sexually enjoy. Over a plate of good food and some fine wine, not to mention candlelight, sharing with each other the specifics of your sexual wishes can turn into a tantalizing couple of hours. Shy? Then look on it as an interview. You're interviewing this person to see if you're sexually compatible. Just as you would interview a new acquaintance to see what you both have in common, you can do the same with someone you have chemistry for. Even if what they like doesn't turn you on, it's not going to bore you to hear about it. Fantasies over food are wonderful entertainment. Isn't hearing, "I dream of walking through an undulating field of soft golden breasts," more interesting than gossip about the latest Young Democratic Lawyers meeting? And it's easier for you to say "I love a long massage" here than in the middle of the seduction. Cue your lover ahead of time. It makes for a more sensual session later.

In bed you can remind your lover of what you talked about earlier. You can remind him with a touch or a kiss or a few words. But do the bulk of the discussion before making love. You'll be more relaxed and better able to enjoy yourself.

3. *Ask your lover to do his fifty percent.* Women often ask, "How do I get my lover to ask for what he wants?" Once more, ask him.

Tell him that you need to know what he enjoys. You need

feedback—in sounds, words, or gestures. Be specific. "I need to know when you come," or, "I need to know if you like this caress."

By asking for what you want, you have set an example. You are opening love-making to change and to requests. When you take that romantic silence out of sex, you are giving your lover the freedom to ask, also.

If your lover begs off with a headache, says no, or just exhibits a lack of interest, do not fall apart. Part of the risk of asking is the risk of rejection. Remember: If you didn't ask, you still wouldn't get. So the odds are with you to take a dare and make requests.

When he says no, decide if it's the truth or a power play. If you're curious, inquire.

Women are so unaccustomed to asking, so fearful of being turned down, we hesitate to put ourselves on the line. But do it. It's a big step toward becoming equals with men. The more you ask, the more you get. Gradually you'll get over your fear of rejection and come to take an occasional "no" in stride.

4. *Ask for one hundred percent of what you want.* This is the final, and most important, part of asking for what you want. If you don't ask for every last bit of what you want, then you'll end up compromising before you've even begun to bargain.

Too often we think, "I can't possibly get all that"—so we don't ask, we don't even try. No wonder, then, that what we finally get we're dissatisfied with—it's a watered-down version of a watered-down version.

So don't edit your copy beforehand. Don't assume that anything is impossible. Go for all of it, and you'll be surprised at how much you will get.

Loving Alternatives to Heterosexual Relationships

CHAPTER 9.   ". . . Since I've been masturbating I've felt much more centered. I had no idea how much of what I do is connected to feeling good about myself sexually."

". . . I masturbated against a tree during a thunderstorm. I used to think only God could 'make' a tree!"

". . . Since I can give myself my own orgasms I've gotten rid of a lot of 'old hats'; that is, men I kept around solely for sex and security."

". . . I had trouble getting into masturbating. I thought, 'What's the point of orgasms without a man?' But gradually I got into it, and found I could do more by myself, be more imaginative and daring. It's fun!"

". . . I wish my mother would masturbate. It would make her happier."

". . . I thought my angry energy would be uncontrollably violent if I let myself masturbate to orgasm. I was scared to feel strong, passionate emotions because I feared hurting myself or someone else. But I found that masturbating helped me separate the angry energy from loving energy."

". . . I like to masturbate after intercourse. I don't come during intercourse, but I can always come masturbating."

MASTURBATION, LOVING OURSELVES, CELEBRATING OURSELVES

Most of us think of sex and love-making as something that happens only with another person, usually a man. If we touch ourselves alone or have orgasms alone, we consider that a second-rate activity, not truly sex or love-making. When one stops and thinks about this dichotomy it's obvious an imbalance exists. We let others love us more than we let ourselves love us. We find others enjoy our bodies more than we ourselves do. We look for others to turn us on because we feel too alienated from our sexuality to know how to please ourselves.

In truth, we have two equally important sexual relationships: the one with ourselves and the one we choose to share with partners. Masturbation is far more than just "getting off" or something to do as a last resort when we're lonely and frustrated. Masturbating is making love to ourselves. It is acknowledging our sexuality to ourselves, getting to know our bodies and our erotic feelings. It's discovering what we enjoy sexually, as opposed to what we think we should enjoy.

Since the women's movement began we've been creating many new ways to make ourselves whole and strong. One of those ways has been to discover who we are as women. To do this we have discarded the cardboard images men had of us. We have stopped trying to emulate men, and have been re-creating ourselves in our own images.

As women, we discovered, we are fine. We lack nothing—though we have much to learn. We don't feel or think like men, nor are we physically like them. Nor does each woman do things exactly like any of her sisters. Our strength is in being ourselves, and in finding brothers and sisters who love us and support us in our uniqueness.

Masturbation can re-create our sexuality for us. It lets us discover and define who we are. And because sexuality and intimate relationships are so intertwined, the more we discover who we are with ourselves the more confidence we gain in expecting, and getting, intimate relationships with others, of the kind that respect our sexuality, and, therefore, ourselves.

Masturbation offers a very personal way of getting to know ourselves. To allow time to masturbate also gives us time to be alone with ourselves. Such time can be used in many ways: for meditation, for celebrating our strengths, for soothing our depressions. Masturbation can ease our menstrual cramps and our menopausal "hot flashes." It can also bring us closer to our feelings, for the deep breathing and focused attention—the sheer physical exertion of orgasm—often arouse profound sensations of sadness, fear, anger, and joy.

Not only that, masturbating is fun when you're sexually turned on and can't stand it one moment longer! Many women masturbate during or after sex, with their partners, in order to satisfy themselves completely. Orgasms are more than "clit"-deep, one might say.

WOMEN LOVERS

Many women become terribly confused over the prospect of having women lovers. And yet, wherever I've gone to do workshops, ranging from small Midwest towns to huge urban centers, women want to know about the possibilities and considerations of being gay. "Am I gay?" they ask. "Should I be?"

There are two primary reasons women discuss this issue. One is the feeling that they *should* be gay: the sexual revolution and the women's movement demand it. The reasoning here is that since we are in love with our sisters emotionally, since we are so close physically and mentally, often hugging and kissing each other easily, why stop there? After all, if we were in a similar relationship with a man we'd most likely be having sex.

There is a lot of truth in this argument. In some respects, it does seem sexist and unfair to eliminate sex from our relationships with women. The problem arises with that word "should." Many women have already convinced themselves that their lack of erotic feelings toward women constitutes a form of discrimination, an ingrained sexism. And many lesbian women certainly agree with this.

Indeed, it *is* a difficult question: Why am I turned on to women in all ways but sex? The answer is so complex and personal that each woman must trust the rightness of her own feelings, disregarding what is "hip" or fashionable.

Women who have had very bad sexual experiences with men often consider the benefits of being lesbian. As one gay woman told a group, "I think being heterosexual is a very dangerous decision because of the potential for violence by men against women." Women who have been battered by men not only physically but emotionally many times turn to other women for the gentleness, equality, and heart-felt loving they cannot find elsewhere.

Women also consider having women lovers due to what they call the "man problem." Women have noticed that most men are so slow to acquire a feminist consciousness there's a definite time-lag between female and male consciousness; and, consequently, there aren't many men around who aren't sexist. With this shortage of available males, it is only logical that many women are feeling turned on to other women because in the profoundest sense they already love them.

Since men, in general, have admitted no sexual problems, they have not organized groups to work together. By contrast, women working in groups have not only solved most of their sexual problems, but re-defined their relationship needs as well as their needs from men. They are acutely aware of sexism and sex roles. Deciding they cannot accept such stereotypes any more, they have said: "I want men who are friends first, who treat me as an equal. I want a man who can talk about his emotions and his feelings—not only about sex, but about everything." Consequently, women find there are few men who interest them. At first they feel angry about this gap. Then disappointed. Then desperate. Inevitably, someone comes up with the obvious: "I wish men were like women. When I meet a woman I like, we feel *simpatico* right away. That doesn't happen with men. Why am I emotionally turned on by women but physically turned off by men?"

What about being gay, then? Is it a viable solution?

First, though, let's explore the pros and cons of deciding to be sexual with another woman. The question here specifically involves one woman's wish to be sexual with another woman, and not the far more major decision to be gay. There is a big difference. Forget the myth which says that if we are turned on to women and have a couple of homosexual experiences we are lesbians for life. This myth prevents us from fully exploring our own feelings about other women. Yet we must be free to do so, without ever feeling that this forces us to assume a whole new lifestyle and philosophy—that of being gay. The latter is another question, entirely; one I am not qualified to write about, since I myself am not gay.

I am qualified, though, to explore the considerations involved in deciding to have a woman lover. (Does that make me bisexual? Such labels are terribly restrictive.)

First of all, why do it? Well, for one thing, it's fun! Beyond that, making love with another woman is in many ways like making love to yourself, which is a very beautiful and self-accepting experience. It's easy to relate to a woman sexually. You know what to do with each other because you know what women like. You do to her what you enjoy yourself. Women instinctively understand each other's sexual needs; and, in this way, there is less of a sex-gap to be bridged.

Many women recall the sensual good times they had playing with their girl friends or sisters when they were very young. Before we learned it was "bad," many of us discovered our first sexual pleasure with another girl in a "let's-play-and-ain't-this-fun" sort of way. As grown-up women we can enjoy each other in the same manner, if we so desire.

Many bisexual women like to point out that feeling free to

make love to women opens up a whole new world of sexual intimacy to them, and eliminates the panic about Saturday night. It's a great relief to know you can enjoy a date with a woman as much as a date with a man, especially during these times when relationships between men and women seem so unsettled.

But not everything recommends having a woman lover. The fact that today's sexual revolution predicates a "should" about being gay must also be considered. Because the liberated women is expected to be *totally* liberated, it is easy to reason, "I *should* be gay to be liberated." Proving our sexual freedom by having sex with another woman because we feel we ought to, rather than because we feel turned on and want to, causes hurt feelings and can ruin good friendships. What's more, this is the same sort of adapting we have previously done with our men lovers—and it didn't feel good then, did it? We are not liberated when we respond to "should's," no matter how radical they appear to be.

Some women also state that our romantic sex-role conditioning can make sexual relationships between women difficult. This conditioning tells us, against our better judgment, that having sex with someone also means having a relationship with them. Commitment is expected because we shared sexual intimacy. Women do not traditionally have the freedom of dalliance men exercise and enjoy. So if two women make love, there is often the expectation that this is it, a relationship; when in fact what either or both might have been seeking was a brief encounter. It's a good idea to discuss this problem ahead of time so both of you understand each other's expectations.

When we think of being sexual with another woman, many social injunctions come to our minds. We have already mentioned the "gay-for-life" myth. There are also the old taboos about homosexuality: that it's a "perversion," that it's "sick" or "weird." We grew up with those, and they will not be overcome in a few weeks or years.

With a woman lover we cannot be affectionate in public except in certain permissive parts of the nation. This creates a certain tension that is not pleasant. We have to hide our feelings from our family and some of our friends; perhaps even create subterfuge in our job. It is difficult to feel positive about a love affair when we know that to reveal it would make us social outcasts.

An added complication is that many women first make love to each other at the instigation of some man. For many men, the ultimate trip is being made love to by two women. Unless all members of a *ménage-à-trois* feel equal in their roles, and the women are as turned on to each other as they are to the man, this can grow into an uncomfortable and sexist situation. Sexist because it is always safer to focus on the man and make sure he's satisfied: after all, we know how to do that. Still, with just one penis to go around, the two women can be left dangling, unsure with one another, and not at all certain they want to remain here fulfilling some guy's fantasy.

Many women believe becoming gay will solve their orgasm problems. They assume that the sexual and relationship problems they experienced with men will automatically clear up once they are relating to women. This is not true, as women in groups have discovered. Gay relationships have the same problems as heterosexual ones: poor communication, reacting to paranoias rather than facts, unclear expectations, one person being more aggressive than the other. Stereotypical relationships are sexist—no matter what the sexes of the participants. If a woman doesn't know how to have orgasms before she has sex with another woman she will not automatically become orgasmic just because she's with a woman.

And yet, as Woody Allen says, "Being bisexual immediately doubles your chances on Saturday night." More and more women are considering having women lovers. It is a freeing, loving, exciting alternative. If you choose a woman lover, however, do it only if you are truly sexually excited by her—and not just feeling you ought to be.

Heterosexism in Sex Therapy

It is generally assumed by both women and men that women want and prefer male lovers. Not only is this a sexist assumption, but it's also not always true; and, in fact, reflects our cultural norms, prejudices, and fears.

In every group I make sure to stress right from the start that having sexual feelings towards other women are as important and as normal as having sexual feelings towards men. How can a woman feel free to create her sexuality unless she receives support from her group leader and co-workers to be whomever she wants sexually, even if that means being bisexual or gay?

This is doubly important because another fact of heterosexism is that women are not considered valuable as lovers; certainly not as valuable as men. As we explore our sexual feelings and open ourselves to the various possibilities of expressing our sexuality, it is important to consider our sisters as lovers, too. I am not saying we *should* have women lovers; I am saying we should not automatically close ourselves to such prospects due to prejudice, fear, or social conditioning.

In the beginning—and it still remains so for the majority of sexual-therapy situations—all groups presumed that women were interested in solving their sexual problems exclusively with men. This bias brought about two problems that are as yet unsolved: Lesbian women are discriminated against in these heterosexual therapies; and, because of this, many have had no choice but to solve their own sexual problems working exclusively with other gay women—or not at all. This heterosexism keeps gay and straight women isolated from each other on a subject that, ideally, unites us. Gay and straight women alike have female bodies, female sexuality, and female orgasms. Whenever we have shared our experiences in group, it has always proved helpful to both gay and straight women, and the group receives the additional benefit of women understanding each other regarding a life-style that had once seemed so threatening and mystified.

In turn, lesbian women discover their problems are similar to those of heterosexual women—lack of information, oppression by certain myths, inability to communicate clearly. The heterosexual bias of our culture still regards homosexuality as a neurotic response needing correction and rehabilitation. Thus, even if a gay woman finds approval for her sexual choices, she may still be unable to find sexual help from women who have no personal experiences or political understanding of the problems of lesbian women.

Complicating this heterosexism is the backlash of reverse homosexism coming from some gay women. For example, a woman may appear at group and state, "I'm not feeling turned on to men." Her problem could be understood in a number of ways. If the therapist is heterosexually oriented, she will advise the patient how to feel turned on to men. This is a standard heterosexist presumption, of course. And yet the reverse, equally damaging, is to assume that the patient is actually turned on to women—"as well she *should* be in our sexist society"—and counsel her accordingly. In actuality, the woman may just not be turned on, period. She is probably so alienated from her sexuality that she doesn't even know what interests her. The myth of the "latent lesbian" or "politically correct" lesbian may have her believing she is gay. Being pushed to identify her sexuality in terms of men or women keeps her from experiencing what a group without either bias would enable her to do: make up her own mind; and know that the group will happily support either—or both—her decisions.

HIGHER CONSCIOUSNESS CELIBACY

Just as fasting helps rejuvenate and cleanse the body after too much eating, celibacy affords the soul respite and refreshment when sexual energy needs to be understood. Many of us, men and women alike, give away our sexuality too casually. There are many reasons for this: we are adventurous; we think sex is our only substantial power; or we just can't seem to muster up the strength it requires to make our sexual situation suit us and thus we continue to take whatever is available. If we don't enjoy what we're doing, after a while our sexual energy becomes dissipated, leaving us empty, with many gaps in our souls.

Sexual energy has many uses and many ways of being expressed. We are accustomed to thinking that it is genital and can be felt only with the inspiration of someone else. When we share it, we want our affection, love, fun returned. We expend a lot of our energy trying to get payoffs from sharing our sexuality. We don't think we can survive without sex, a man, and "that sort of love." We may want it so badly we begin to lose touch with what our sexuality really means as we scatter it about with desperate abandon. It takes waking up one morning overwhelmed with desolation, or laid low with physical illness, to make us realize we're exhausted, off-center, and in need of rejuvenation.

If you've reached this point, take a break! An excellent, sure-fire way of getting your sexual energy back under control is to take a celibacy break. Do it with higher consciousness, as a positive action you've chosen for a certain determined period of time. By higher consciousness I mean staying in touch with yourself while you refrain from sharing your sexual energy. Don't just flip into neutral and coast; watch and feel what happens to your sexuality day by day, analyze your moods, and begin to pay attention to those glimmerings of emotions that point you in the direction of what you sexually enjoy. Notice how the energy you used to squander for small returns can be channeled into taking care of yourself. Many women realize how much career work they get done in those periods between lovers. And why not? They have all this extra energy to invest!

Celibacy, traditionally, means not having sex. It means you are weird—uptight—perhaps ready for a nunnery, probably genetically defective, and most certainly in deep trouble psychologically. Celibacy means no orgasms. It means being uninterested, disinterested, or incapable. Announce to your friends or a lover, "I'm being celibate for a while," and they look at you with pity. This is usually followed by a long confused speech that begs you to reconsider. When that doesn't work they decide you've gone quite mad.

And yet, for all that, periods of self-initiated sexual celibacy can prove quite meaningful in our lives. Such times provide us with centering. They are self-energizing and self-defining periods—be they a month or a year long. When our sexuality goes out of control, when we feel we're using it without pleasure and engaging in it without meaning, stepping back and choosing to re-define what we're doing by opting for celibacy is a way to return our sexual energy to us. It gives us space and freedom to study ourselves, and our sexual feelings.

Being celibate does not mean being non-orgasmic or devoid of sexual energy. Celibacy is not intended to be suppressive; rather, it is a time for experiencing sexual energy profoundly, but reserving such feelings for oneself. Masturbation during this time is truly making love to yourself. It is an enlightening, nurturing part of being celibate and becomes an even more effective means of meditation than humming "Om." Higher consciousness through masturbation? The gurus might stamp that as unorthodox, or even blasphemous. But sexual energy is powerful; and, channeled for self-exploration and self-appreciation, it's a potent antidote to murky emotions and confusing assumptions concerning relationships.

Celibacy means taking time to be without sexual partners. It is a time to explore your own sexuality for yourself, to implode an energy usually directed outward. It is also a safe way to take a break from boring or self-defeating sex games.

How do you know when your situation warrants a period of celibacy? Here's how one woman determined it:

"My first celibacy period happened because I could no longer go on. I had been so sexually 'groovy' and assertive and liberated I got sick. One day I was still bouncing from bed to bed assuming I was having a wonderful time (so what if I didn't have orgasms and cried myself to sleep with loneliness after these 'fun' encounters . . .) and the next day I was in my gynecologist's office in a lot of pain. I had endometriosis. My Fallopian tubes were inflamed. Having intercourse hurt. So I took a break from my lovers. Then I began to wonder why my genitals had decided to become ill. As time went by I realized I didn't miss sex. As a matter of fact, I was surprised to discover I felt relieved to be without it. My medication being high dosages of birth-control pills, I was very turned on most of the time. I found places to masturbate that really tickled my fancy—in my classroom, in my car during a traffic jam, in the park, in the tub—I loved it!

"I felt very guilty about my enjoyment of solitude. I had to ask my women's group for permission to be celibate. The women were supportive, but I did lose men 'friends.' The longer I was alone, the more I realized that my sexual relationships and my use of sexual energy had been making me unhappy, but I had been too proud and too scared to admit it. In my solitude, I was, much to my surprise, rediscovering the joy of my sexuality. I remained celibate for six months. During that time I got rid of endometriosis, much to my doctor's surprise. I think I cured myself by masturbating.

"For the first time I felt I had control over my body. I'm a very physically active and strong woman, and my sexuality had always been close to the surface. I didn't realize until I was celibate how much my sexuality had changed over my years of sexual exploration—and not all of those changes I liked. Now, with the pressure off of me to be doing sex with or for somebody else, I began to get a grip on that profound energy I had always felt.

"Listen to your body, follow where it leads, I told myself. This proved an exhausting experience. It strained me, like trying to distinguish a soft animal sound in the woods from the howling wind in the trees. I felt like an Indian tracking my own internal animal—not to capture it but to be able to follow it, admiring its beauty and spirit. As I trusted myself more, the soft animal sounds became louder and clearer; and I began to heal, both psychologically and physically.

"For months I had been torn between two relationships, both of them sexual. Listening to my body, my gut contracted each time I thought about having sex with either of them. I spoke with both of them, and stopped the sex. I figured that when my body wanted to be aroused again, it would let me know. I didn't panic that I would be turned off forever. As I discovered later, my intuitions were right: my body still had its fire, only the flaming situations were different from what I expected them to be.

"My sexual energy, my life energy, multiplied and expanded. I found it in new and odd places. I particularly noticed how sexual I felt when I felt powerful. A good day of work, the realization that I'd had a strong effect on a situation—any situation that I felt powerful in also turned me on. That way, my masturbation and celibacy became self-celebrating. I really loved to make love to me because I felt in love with myself. Naturally, I felt a little guilty about all this so-called narcissism. 'You stuck up or something?' one of those infernal internal voices would ask. But I didn't feel narcissistic or stuck up—for the first time in many years, I felt *good* about myself! I never wanted to lose those feelings. Yet I knew I would—moods swing and situations change.

"So I wrote down in poetry and prose what those feelings felt like. I tried to embroider in my heart the recipes and formulas that created them. I wanted to be permeated with a sense of how they happened and what they felt like, because, when they slipped away, I wanted to know what it would take to pursue and re-create them.

"During this time, I was very productive in my life. I started an organization, I made many new friends, I quit smoking and began to take good care of my body. It seemed to me that all of that sexual energy I had been using before to try and make myself happy and make people love me had been squandered. Like a millionaire blasé about money, I hadn't understood the value of sexual economy and had squandered orgasms without giving any thought to what I was doing, certain that there would be enough to last forever. Suddenly experiencing my sexual energy as an energy to make me happy and enable me to feel fulfilled was a stunning, enlightening experience.

"It didn't always go smoothly. Sometimes I felt very lonely, afraid that my current disinterest in sharing sex was a permanent condition. I lost some men friends, and some women lovers dropped away, too. I was often confused over my purposes, and got scared at times that the only way to make and keep friends (especially men) was through sex.

"The curse of invisibility struck me deep with fear. I had been known as a sexy woman. When I changed my sexual energy from outward to inward, many people assumed it had died—that I had no sexual appetites. They walked around me at parties, kissed and hugged me perfunctorily, as if I was a Martian.

"Every now and then I would feel twinges of being turned on towards another person. In my pre-celibacy days, I would have assumed those twinges meant 'Big Arousal' and I'd have madly pursued the object of them. Now I had the opportunity to be more discerning, and I began to notice differences in what turned me on. Intensity and duration varied. Some people turned me on for two seconds. Others I spent weeks fantasizing about—realizing, however, that I didn't want to ruin my daydreams with a sexual reality. Some people appealed to me sensually, not sexually—a distinction I had never made before. Freed from the need to always Do Something About Those Feelings, I was able to track them, note how they developed and waned. I came to understand my sexual chemistry, and to trust it to react accurately to sexual stimuli. Thanks to this knowledge, I could let myself react sexually to every person and every occasion. I didn't have to Do Something—I could enjoy the feeling, and that in itself was fun. It enabled me to be loving and nurturing, and not get tied in knots due to performance fears.

"I quit being celibate when my chemistry knocked me

over one day. This time I met someone who really turned me on. I was able to recognize it, and was able to decide with confidence that I wanted that person sexually. 'Yes, indeed. That's quality!' I said to myself, feeling assertive and powerful, in control of sex for the first time in my life.

"Since that affair—which was a brief, intense summer love—I have continued to be as concerned with chemistry and quality. I would rather have one good sexual relationship a year than a series of so-so's, who keep the bed warm but leave a cold morning.

"Whenever I begin to feel strung out, or in pain over my sexual relationships, I return to being celibate for a while to sort out what's happening. As supporters of Tantric yoga note, sexual energy rises through the body, clearing the mind and illuminating the soul. Ecologically speaking, I feel it's using a natural resource to its fullest. I never am not sexual: I am using that energy in many, many ways.

"Higher-consciousness celibacy enables me to maintain my independence, a difficult position for any woman. I fear losing myself in a comfortable, secure relationship which offers only that: comfort and security. I want lots more from my sexual relationships. I myself can provide the comfort and security—what I want is fun and play and passion.

"I feel secure with myself, knowing that my periods of celibacy are not lonely or isolating; but, rather, an extended meditation. I enjoy my own company. I can masturbate when physical sexual expression is what I want, and I'm always feeling loving and sensual with my close friends. I know I am a very sexy, very sensual person, although I may spend more time during a year being celibate than being with a partner. My sexual energy and me are very close."

PART 3

---

practical exercises and questions

Masturbation

CHAPTER 10. Now that we have explored the ramifications of sexism and discussed the various ways to change the status quo, it is time to get down to specifics concerning our bodies and its manifold pleasures.

We begin this chapter, then, with a series of exercises to help women become orgasmic—by themselves and for themselves. From there it is but a short step to becoming orgasmic with a partner.

Remember: these exercises are not absolute. They are for your enjoyment alone. Employ them as a foundation, building upon them according to your own private fantasies and goals. It is important not to get caught up in a lot of life-denying "should's." Rather, flow with your desires. Let them lead you. Create pleasures of your own.

Above all, realize that sex is fun!

THREE STEPS TO ORGASMS

STEP 1: TIME AND PLACE = SETTING
THE SCENE FOR THE SEDUCTION

Learning to give yourself orgasms means throwing out a lot of old ideas about what orgasms constitute, and also means changing your attitude toward your sexuality. These exercises are geared to help you do both these things, with a maximum of pleasure. Because much of what you will be doing is new and unique to you, a good way to think about it is as . . . a seduction of yourself. Think of doing these exercises as if you are planning to satisfy your favorite lover's most profound sexual desires. I know that may sound a little silly; but part of doing anything new and different means having to feel a little silly. Don't expect the "seduction of yourself" concept to work immediately, either. Just tuck it away in the back of your mind as an over-all reminder of your mood on this journey to orgasm. You are, remember, learning to make love to yourself—and falling in love requires a bit of fantasy.

Now, about time. This is the biggest bugaboo of all. The most frequently heard complaint from pre-orgasmic women is: "An hour a day with myself? Alone? I don't think I can spare the time . . ."

Taking time is the most important requirement to becoming orgasmic. The main reason you are pre-orgasmic is because you haven't taken the time to figure out how to become orgasmic. And usually the reason you haven't is because someone told you that orgasms happen quickly with the right partner—and, besides, who'd ever think of devoting an hour a day to masturbation? Consequently, taking time is the most persistently difficult requirement for women. Why, just look at your schedule! Where would you fit in an hour or so?

Traditionally, women don't consider it proper to take time to be alone with themselves. Work schedules, study schedules, and motherhood schedules gobble up all of our available hours. We are so accustomed to being givers of time rather than takers that we don't even notice how little time we spend with ourselves—which we need to get reacquainted and refreshed with our own minds and bodies. Typically, we leave for ourselves only whatever few minutes remain after we have helped our family, friends, and lovers. If we have a job or attend school as well, those minutes diminish into seconds.

As Barbara put it, "I'm actually afraid to spend time alone.

What will I do? I feel useless when I'm not taking care of someone or something. Besides, what if I find I'm bored with myself, that I don't have any personality, really? Suppose, creatively, I'm a dud? I don't want to spend time alone because I may not like the person I'm spending that time with!"

Lyn and Marsha agreed that time would be their biggest problem, too. Marsha feared graduate school would demand too much attention; and Lyn, though she had empty hours on her schedule, feared procrastination, her favorite way of avoiding things.

Kathy, a young mother, reckoned she'd have to break her "motherhood habit" as she called it. "I always put myself last. And who will take care of the baby?"

Over the years of doing these groups I have seen some very clever excuses involving time conflicts used to sabotage becoming orgasmic. These conflicts sound legitimate superficially, but a little scratching beneath reveals their subversiveness. Graduate programs, children, communes, lovers, drafty bedrooms, mothers, community activities, crowded bathrooms, jobs, ill health, babies—you name it, all these can take up too much time to come. And these things can prevent you from becoming orgasmic—forever. In fact, the true test of whether or not your schedule allows you enough time comes down to one thing: How much do you want to be orgasmic—truly? If you don't feel like it right now, you won't have the time. But if you do really want it and, in fact, feel it's long overdue—then you will have the time.

Setting Up Your Hour

In a group women make a contractual agreement—like a legal contract—to spend an hour a day with themselves doing the suggested exercises, or "self-work," as many prefer to call it. You can make the same agreement with yourself, or with anyone else with whom you may be sharing this work.

Keep in mind that no one is perfect and that you won't be

able to put in an hour a day every day. However, because time is the most important factor in discovering your way to being orgasmic, don't let too much time slip by. If you are spending less than four hours a week with yourself while learning to be orgasmic, you will have a difficult time because you are breaking up the momentum of the work you're doing.

Be gentle with yourself, though. When you skip an hour, do it with "higher consciousness." That is, instead of kicking yourself and feeling guilty, understand why you skipped. An exam? Your in-laws? The kids? Or did you just not want to do it today? Figure out why, and determine if it's sabotage or a real conflict. But keep in mind that these exercises work. And the failures are due to only two things: not enough time put into the exercises; or a decision that now is not the time to become orgasmic.

The establishment of your hour is a big step. If you live with other people you're probably shy about announcing at the dinner table or at a house meeting, "Listen folks. I'll be needing the bathtub an hour a night from now on to masturbate." (Of course, if you're an exhibitionist at heart you might find this quite exciting!) However, more subtle methods are possible for those who are a bit shy.

Marsha, for instance, told her household she was learning to meditate and wanted the hour between nine and ten each night as her time in the bathroom. Lyn preferred the morning hours, and chose a period when the house was empty. Consequently, for her the problem of privacy never came up.

What to tell a lover? If you don't live with them, you can decide whether or not you want to tell them anything at all. Be careful about committing yourself to a sexual performance, particularly if you are doing this work at a partner's encouragement or insistence. If you are becoming orgasmic primarily for your own pleasure—great! If you are doing it because your partner wants you to and you aren't that excited about it, stop right now. Time and again group experience has proven that women motivated solely by their partners, and not by themselves, remain unorgasmic. I remember one young woman who joined a group, paid for it with her fiancé's check, and after a few sessions disclosed to us she was doing this work because, "Unless I have orgasms he won't marry me." She was unable to become orgasmic until an accidental separation from him took the pressure off. Then she was able to determine what was for her and what wasn't.

It is O.K. to keep secrets. Not everything has to be revealed. You can have private things in your life. Many women find that even after they are orgasmic they like to keep it to themselves for a while just to savor the new sensations.

If you do want to tell a partner, you can show them this book and then ask for his or her cooperation. Frequently partners feel left out. Suddenly they are ejected for an hour (a whole hour!) from the bedroom or bathroom. Point out the value of this time to your lover and encourage him or her to use it as creatively as you are. Kathy's husband, for example, volunteered to provide child-care to assist her. He also agreed to leave the house during that hour so she wouldn't feel pressured. Kathy noted that her partner confided he was a little concerned about being left out. He feared she'd learn to masturbate and prefer that to him—or, even more frightening, that once she learned to be orgasmic she'd want to have other lovers and he would lose her. He also confessed that he had prejudices about masturbating, and a part of him thought she was kind of strange for taking time to "beat off," as he put it. Kathy discussed masturbation as self-loving and he agreed to try and think of it that way, too, even when masturbating himself. To keep him from feeling left out, Kathy agreed to do her hour alone before spending time with him in the evenings. She liked that because "I come first, but I still get my cuddle and talk-time with him."

To insure a successful use of your precious time, here are some typical problems to avoid:

Your partner timing your hour. Having your lover panting outside your door, awaiting the sweep of the second-hand so he or she can yell, "Time's up!" is a pressure situation. Time yourself.

Answering the phone. Telephones provide a great excuse for saying, "But, but, but I got interrupted." Although one practiced masturbator I know actually programmed herself to reach orgasm when the phone began ringing, racing to see if she could come before they hung up, this is not an advisable practice for the novice. On the contrary, many an orgasm got missed because the phone came first.

Letting your children interfere. Many mothers secretly feel chained to their children, so when it comes time to take an hour off for themselves they grow guilty. Use your masturbating as a first step in liberating your children and yourself. Arrange care: leave the kids with a neighbor, hire a teenager, ask your husband or housemates to help. After all, it's only an hour.

Your partner sharing your hour. Sure, it's fun to bathe together and massage and snuggle and "talk kinky." Besides, partners can act pitiful when you take off for that hour without them. You also may be feeling a little lonely and strange by yourself at first. But sharing your hour with someone else sabotages the work. The point of it is to get into you, and you alone. Divided attention is one reason women are not orgasmic, so don't perpetuate the situation. When you become orgasmic, there will be lots of time to share.

Setting Up Your Place

Be it bedroom or bathroom or backyard, make it cozy and sensual. Take command of your environment—a new experience for many of us—and set your own mood. This is a great time to truly plug into your imagination.

Replace harsh white light bulbs with sexy red or pink ones. Burn incense, play music, light candles, surround yourself with plants—go to town on atmosphere.

Privacy is most important, particularly at the start. Put a lock on your door; hang a curtain over the window; patch up the peep-hole in the bathroom door.

Warmth, or rather the lack of it, is a common complaint. Buy a space heater or a thermal light. Use your electric blanket. Or adjust yourself to include a sheet, blanket, or warm gown.

A warning: Don't do this work in a place where you've tried to masturbate before and failed. Such spots are depressing, psychologically. Particularly since prior to now you may have felt bad about masturbating and chose spots in keeping with your feelings. Marsha, for example, had to be coaxed out of a dark closet where she would huddle among the coats and shoes trying to masturbate. As for Barbara, she had tried sitting on the toilet, which was most uncomfortable and restrictive. I recall one woman who had such a dreary history of trying to masturbate on her bed that she now thought of it as a cold and lonely zone. She stayed away from it, and wisely turned her attentions toward her bathtub instead.

The point of all this is to start taking control of your environment. Women are not accustomed to actively creating their own settings, particularly sexual ones. So indulge your territory with your personality and sensuality. It's a big step toward helping you feel in control of your sexuality.

Established your time? Got your place in mind? You're ready for getting down to some real physical pleasure.

Beginning with Step II, the self-work exercises are given by the hour. Each set described takes at least one hour to do. Often you are asked to repeat an exercise in order to feel comfortable with it, and to become increasingly familiar with yourself.

There is no set time for completing these pre-orgasmic exercises. In a traditional group these exercises extend over a five-week period, and most group members become orgasmic sometime during the second or third weeks. However, you may move faster or slower depending on how you feel. Don't push yourself so hard you get exhausted or scared. And don't go so slow you lose momentum and get bored. Pace yourself for pleasure, follow the pleasure, and gently dare yourself to experience more and more.

STEP II: EXPLORATION AND HISTORY

It seems almost instinctual, but the first thing women do when told they can talk about sex is to tell their histories. And, each time, women are amazed at the similarities, even though the events themselves may be radically different.

Kathy, Lyn, Marsha, and Barbara learned this at their first meeting. Each was sure she had the most unhappy, isolated, unsuccessful sexual past and present possible. But to their surprise—and great relief—they all found much in common, both tragic and funny. Fascinated, they devoted that entire first meeting to the subject. "I never told these things to anyone before in my life!" marveled Kathy, after admitting she found intercourse boring. "I thought I was the only one who felt that way, and I'm not. What a relief!"

All four discussed how they first had learned about sex, and what their first sexual experience was like. Each told how she had first heard about masturbation and what her present opinion was of it. Each described her most significant love affairs and how these had affected her sexuality. Traumas, tribulations, jealousies, abortions, pregnancies, and broken hearts filled the warm air of the room.

Hour #1: *Self-Work*

Write down or verbally share your sexual history.

After doing so, take a look at the list of problems compiled from the histories of many women doing just as you've done. See how much your history has in common with theirs, and, remember, these women are now orgasmic. You can overcome . . .

FIFTEEN COMMON BLOCKS TO ORGASMS

1. You have never associated sex with pleasure, and no one ever told you this was possible.
2. Your religion, parents, lover told you sex is bad and orgasms immoral, difficult, or unimportant.

3. No one told you orgasms exist or what they are truly like.
4. You are unhappy, angry, dissatisfied (pick one or all) with your lover(s).
5. Your sexual past consists of unhappy, boring, or frightening experiences.
6. You believe you are genitally non-orgasmic, or that your clitoris and body are "broken."
7. Your body feels pain when you get aroused, frustration hurts, intercourse hurts, sex hurts.
8. You think masturbating is for the ugly, weird, or lonely.
9. You don't know how your body works sensually and sexually.
10. You've been using a vibrator and now your fingers don't seem to work.
11. You believe you have psychological hang-ups.
12. You're afraid of being out of control sexually if you have orgasms.
13. Your lover wants you to "shape up or ship out" and you know if you don't come soon you'll have to go.
14. You're basically a romantic and believed all these tales of love and romance, particularly the ones about Prince Charming.
15. You didn't think it was important until now.

Rx: The "cure" for these blocks is to recognize them, acknowledge them, and then kick them aside. Think of them as tricks to keep you from enjoying yourself. Have a day of mourning for your sexual past, and then decide to bury it. It won't happen all at once. Let it go slowly, like the slow leaking of air out of a balloon.

Psychoanalysts, doctors, and therapists would have us believe that we cannot overcome unhappy, paralyzing sexual pasts. The fact that 95% of the women going through groups become orgasmic belies that. Yes, I know what you're thinking: "I'm in that other 5%." You're in that other 5% only if you're not sure you want to be orgasmic, and only if you don't give yourself enough time to be. As you will see, these exercises concentrate on your body and your physical pleasures. This is done purposefully to avoid the "head-tripping" involved in the Fifteen Common Blocks. In this work, it's body over mind, a proven way to put old heady feelings to rest.

Hours #2 and #3: *Into Your Body*

Now that you have established the time, the place, and your past is getting put in its place, you're ready to meet your body.

—*Begin* your hour by running a warm, luxurious bath. This exercise will be part of every self-pleasuring hour you do. If you want, add bubbles or oil to the tub. In the bath, caress yourself with the soap and concentrate on *feeling* the touch of your hand on your skin. Put all other thoughts out of your mind—just *feel*. Breathe deeply as you do this, inhaling as you start a touch and exhaling slowly as you complete it. Go slowly and sensually. Notice which parts of your body are particularly sensitive.

Do not get aroused. Just notice what feels good and where it does. (Women have been told that specific areas should feel sensual, such as that touches upon the thighs and breasts should make us swoon. Not always. You're unique, remember, and you'll have different sensual spots.)

—*After* your bath, study your body in a full-length mirror (or the closest thing to it you can find.) Move, dance, bend. Notice what you like about your body and what you don't. Whisper your likes and dislikes aloud to yourself.

Watch out for "fat monsters," those corpulent creatures who invade our minds and convince us a dimpled thigh is a "fat one," a womanly hip expanse "too broad," and a curvaceous belly "obese."

Some women find it difficult to find what they like about their bodies because they don't conform to the media standards of beauty. This can get quite extreme. I recall one woman in group who went into incredible detail concerning the blemishes on her body to such an extent that the only part she even vaguely liked were "my ankles." Begin freeing yourself from the emaciated skin-and-bones fashion-magazine image by paying particular loving attention to those thighs, hips, and breasts that you may feel unfriendly towards.

—*Now* rub yourself all over with a body lotion or oil you particularly enjoy. Make sure it is non-alcohol and nonpetroleum based. Once again, be indulgent. Shop for a special oil with a favorite scent. Some women even prefer to use silky corn starch. Rub the lotion on with feeling. Don't slap it on—take time to feel. Notice what parts of your body respond most to your touches.

Include your genitals and breasts in this massage. Don't get turned on—just get acquainted. Using a hand mirror and a light, take a look at your genitals. If you've never looked before—a very common experience—you may be nervous or even feel slightly repulsed at the idea. Women have been told that their genitals are extremely ugly and quite odiferous, so not feeling good about them is very common.

Some women say, "I look at them all the time when I put in a Tampax." That's not really looking. Go back and do it for aesthetics, not practicality, this time.

—*Use an illustration* of the vulva in any good women's health book to guide you here. (*Our Bodies Ourselves* is a good one.[1]) Identify all your features, and touch them as you find them. Sometimes the urethra is difficult to locate, so look closely. For fun, notice your hymenal remnants. They resemble lacy frills around the opening to your vagina. Notice your colors, and the sizes of your labia. Touch your skin and notice the textures. Begin to get comfortable with your vulva. You won't resemble this illustration exactly, of course. Genitals are as different as fingerprints or snowflakes: no two are alike.

Begin now to think of positive metaphors for your vulva and see its shape in nature. Seashells, succulent fruits, nuts, jungles, knots in tree trunks—vulvas are all around us.

---

[1] *Our Bodies Ourselves: A Book By and For Women,* by the Boston Women's Health Collective (New York: Simon and Schuster, 1971).

Kegel Exercises

Muscles make orgasms; and, if your muscles are out of shape, your orgasms will be, too. This little exercise—the Kegel (rhymes with bagel)—is like a vaginal push-up. Doing so many a day will put your abdomen in good physical shape for orgasms.

Kegels were invented by an American doctor in order to correct urinary incontinency in post-hysterectomy women. To everyone's surprise, many of these women began having orgasms for the first times in their lives. So, for obvious reasons, these exercises are added here to your self-work. You should do them for the rest of your life.

How they work: A set of muscles, essentially the pubecoccygeal muscles, support your abdomen. Some of these muscles connect to the clitoral hood. Thus, when you squeeze these muscles, contracting and expanding them, the clitoral and vaginal areas are stimulated. The stronger these muscles are, the stronger your orgasms can be.

When these muscles are flaccid, orgasms are difficult—particularly if you have had children. It's so simple; and yet many women are without orgasms simply because their muscles are out of shape.

How to do Kegels: These are the same muscles you contract when you want to stop urinating. Find them by sitting on the toilet and intermittently contract to stop the flow of urine. Feel those muscles?

Do your Kegels daily:

1. Do 10 contractions rapidly, in a set of three. That's 10 contractions with a pause after every set of 10.
2. Then do 3 contractions and hold each to the count of 10.

These may be difficult at first, but you'll get more coordinated with experience. To check your progress, before starting stick your finger in your vagina and contract. Repeat this again after a couple of weeks, and see what a difference you can feel.

If you've been doing your daily push-ups, you'll feel a difference in strength and tightness.

Have trouble remembering to do them? Coordinate your Kegels to a common occurrence. Lyn did hers at every red light. Barbara remembered hers when she noticed a turn indicator on the car in front of her, and Marsha while talking on the phone. Because you can't be seen doing them, you can do them anywhere.

As for your general health, these exercises will help you get back into shape after childbirth and, as you age, these exercises will keep your abdominal muscles firm. This prevents those uncomfortable occurrences our grandmothers endured, like sagging bladders and uteruses.

Hours #4 and #5: *Into Your Body More*

—Again, and always, precede your hour with that luxurious bath and a sensual creaming of your body using your favorite lotion or oil. This time, though, include your genitals in your caresses. You've been touching them and becoming acquainted and friendly. Now, begin to discover what touches they enjoy. You aren't trying for an orgasm. You're just discovering what feels good and what parts of your genitals are sensitive.

Make sure you use plenty of oil or saliva as lubrication. It enhances sensitivity. Be gentle in your explorations. Learn to become specific in describing what and where it feels good. Don't just say, "My clitoris feels good." Say, "My clitoris feels good when I touch it to the right. Not directly, because that hurts. I like to rub around it, using this sort of rhythm, and at the same time I like having a finger in my vagina." Be specific. Notice pressure, rhythm, style, and precisely what parts of your genitals respond to precisely what sort of stimulation.

—An important part of these hours is tasting and smelling your secretions. "Yucko!" you may think. But as every woman in group has discovered, both are surprisingly pleasing.

You might want to taste yourself right after your bath when you're freshly washed. Because there are so many terrible myths about the filthiness of our genitals the thought of tasting or smelling anything "down there" can seem repulsive, particularly if you've been plagued with yeast infections or vaginitis and have used gooey medicines.

Genital fragrances, each unique, are as exciting as a special perfume. They are *your* perfume. Dab a little behind your ear, as Marsha did in a moment of wild abandon.

As for taste, it is surprisingly light. Lyn reported, "I taste a bit like sea water," a pleasant comparison. And Kathy said hers was a bit "acid on the palate—but nice." That's not surprising, as the vagina is an acid environment.

—Make a list of reasons you like yourself. For example, Barbara wrote, "I love myself because I'm always changing." Do it on a big piece of paper and use bright colors and crayons. Hang it in your room as a constant reminder of why you deserve to be loved.

Orgasms as a Path

Women have been discouraged from being orgasmic by being told orgasms are magic, an unpredictable phenomenon. This is not true. In fact, every woman has a precise path to her orgasms; and that is why I stress being absolutely specific in determining what feels good and why. As women become more experienced with their orgasms, they will be able to discover more and more paths toward them. But, right now, you are trying to discover your first one. That's why it's important to remember what feels good and stay with it.

It helps if you think of your orgasm journey as climbing a mountain you've never climbed before. You want to get to the top. In order to do so you must forge your own trail. You have plenty of time—you made sure of that earlier—so the goal is not merely to reach the top but also to enjoy the trip up there. Notice flowers along the way, different trees, the changes that occur with the differences in altitude. Sometimes you head into a clearing only to discover it's a dead end, impassable. Other times you find a good path. As you connect all the routes together you get closer and closer to the top, full of remembrance of vivid beauty and special natural delights. When you get to the top you are breathless, but not exhausted. You can look back and think, "That was really fun!" Orgasms are like that. Notice the various sensations along the way. Give yourself time. Remember you are blazing a new trail.

Anatomy and Physiology

You've been feeling pleasure and sensualness for a while. Now find out why. During one of these hours read a woman's book on your sexual physiology and anatomy. (I suggest Barbach's *For Yourself*[2] or *Our Bodies Ourselves*.[3]) If you have a partner and want them to know how you work, ask them to read this section, too—after you.

BEFORE MOVING ON . . .

By now you have spent a week and a minimum of four hours pleasuring yourself. You have an idea of what feels good and how to create those feelings. You know what your genitals look like, and you know how your body physiologically responds to sexual pleasure.

You also have an idea of what it's like to spend time alone and be with you. By now most women find they are enjoying it and really look forward to those luxurious hours alone. We must have our indulgences. Making time for you isn't easy—but it sure pays off.

Having some problems getting into it? Don't feel like

---

[2]Lonnie Garfield Barbach, *For Yourself: The Fulfillment of Female Sexuality* (New York: Doubleday, 1975).

[3]*Loc. cit.*

you're really involved? Here are some common reasons why. Check the list. If you have any of these difficulties, don't go on. You'll only be sabotaging yourself. Clear these up first—then proceed.

1. You're not making your environment as comfortable and private as you need.
2. You are choosing a time to do these exercises when you're too exhausted or preoccupied to concentrate and enjoy.
3. You're permitting interruptions of your hour.
4. You're not engaging your imagination and childlike curiosity and fun in making this work enjoyable, so you feel bored and wooden.
5. You're concerned about the reaction of a housemate or lover and you need to resolve it with a discussion or a decision.

If these sorts of problems have kept you back, take another hour or two to repeat the pleasuring exercises that feel best to you. It is hoped you can eliminate these encumbrances by letting yourself experience sheer, simple physical enjoyment. Talk with a friend if you need some verbal relief and reassurance.

Before going on, think back on what you've learned about you thus far. What's been most fun, most pleasurable? The bath? Moving your muscles in front of the mirror? How's your clitoris feeling? What's that particular spot on your body that gives you goosebumps? *Concentrate on what feels good.*

It's so easy for us to remember only the bad and negate the good. That way we can give ourselves the impression that only bad things are happening, and nothing pleasurable. Focus on the positive.

—*Celebrate getting acquainted* with yourself by doing a self-portrait—of your genitals. Let it be a modern abstract, or scientifically realistic. Don't worry about being an artist—just have fun. Kathy, Lyn, Marsha, and Barbara did their self-portraits in the group, then took them home to hang in their own rooms. "I want to see if anyone recognizes me!" said Marsha.

STEP III: STIMULATION AND ORGASM

Hours #6 and #7: *Getting Warmer . . .*

—Following your bath and lotion, focus on your genitals and see if you can create a feeling of low arousal. Begin finding your orgasms. It's O.K. to feel as turned on as you can—and don't hold back. Have an orgasm whenever you want now. Spend at least 15 to 20 minutes touching your genitals. Begin to discover how to touch your genitals so you feel turned on. Remember to use plenty of lubrication. Tease yourself. Get excited, and then go away from that touch for a minute. You know how a bit of a goody makes you hungrier for more? Do that with your touching now.

If you are bored or discouraged with your fingers, you may want to try using water. Frequently women who have tried unsuccessfully to masturbate with their fingers feel psychologically defeated. Using water can circumvent this. And it is easy to have orgasms with fingers after learning to do so with water. Faucets and showers do have their own special charm.

If you find you're getting *too* excited—and by that I mean that you feel uncomfortable being that turned on—stop playing with your genitals and return to caressing other parts of your body. You may want to get up and walk around, or dance a bit to work off the tension. It's fine to take a break. You'll discover an interesting thing about getting turned on: it's hard to lose it. After your break, go back to touching yourself, and you'll see how rapidly you can get stimulated. Not bad, huh?

Recall the "Orgasms as a Path" metaphor as you stimulate yourself. When you find a good route, stick with it. As soon as you find the pleasure fading, move on to a more rewarding spot. Don't jump around too much, though, or you won't have time to feel. Stay in the NOW with your fingers and don't anticipate. Your body will lead you where you want to go if you listen to it.

Spectating. This can be a problem at this stage. Spectating means what it sounds like—that you are *observing* yourself doing this work, rather than feeling yourself doing it. For example, when you touch yourself, you notice you're touching yourself, rather than feeling the touch. The way to avoid spectating is to stay in the present, the here and now, with your feelings. Don't think of "what I *should* be feeling" or "how come I don't feel otherwise?" Notice what you ARE feeling and heighten it bit by bit.

Hours #8 and #9: . . . *and Warmer* . . .

The best part about these two hours is: You get to add a prop to your masturbation. This is another place where you can really use your imagination and add some pizazz to your love-making. Add anything you want (except, of course, your partner . . .). Be silly and inventive and daring. Add something you may never even dared consider before.

Lyn gave vent to her Toulouse-Lautrec *femme fatale* fantasy and costumed herself accordingly. At a flea market she bought a big floppy picture hat with a red feather, added a garter belt, black stockings, and jewelry. "I shut myself in my room and paraded around before my mirror. I absolutely knocked myself out. It was great!"

Barbara bought a fur-piece with which she did some erotic tickling while rolling about in her favorite silk kimono. "My skin *loves* that cool touch!"

Kathy picked a zucchini from her garden, creating what she termed, "My organic dildo. I like something in my vagina. I found hot dogs too greasy and plastic dildos too hard. Zucchini is perfect." The group suggested that serving it later in a dinner salad would be both fitting and delightfully naughty.

Marsha combed bookstores and pornography shops. She discovered that reading an erotic study stimulated her fantasies and greatly enhanced her masturbation.

The only limitation on a prop should be its harmfulness. One woman, after much embarrassment and hesitation, said the only prop that really turned her on was her husband's hairbrush. "Hairbrush!" the group gasped in horror, thinking of course she meant the bristly end. "No, no—the handle," she corrected. "I want to use the handle in my anus." We cautioned her not to hurt herself, but other than that give free sway to her fantasy. Some women become enchanted with the various possibilities of electric toothbrushes. But a word of caution here: overheated motors can burn your tender lips.

Vibrators, Drugs, and Liquor as Props. As for myself, I have a bias against vibrators—probably because technique-happy therapists have over-prescribed them and because they are not a fool-proof method. I would suggest a woman learn to give herself orgasms with her fingers or with water before she uses a vibrator. Time and again I've had women come to group who call themselves "vibrator junkies" because they cannot have orgasms without resorting to these machines. When they want to switch to using their fingers, they feel all thumbs, so to speak.

The problem with a vibrator is that it does the work for you. It's not as subtle as water, not as intimate as fingers. Therefore, it's harder to slow down and learn to use fingers or water after the easy luxury of vibrator orgasms. In addition, vibrators are not always successful. In this age of "give-her-a-vibrator" sex therapy, these appliances have earned a reputation as a guaranteed cure-all. Not so. I've worked with many women who found vibrators not only unsatisfying, but unpleasant.

So, I caution their use, though I won't condemn them outright. If you aren't particularly concerned about manual stimulation and if you are really set on having orgasms with a vibrator, then go ahead. But if you want to be digitally proficient, consider holding off on the vibrator until you've succeeded with your hands. Of course, some women have found that a vibrator works better first, and then come fingers. Try fingers, try water, then try a vibrator.

It's also appropriate here to talk about the most traditional sexual prop for women—drugs and liquor. In group Barbara was worried about the fact she enjoyed having a "little drink of wine" before relaxing to enjoy her bath and stimulation. "Little drink" is a tricky phrase. How much is "little?" A glass of wine or sherry—or a short bit of grass—is fine. Any more than that and it's worth worrying about.

A major part of this work is getting in touch with your feelings, both sexual and otherwise. Even though they may be disquieting or confusing or frightening. Drugs are a crutch in that they mask emotions. If you find yourself relying too strongly on dope or drink, stop using these props and analyze what is going on. If you decide you need help, find a feminist-oriented counselor to advise you.

How to Use that Prop: Whatever you chose, use it for at least 15 minutes.

In addition, during these two hours increase the time you spend on your genitals to at least 30 minutes. See how excited you can make yourself!

SOME POSSIBLE PROBLEMS AT THIS POINT . . .

Getting aroused can bring on some strange and disconcerting emotions. You may be feeling a little discouraged by now, bogged down in difficulties and questions. Don't give up! You're almost there. Truly! This is the hardest part—next to making time. Because now you are really encouraging yourself to feel and get aroused. And doing this can lead to some heavy, difficult feelings.

At this point, the women in group shared their problems with each other. What they experienced is typical of every woman. Read this section on problems and solutions, but keep in mind that all the talk in the world can't get around the essential ingredients for learning to have orgasms: experience and daring. Like any new skill, orgasms require concentration and effort. And they are not a vicarious experience—no one else can do them for you. Plug your imagination in, vow to be a stubborn hedonist. Remember you deserve it—and keep on rubbing like Aladdin did his magic lamp! Yes, you're taking some chances and you're out on a limb and dangling there. You aren't sure where you're headed, and have only the vaguest idea how to get there. So take a chance, for once—and follow your lead up the Path to Mount Orgasm. You *can* do it!!!

By now the women had met with each other four times. The mood of their fifth meeting was despairing. All had found they were having difficulties relaxing and feeling excited.

Kathy expressed fear of not being able to come, Barbara complained getting aroused was painful, Marsha was having roommate problems, and Lyn felt out of control. Then they took a deep breath and plunged in, assuring each other they could find solutions.

Kathy began. "I'm really afraid I won't be able to come. I'm going to be the loser. I've been feeling discouraged doing this homework. I doubt I can do it, and I'm scared I can't. All the other times I tried, I failed."

In doing groups women have found that the best way to overcome such fears is to resolve that this time is a rebirth, a whole new sexual experience. Forget about the earlier failures and start anew. By affirming to yourself your right to sexual pleasure, and reminding yourself that this time you have a better idea of where you're going (you have this book, and you have, one hopes, the support of friends)—you can be sure that this is truly a *new* experience.

We have also found that women who go through these exercises and remain pre-orgasmic have, in some fiber of their being, made a decision to remain so. A group can ask questions to determine what constitutes such a decision. Usually the decision is "I'd prefer my lover to make me orgasmic" or "I'm not ready yet—it still scares me." The point is: there was a decision. It's not just sheer chance that makes one woman orgasmic and the next non-orgasmic. Orgasms involve making a decision to have them. "I want them!" must be felt and said and pursued. You must make it happen.

Then, too, women who feel bogged down with fear are often surprised at how much "work" having an orgasm is. They're fun, they're great, they feel good—but they don't just happen. If you aren't used to concentrating on yourself, focusing on your body feelings, and stubbornly striving for what you want, you first orgasm may mean a lot of "work." Remember: It's worth it! And it will get easier with practice.

Barbara expressed fear of getting turned on any further because: "It hurts." She explained she experienced strong muscle tension that was so painful and frustrating it kept her awake nights. "I've felt this for years, and solved it by refusing to let myself feel turned on. Now I'm turned on again, and I'm afraid of it. What do I do?"

All women experience muscle tension when they get aroused. It's called myatonia, and is necessary to have an orgasm. After all, an orgasm is the release of tension created by blood congestion. However, some women experience more myatonia than others; and thus they find it more frustrating not to be able to dispel it with an orgasm. Some women describe this frustration—which lasts up to seventy-two hours—as being little more than indigestion and a cranky mood while others, like Barbara, find it so painful they want to avoid it at all costs. Keep in mind that whatever muscle tension you create, an orgasm will relieve it. Like a roller-coaster ride, the thrill on the way down is due to the tension on the way up.

Change your attitude about this tension. You can relieve it—the relief, as we've said, is an orgasm. Begin to understand this tension as a signal of sexual arousal, of extreme proximity to orgasm. Myatonia occurs in the plateau phase of arousal—and that's right before the "Big O" herself. It's not anxiety, it's sexual tension. And if you have it, that's good!

You can relieve it. Get up and walk around. Move, shake, or jump to music. Then return to masturbating. Let this tension guide you—don't let go—and you'll find yourself sliding over the edge and experiencing the relief of orgasm.

Marsha told the group she felt a little silly about her problem, but, all the same, she realized it should be brought out into the open. "My roomate and I talk about this group and she told me she felt jealous of my being here. She's not able to have orgasms and wants to learn how. She makes me feel guilty that I'm getting so turned on. I worry that if I have an orgasm she'll feel left out and hurt, and then I'll lose her friendship. I worry about that same thing with all of you here. I'm really getting turned on, but I keep holding myself back from going all the way. I'm afraid to be the first one to come. You might get jealous and not like me—I'd lose my friends because I solved my sexual problems! What a mess!"

Marsha's heart is in the right place, but her actions aren't. Proving loyalty by remaining unsuccessful helps no one. Still, there is truth in her feeling that competition can create confusion about success. Studies have shown that small children in play-groups tend to harass and exclude the most creative and successful member. Our society encourages us to compete, to win, enforcing this idea by making us believe there isn't enough success to go around. That certainly isn't true with orgasms. There's plenty of them—and each woman has lots of her own. We need to learn to support each others' successes—not continue with the old female habit of sympathizing with each others' losses.

Lyn said, "I feel what I'm experiencing is too much for me. I feel like crying when I get excited and that scares me. So I stop masturbating."

I remember when I first began letting myself experience the feelings that accompany sexual arousal. I felt many emotions I hadn't expected and didn't really want to have. I realized from having done deep-breathing exercises that what was happening was a normal phenomenon of deep breathing—it brings all kinds of emotions to the surface. I decided to let myself experience whatever was there, because when I stopped feeling them, I stopped feeling everything. I'd cry a little and then diddle a little. It turned out to be a cleansing, relaxing experience and accustomed me to the fact that my feelings, no matter what they are, are normal. I even began to use masturbation to get in touch with feelings I couldn't quite fathom. My anger, fears, unhappinesses would suddenly all come into focus this way. I still find it a valuable meditation in this respect. As Lyn discovered, after a few sessions these feelings aren't so overwhelming anymore and the pure pleasure comes through. All the same, when a bit of a fear tries to sneak in, let it. Experience it. And then proceed with loving yourself.

Women discover other difficulties at this stage of the journey and knowing how common they are can help you keep the faith:

"My lover does it better." Sometimes a woman finds doing this work difficult because it is hard to learn to focus on herself and grant herself pleasure permission. When this happens she often recalls love-making with her partner, remembering that she was at least turned on with him or her—though not orgasmic—and comes to the conclusion that her lover knows how to excite her better than she does herself. To prove the fallacy of this, ask yourself the question: "If they were so good, then why didn't I have orgasms?" More important still is for a woman to assure herself there is nothing her lover does that she can't do for herself. Want to hear sweet nothings whispered? Say them to yourself. You'll find it difficult at first, but exciting as you get used to it. One woman even made a list of what she wanted to hear said and kept it with her as her erotic literature. Want some cuddling? Surround yourself with pillows for a cozy, secure feeling. Want a little excitement in the touch? Do to yourself what you'd want your lover to do. You'll find it even more exciting because you know your body better than even your most intimate lover does. As you get closer to orgasm and more proficient at knowing your body you'll discover that you have a lot to teach your lover.

"I'm having nightmares." Whenever we go through intense and significant changes and start to confront areas of our lives that have been intimidating us, our subconscious will invariably respond. It is not unusual to have disquieting dreams or even nightmares while you are changing your mind about your sexuality. Opening yourself to orgasmic pleasure means throwing away a lot of "don't's" and "should's" you were socially

indoctrinated with. The dreams will pass as you become more comfortable with your masturbation. Don't let them stop you.

"I'm not feeling much of anything. I can't get any further." Then you're not *really* doing the exercises. You may be going through the motions, but you're not truly feeling them. If you are feeling nothing, or feeling bored, or seem to have hit a plateau and can't go any higher, consider why you are resisting these experiences. Sometimes women discover they keep hoping Prince Charming will show up and do the work for them. Others discover they aren't using their creativity and imagination to augment the exercises. Some are continuing to spectate. And others fear going too high for losing their sense of control. Whatever your reason, figure it out. If you decide you're not ready to become orgasmic quite yet, take a break and come back to it when you feel you're ready. Orgasms are not meant to be "should's"; they are big "want's." If you make a definite decision to be orgasmic and stick with it, you will find these exercises working for you.

"My fingers get sore." Of course they do. You haven't used them so much before. Keep using them—and you'll build up those muscles and reap the rewards. Don't concentrate on aches. Concentrate on good sensations.

"My genitals are sore." You're rubbing too hard, and you're not using enough lubrication. Don't ever hurt yourself doing this work. Take it easy. Be gentle.

"I'm afraid of losing control." We used to show our groups a movie of a woman masturbating. She was named Estelle. I think Estelle's convulsive, twisting, backflip, sidekick, somersault orgasms scared more women than any other thing we did in group. Ashen-faced group members whispered nervously, "She looked like she was having an epileptic fit. I don't want to do that!" We stopped showing the film. Thanks to such cinematic stereotypes of female orgasm, which can also be found in many novels, some women think an orgasm is like a convulsion or a fit—a coma that puts them totally out of control.

The grain of truth in this exaggeration is that orgasms *are* powerful reactions. But they are not so powerful as to knock a woman out of control. As a matter of fact, a woman is always totally in control of her orgasms. She can even stop having an orgasm in the middle of one. Orgasms do not come out of the blue and strike like lightning. You search for them, you build them, you create them. That's what you've been doing with this self-work. And that's why you are in control of orgasm.

If you're concerned about wriggling and moaning and thrashing about, make sure you've got pillows on your bed to protect you. In your bathtub, make sure you're lying down and that the water is not too deep.

"I think I'll look ugly." When we've been told, since sixth-grade charm classes, to be as poised and cool as mannequins, the image of ourselves in orgasm can unsettle us. Women worry that the muscle contractions "will make me look awkward" or that the facial expressions "make me look like I'm in pain." Again, this is a matter of changing our image of what is woman. The actions of orgasm aren't awkward or ugly. Actually, the body appearance is one of intensity and concentration and strength—a kind of beauty not many of us were ever told about.

You can accustom yourself to these looks by sitting in front of a mirror and imitating them. Grimace in orgasmic ecstacy—as best you can imagine—and you'll see your face expressing strong feelings. And that's not ugly—it's emotion and it's you. The same with your body. One woman turned a phrase to feel good about her orgasm movements. She called them "erotic wigglings" and found orgasm impossible without them.

"I feel like I'm in a movie watching myself." Again, this is spectating. It's an easy way to remove yourself from the situation. Intellectual women are particularly prone to spectating. Circumvent it by concentrating on the physical sensations happening *right now.*

"I'm not responding like I should," or, *"I'm not responding like I thought I would."* Many of us have a preconceived notion of

"What My Orgasm Will Be." Some of us anticipate explosive-ness and fireworks, others search for a sweet and melting sensa-tion, still others wait to be thrown off the bed and onto the floor by its punch. Whatever we think it should or will be interferes with what it actually is. Remember, your body's feelings of pleasure and arousal should lead you in this work, and not your heady preconceptions. If you find you are fight-ing your responses and trying to change them, you are sabotag-ing yourself. For example, one woman found that she much preferred the shower in her bathtub to using her fingers. The shower excited her, the bathroom atmosphere pleased her, and yet she kept stopping herself. Just as she would be on the verge of an orgasm, she'd stop. And the next night she'd climb into her cold bed, refuse to take a bath, and try quite unsuccessfully to masturbate with her fingers. She explained this by telling me, "If I don't know how to use my fingers I'll never be able to have orgasms with a partner. I don't think the water was a good idea." She felt nothing with her fingers, kept pushing herself to enjoy her bedroom—a "should"—and avoided the obvious success possible with her shower. I assured her that "water babies" are as successful with partners as "finger ladies." And, as a matter of fact, many water babies prefer cunnilingus with their partners and find it easy to enjoy because it's similar to using water. That night she went home, climbed in her bathtub . . . and had her first orgasm.

There are no right ways or wrong ways to have orgasms. And no two women's orgasms are alike.

"The way I masturbate is just too weird." If you're holding yourself back because you think your pleasures are strange—don't! Women masturbate in every conceivable position and under every imaginable stimulus. Pain and tissue damage are the only "pleasures" to question. Otherwise, nothing is taboo. Just to loosen you up a bit, here are some true stories: One woman came to a group to learn how to use her fingers to masturbate. The only way she could presently have orgasms was by hanging from a chin-up bar at the YWCA. Hanging by

her arms created abdominal pressure that enabled her to come. Yet, as she pointed out, "As satisfying as it is, my method is not too adaptable for bed and partner use." Another woman, after being in group and trying to find the right stroke on her clitoris, accidently discovered that she was orgasmically sensitive at the small of her back. She lay on her stomach and caressed the tender area and found it both exciting and rewarding. Other women discover they need no genital stimulation, or very little: their breasts are extremely sensitive and, when touched, lead to orgasm. I've already mentioned the woman who used the handle of her husband's hairbrush, not to mention the women who employ electric toothbrushes. In one group a woman used what she called "The Double Vibrator Method." She used two vibrators at opposite ends of her vulva—one on her clitoris, the other in her anus—to stimulate herself. She was in group to get support to introduce this technique to her lover. Much to her surprise, he found it most exciting; and they incorporated her equipment as a third party to their love-making. A couple of women I know find that certain yoga positions create the right tension to give them orgasms. Others enjoy masturbating before mirrors, finding it exciting to watch themselves become aroused. Some women curl up in little fetal balls and hide their heads under the pillows while they masturbate. Others balance on their knees with their buttocks high in the air (this position also creates good abdominal tension). Others leave the bathroom door open a crack to stimulate their fantasies of "What if I get caught" which excites them. Some women need such fantasies—others do not. As you can see, there is no end to the ways women make love to themselves.

Keep in mind that your style will change over the months and years. You may like the rug on your bathroom floor right now, but in a couple of months—or years—abandon it for your hand and the quilt on your bed. That's why it's important to not censor yourself. Do it! Experience it! It all adds to your repertoire and gives you confidence to try other ways.

Hours #10 and #11: *Getting Hot . . . Getting Closer . . .*

During these next two sessions, following your bath and lotion, increase your genital concentration time to 45 minutes. No kidding! We've found that it takes a woman an average of 45 minutes to have an orgasm when she's going from absolutely cold to positively hot. So give yourself plenty of time—and really focus on your vulva. If you rub it right, it works!!!

Work hard to overcome any problems you may be having. Quit procrastinating. Become absolutely self-indulgent. Remind yourself how much you deserve the *so* good feelings of orgasm.

This is where learning to be selfish pays off. "Being selfish?" I can see you shaking your head. I use the word "selfish" purposely here because women have been taught that thinking of themselves first is a selfish thing to do. Consequently they squander a lot of themselves away. Remember how much trouble you had even reserving time for yourself? Having orgasms requires a "selfish" focus on the self. Actually, this isn't being selfish at all—it's taking care of your wants and desires.

In your masturbation, be Selfish. Stay in the bathroom all day if you want. Barricade yourself in the bedroom with the stereo and candles for an hour and a half. Be unmerciful with negative voices in your mind that keep you from letting go and enjoying—kick them out. And do the Yes and No Exercise described below:

For the next week say Yes to three things you would normally deny yourself. In turn, say No to three things you would normally feel obligated to do. And make one of each of these a sexual Yes or No. For example, if you usually say Yes to washing the dishes because no one else will do them, this week say No and let someone else worry. Or, if you disagree with someone and you normally say No to getting angry and voicing your differences, this week say Yes to sticking up for yourself. Sexually, if you usually say Yes to giving your partner an orgasm when he or she wants it, whether or not you want to or not, this time think of what you want first, and only then decide Yes or No.

Note: Don't say Yes when you usually say No because you feel guilty for saying No all those times. That's a "should"—and this exercise is meant for "want's," not "should's."

The Decision to Have an Orgasm

Through the years of doing groups I have found that a most important step is: to actually Make the Decision to Have an Orgasm. There seems to be a pattern towards this decision. When a woman first starts this work she is hopeful, at best, about becoming orgasmic, and despairing about her success—which, so far, has been *zilch*. She is teetering between "I can do it!" and "I just can't."

As the work proceeds, bit by bit she becomes more confident. Her attitude begins to change as she quits focusing on her failures and starts noticing her successes. She feels more, experiences greater arousal; she comes to grips with her feelings about her sexuality and begins to talk to other women about theirs. She gains more sense of identity. Her confidence increases.

However, she is still teetering. After all, she has yet to take that plunge from high excitement into orgasm. And that can feel like jumping off a cliff to land in complete darkness who knows where. To make such a leap into the unknown, a woman must, first, consciously decide to do so. Rarely do women get taken by surprise with an orgasm. The majority find themselves very excited—on a scale of 10 they feel they are at 8 or 9—and then, for some reason, they stop themselves.

They must analyze why they are stopping. After deciding why, they are then faced with the decision: "To come or not to come." Most women are so tired by now of being on the edge they clench their fists, set their minds, and vow, "I'm going to have an orgasm." Then they go home and do it.

The point of all this is that having an orgasm is an aggressive, assertive, conscious decision a woman makes. And that decision is what carries her over the edge from excitement to orgasm. It's not magic—it's you! During these two sessions it is to be hoped you will decide to make the Decision to Have an Orgasm. You have all the information by now. You know all about your body, and you've gotten very turned on. You can do it—you *can* take that leap now.

When you decide, remember: Don't push your body too fast. Make sure you let your body lead you. You can tell if you're forcing feelings because, if you are, you will feel frustrated or anxious. Also, you'll be doing many things but not feeling anything very much. Slow down! Keep your confidence! Tease, stop and go, keep feeling aroused, let your body take you there.

I've talked you as far as I can. The rest is up to you. Orgasms are not a vicarious experience. When they happen, it's because *you* did it!

About Orgasms—A Little Demystification

Orgasms, like all good things, come in all sorts of sizes, flavors, and forms. They take varying amounts of time. No two are alike, not even with the same woman.

There are a few things all orgasms seem to have in common, however: There is a period of mounting physical sensation, of tension and excitement. The mind gets a little fuzzy, devil-may-care space-y. Either quite suddenly or very gradually this tension ends, to be replaced by a feeling of well-being, relaxation, and satisfaction. If you've had this feeling, you've had an orgasm.

Women describe their orgasms differently. Some say, "It was like being swept away on a wave." Others report seeing vivid images and bright colors. Others experience a sweet sense of well-being and relief, sometimes so gentle they're not even sure it was an orgasm.

However, because of the myths surrounding orgasms, sometimes it can be hard to recognize them when they happen. There are a number of convenient ways to discredit them as more than one woman has discovered:

"Dr. Reuben Sez." Barbara came to group, described her orgasm in great detail and with ecstatic relish, but never called it an Orgasm. "Did you have an orgasm?" the group asked. "Well," she said, "if I'd been able to feel my vagina contract I would call it that."

There are many so-called authorities who purport to have the last scientific word on female sexual response. Women read their books and follow them word-for-word. If one expert says, "Nipples will be erect at orgasm," women eye their nipples to find out if they are turned on or not. Although the scientific research of William H. Masters and Virginia E. Johnson is important, women and their partners seem to have read their findings as they would a car manual: if it does this, then it's working right. Thus muscle contractions, amount of lubrication, pulse rate, skin color, response time, and technique are all rigidly defined. Doing this disregards the uniqueness of each woman's response. Nipples don't always get erect, lubrications vary, and responses can't be predicted. Barbara couldn't feel her vagina contracting because she was feeling every muscle in her body contract when she had orgasms. It took her some time to distinguish her vaginal contractions from her over-all body ones.

It's your feelings that count. Look for that sense of happiness, relief, and satisfaction which follows tension. You can get into the more sophisticated responses, like vaginal contractions and nipples, after you've recognized your orgasm feelings.

"I Have to Be Relaxed to Masturbate." Often women come to group and report an inability to pleasure themselves due to depression or nervousness. There's an idea that orgasms and pleasuring can happen only if "I'm in the right mood"— whatever that is. On the contrary, we've found that this work can put you in a good mood and take you out of feeling depressed. You may not want to get as far as having an orgasm,

but getting into a bathtub and indulging yourself for an hour (without guilt!) is an excellent meditation. Clear your mind of everything but physical pleasure for an hour, and your subconscious will reward you with a fresh outlook.

"I'll Know It When It Happens." Usually this is true. But sometimes, when a woman has a strong idea of what her orgasms should be like, she misses them even when they occur. If she's expecting fireworks, and instead feels a sweet slip over the edge, she may not recognize it. Pay close attention to your feelings. You can intensify your orgasms as you have more of them. But don't discredit those first ones, no matter how "small" they feel.

"Meanwhile—Back at the Group" Kathy, Lyn, Barbara and Marsha were sharing stories of their orgasms:

The week after the meeting in which Marsha revealed her competitive concerns about being orgasmic, Marsha returned, looking joyous. This time she wanted to report a big victory. "I did it!—I had an orgasm!" When the cheering died down, she was pressed for specifics. "It was really simple," Marsha said, shrugging her shoulders. "I just decided I was going to do it, and I did. It took me about forty-five minutes, I guess. I took my bath and I had some music on the radio. Everyone was out of the house so I had a lot of privacy and no concerns about being interrupted. Besides, it was in the afternoon and no one calls me or bothers me then. So, after my bath, I rubbed my favorite musk oil all over myself, particularly on my genitals, because I've found I really like that. And then I began to touch myself in the same old ways I always had. This time I decided not to stop but to just let myself feel as excited as I could. I rubbed my clitoris, never directly because that hurts, but to the right of it. . . . I rubbed here, about this fast," Marsha smiled, demonstrating a quick rhythm, "and after a while I felt very space-y and my breathing got fast and at some point I had to stop touching myself—it was just too much— and then I felt very relaxed and full and content. It was very nice, very satisfying."

Any problems?

"Only that I tried it again the next day and I couldn't do it. That's got me worried. But just a little. I think I was pushing myself too much and anticipating my responses, rather than letting them just come. I got very anxious, however, and panicked. Could the first one have been an accidental fluke? But, rather than feeling depressed, I decided to take a break for a day or so. The next time I tried I had an orgasm again, and I'm sure it was because I felt relaxed and assured I could. So, no—no problems really. Now I want to do it more!"

Although no one else claimed to having orgasms during that meeting, everyone agreed they felt inspired by Marsha's success. "I feel a little jealous," Barbara confessed. "But I'm relieved at the same time to know somebody took the leap and landed on their feet. It gives me confidence."

Kathy looked glum, however, and commented morosely that she "just knew everyone else is going to come but me. I'll be the one who can't."

"Mmm, sounds like you've made a decision," Lyn noted. "Sounds like you've decided you can't come, and so, therefore, you won't. You're still insisting on paying attention to the difficulties, rather than the successes. Look at how far you've come in these weeks. You've gotten more excited than you ever have before, you've been wonderfully creative with that crazy zucchini of yours! I think the only obstacle to your orgasms is your pessimism."

Marsha suggested Kathy think about her desire to have orgasms, and decide whether or not she really wanted to. And Barbara asked Kathy to bring her "Why I Love Me" list to group and read it aloud. "I think you'll feel more confident if you really believe you're good enough to deserve giving yourself orgasms."

The next meeting Barbara and Lyn both reported becoming orgasmic. Barbara even brought a cheesecake to celebrate with her sisters. After a congratulatory handshake and much giggling they each shared their winning with the others.

Lyn began. "Remember I said I felt like crying sometimes

when I get excited? This week, I let myself cry and realized my tears were many feelings. I felt sadness for the years I had felt like such a miserable sexual failure, and for the orgasms and pleasures I hadn't experienced. And I felt anger at men—and at myself—for the lousy sexual adventures I had endured. I resolved I'd never, ever want to have intercourse again if it's anything like it has been in my past—I really hate it! And my tears expressed my fear, too. My fear of 'Where do I go from here?' and 'Who will I ever share these feelings with?' And I longed for loving and knew that it had to come from me before it could come from anyone else.

"So, after this good cry, which lasted most of my hour, I took another bath, and rubbed oil on myself, and decided to treat myself gently. I took a long walk and had an ice cream cone, and realized how cleansed my mind and soul felt.

"The next day I felt eager to do my work. After the bath and lotion, I rubbed myself and kept right on rubbing until I had an orgasm. It felt wonderful! I don't want to be with any men for a while, I've decided. I'm very happy feeling good about my sexuality and my body—for the first time in my life—and I'm not ready to share it. I don't want to ruin it."

Barbara felt calmed by her success. "I spent a couple of hours concentrating on changing my attitudes towards my arousal feelings. They always felt painful to me, like I said before. So I decided to think of them as pleasurable in anticipation of an orgasm, and my masturbating went much easier. Whenever I felt too wound up I would get up and walk around and move to a little music. Not only did it spread the tension throughout my body, which relieved the areas of concentrated contractions, but it turned me on more, for some reason. In one hour I had *four* of those feelings that Marsha described! And I'd say they were orgasms, except that I couldn't feel my vagina muscles contracting or my nipples getting hard."

The group chuckled a bit over Barbara's multiple response and her subsequent attempts to discount her experience with a "Dr. Reuben Sez" question. The group assured her that as she became more accustomed to being orgasmic and more aware of

153

her bodily responses, she might be able to feel such contractions. "Some women feel them, some women don't," they reminded her. And the story on nipples is the same. Some women's nipples have very pronounced erections, others don't. Since the whole breast swells, whatever nipple erection does occur can get drowned by the swelling of the entire breast.

Barbara still looked dubious, so the group told her to go home and have more of those things that felt like orgasms and see if they really were, and to forget for now the needed proof.

Kathy, of course, looked more depressed than ever, although she tried to sound optimistic and cheerful. "I'm glad for all of you. I'm sure I will be next . . ." But she didn't sound convinced. All the same, she'd brought her "Why I Love Me" list and reluctantly agreed to share it with the group. At first she read her list in a monotone. "Read it like you mean it!" Barbara instructed. Kathy picked up the pace, wept a bit in the middle of her reading, but sounded stronger and more convinced by the end. "Do it again!" someone said. "I can't!" Kathy protested, near tears. So Marsha read it for her in as positive and nurturing a way as she could: "I love you for your warm smile. I love you for your great ass. I love you because you take good care of your family. I love you because you write poems." And so on. Kathy began to smile, finally, as the warm words spilled over her; she looked more hopeful than she had in weeks. Finally she read the list again herself, quite loudly. The group sat quietly for a moment in appreciative meditation.

Barbara spoke first. "Kathy, I really want you to come. I think you can do it—I know, because you've come so close. I don't want you to give up when you're this close. O.K.?"

"I thought about whether I want to have orgasms or not," Kathy replied, "and I do. I realized that I'd been scared, and a part of me kept hoping somebody else would do it for me. I realize, too, that having orgasms means growing up in other ways. It means I take responsibility for a big chunk of my life and my sexuality. No Prince or Princess Charming will do it for me. That responsibility has paralyzed me for weeks. But now that I see you are all growing up, I want to, too. And I know if anybody is going to do it, it has to be me. This week, I do my hours!"

It took Kathy two more weeks to have an orgasm. But when she finally did she flexed her biceps like a champ, exclaiming proudly about the rewards of hard work. "This is the most difficult thing I've ever done. And yet, it's the simplest, too. Orgasms are not hard. They require lots of concentration, that's all. I've never concentrated so hard on myself. I suppose it'll get easier, huh?"

"Yes, yes, yes," the more experienced reassured.

"Well, I'm sure glad it's happened. Wow—am I a champ! I did it in the bathtub. Fingers don't work as well for me as water. So I decided to stay with success, and my bathtub and I are now in love! I holed up in there for two hours one night after everyone had gone out or to bed. Actually, though, I didn't care if they were all sitting on the edge of the tub. I felt like I wanted to do it, fate was on my side, and nothing was going to stop me! I built up slowly and easily, then suddenly my body was all tingly. I noticed I was moaning and wondered if anyone was listening, decided 'who cares, anyway?'—and the next thing I knew I was laying there very quiet and content, listening to my heart pound. That must be an orgasm, I thought. What do you think?"

"Sounds like it," the group said. "Do it again, and see if it's so."

"Well," Kathy said slyly, "I already did. And it happened again. I like it. It's not at all what I expected, however. I thought I'd knock myself out on the bathtub tile in a frenzy, or hardly notice anything—but what happened is very sweet and satisfying, and friendly! I want to do it some more. I'd like my orgasms to get stronger. And from what I hear from you all, that'll happen as I do it more. Oh, am I relieved, I'm ever so relieved! I thought you guys were gonna ask me to leave for being such a poop. And I'm relieved because now I feel I can have a relationship with someone—and I never felt I could before because I always felt like such a dud!"

SO YOU DID IT, YES? CONGRATULATIONS!!! AN ORGASM!!!

Whenever a woman in group has her first orgasm, we always take a couple of minutes out for a round of applause and a congratulatory remark. Do the same for you—toast yourself with a glass of champagne, take a celebratory hike—whatever appeals to you; but mark the occasion with special ceremony.

So how do you feel now? Has the world changed? You're probably noticing it hasn't. But *you* have—feel a bit more relaxed? Relieved? Like yourself better?

Although you have had an orgasm, the more you do them the better they get, and the easier they come. So before moving on from your present sexual relationship with yourself, continue to have orgasms just with you for a week or so. The purpose of this is to make sure you know exactly what you need to have an orgasm, and to give you confidence that you can do it whenever you want to. This also furnishes you the chance to begin determining your own special rhythm, to see precisely how and when you like to be sexy, and to convince you that you and your body are sexually healthy.

So where do you go from here? Many women want to share their orgasms with their lovers. If so, Chapter 13 will tell you how to do just that.

Other women want to continue to enjoy their sexuality for themselves, either because they have no current partners or because they have made a decision to be celibate for a time. If you are one of these women, the previous discussion in Chapter 9 on the positive aspects of celibacy (pp. 109–115) should have given you some ideas on how to preserve a creative sexual identity.

Some Specific Answers to Masturbation Problems

CHAPTER 11. Masturbation is important to women. This has been proven time and again by the many stories brought to us in group. A woman who knows how to masturbate will also have a better time with her lover. Perhaps even more to the point, masturbation affords a kind of self-awareness and is quite pleasurable.

What follows, then, are some of the most frequently asked questions concerning this subject that have come up during various sexual problem-solving groups. Since female genitals and orgasms are related, we have also included questions on these subjects as well.

Should I Masturbate in Order to Be a Liberated Woman?

First of all, any behavior with a "should" attached to it is not a good idea. If you think you should masturbate, the chances of your being successful and enjoying it are going to be limited.

Secondly, there is more to being a liberated woman than just being able to give yourself orgasms. Personally, I think it is important. After all, men have been controlling women's sexuality for years, not only in bed, but psychologically, and by setting up standards. Masturbating and finding out we can give ourselves orgasms is an important move towards independence, somewhat akin to demanding and getting equal salaries, equal jobs, equal privileges. All the same, giving yourself orgasms does not necessarily mean you are liberated. Nor, conversely, not giving yourself orgasms does not always mean you're not liberated.

Do not "should" yourself about masturbating. Do it for fun and self-celebration. Do not do it because you have to in order to prove something. We have found in group after group that women who try to masturbate because they "should" rather than because they "want" have a high fail rate.

I've Masturbated Like Crazy and Still Feel Nothing. It's Hopeless. Any Suggestions?

Yes. Read the previous chapter which gives you step-by-step suggestions on reaching orgasm through masturbating. Go slow and pay attention to every touch.

Keep in mind that there is no such thing as feeling "nothing." You are feeling *something,* even if it's not strong, or doesn't feel good, or is only vaguely pleasurable. When a woman in group says this we ask her: "Well, did touching your genitals feel different from touching your elbow?" Naturally, it did; and she can go on from there to be more articulate about those differences. Ask yourself, "Does the mons feel different from my lips? Which feels better? Do I like to touch my clitoris directly, or on the hood? Where does it feel best to touch my genitals? Where does it feel blah? Where is it uncomfortable?

Finally, it is not hopeless. You are learning a new skill and, like anything new, it takes time to get it down. So be gentle and patient with yourself, and follow only the good feelings, no matter how just barely good they feel.

How Can You Feel Good About Your Body When You've Felt Bad About It for So Long?

In the masturbation exercises in the previous chapter every woman is asked to stand in front of a mirror, move about, and observe her body, seeing what she likes and what she doesn't like. Some women find this difficult. Just as we can point out every pimple on our face, so we can tell you every unsightly bump on our body. We've usually been putting ourselves down for years, comparing ourselves point-by-point to all those emaciated ladies in the magazine ads. Hence, being asked to turn your opinion around about yourself overnight seems an impossible expectation.

You are not asked to change your opinion overnight. It is a gradual process: to go from negative, to accepting, to positive, to loving. The way we do this in group is to allow one group meeting for women to share all the ugly feelings they have about their bodies. Everyone sits and tells all the "awfuls" and "terribles," in one monumental dump session. But, after that, women are expected to think positive. During the rest of the group they are permitted to say only good things about their bodies. Of course, some women rebel against this, finding it difficult and image-breaking. They cry it's impossible and insist they can't do it. We stick by our guns. And, sure enough, after just a couple of weeks, women are finding good things and enjoying the changes feeling good about their bodies creates. They feel more confident; they feel more sexually turned on; and they feel more beautiful. Scarfs that covered hair come off, sweaters that concealed lovely breasts are shed, skirts that hid "fat" legs now give way to shorter skirts and flattering tights.

You will feel good about yourself. Change your thoughts from negative to positive. Help yourself by hanging a note up in your room to remind yourself what you like about your body. Whenever you notice yourself muttering, "Fat, Fat, Fat" or "not right—too this or too that," read your positive message to self. Also, don't discount their compliments when friends and lovers, men and women, tell you what a beautiful body you have. Listen to what they say. Remember their words, repeat them aloud if you have to, and then write them down on that positive list. If you think they're just "jivin' you," tell them that and ask them to be sincere. Don't automatically chalk it up to being "another line." Gather ye compliments where ye may—and don't insist on being a changed woman overnight. Go easy on your change of identity from plain to gorgeous.

Men Will Be Turned Off to Me If They Know I Masturbate.

This has, indeed, happened to some women. They confess how they told a partner they would like to masturbate with him and he went, "Ugh! That's just too weird!" Fortunately, the women who told me these experiences had enough self-confidence to put on their panties and say, "So long, Charlie." If a man is so Neanderthal that he feels this way, he's not worth your time—and certainly doesn't deserve the pleasures of your sexuality.

On the other hand, most men are excited by a woman masturbating. Have you ever watched a lover masturbate? Did it turn you on? Try it and see what you feel. It may scare you a little at first, but most women say that later gives way to feeling turned on. So that is how your lover will feel, in all likelihood, about your masturbation.

Men are often pleased to know a woman masturbates because it indicates she knows what she likes in sex. That takes the performance burden off him. He knows he's having sex with someone who can take care of herself, so he can relax and enjoy and not worry about her orgasms.

If you're curious or concerned, ask your partner how he feels. Also, ask other men how they feel about women masturbating. I've found most men are happy to tell you, and at great length. Anyway, it makes for instructive and fun conversation, for both you and him.

I Shouldn't Masturbate During My Period, Pregnancy, or Menopause.

Not true.

Many women purposely masturbate during their period because they find it relieves the cramps. Others are sexually turned on during their period because of the abdominal congestion created by the menses. Orgasms contract the uterus and sometimes help a reluctant period to flow along a bit more smoothly.

As for pregnancy and masturbating. Check with your doctor, of course, but many books and women say that masturbating was good because the uterine contractions exercised the womb, thus preparing it for childbirth.

Finally, more than one woman has recommended masturbation to relieve the "hot flashes" and depression of menopause.

Orgasms are a perfectly natural body function, and, like any form of exercise and happiness, are usually good for the body and soul and mind.

My Partner Is Jealous of My Masturbation Time. He Interferes and Seems to Be Pouting. What Can I Do?

Ask him what's going on. Sometimes men are worried about women learning to masturbate because they fear they won't be needed anymore. Your partner needs reassurance that he will still be a valued lover even though you can give yourself orgasms. He also needs to be made aware that your desires and needs will change, and this will also require some changes on his part. For instance, he's going to have to learn that sex is more than a penis performance and more than just orgasms.

To be absolutely honest with you, in some groups women who have encountered this sort of interference from partners have decided to end their relationships. They have discussed the problem with their lover and found his attitudes unacceptable. This was not an easy or quick decision, and the group was always careful not to make such a decision for the woman. At any rate, you should be aware that some women have found their partners' lack of cooperation more than they are willing to tolerate.

But if you want to work it out with your partner, take time to talk straight to each other—and be as gentle and nurturing to each other as you can. Gaining your sexual independence will change the nature of your relationship for sure, so keep that in mind and be prepared for some ups and downs. Again, that's one reason it's good to have women to talk with about the changes. They've been through them, or are going through them, and can give you support and encouragement.

When I Learned to Masturbate and Realized How Men Had Kept Me From Enjoying My Sexuality, I Became Angry at Them. I Still Am. Is That O.K.? How Do I Cool Off?

One of the difficult things to do in a group is to keep an even-handed view of men when women realize how much they've been missing and how much men haven't been missing. It's easy for a group to decide that *all* men are creepy and not O.K. and then spend too much time talking about how awful they are. Granted, men have had a better deal sexually than women have, and women's anger is more than justified. However, it's a waste of woman-time and group-time to focus on how bad it all is. It's more important to put this time and, energy into planning how to make it better.

Use this anger to stimulate yourself into better relationships with men. Decide what you want to do with them and stick with that decision until you feel like making another. For instance, if you decide you don't want to have sex with men for months, that's fine. Don't. And don't have sex until you meet a man you think you'll enjoy it with, someone you've decided you want to share your sexuality with. Use that anger to insist that men take you seriously, be your friends, express their value of you in ways other than sex. Turn that righteous anger into being independent of men. Often those most angry are those who depended on men the most. Depend on you yourself and other women for some time, and find out how freeing that is. Use that anger to tell men that you want them to be as nurturing and kind to you as your women friends are.

If you're so angry you don't want to ever see a man again, then stay away from them. Spend your time and emotions with women, and from there decide how you feel about men. Maybe you'll find you neither desire them nor need them. Or maybe you'll redefine your relationships with them so you are an equal.

Be aware that this anger at men can run deep. Again, it's a process of gradual awareness in deciding what to do about relating to them. By learning to have orgasms you awaken yourself to stage one of the awareness of inequality. Over the years you come to realize others—realize how you collude, learn how to fight it, and your life changes accordingly. It's taken most of us years to figure all this out, and just when we think it's finally settled, another problem comes up. Perhaps that's because our anger is all wrapped up with our cultural needs for men and our deep fears of not being as well-off without them. It's not a simple question. And there are no simple answers.

Personally, I've handled my anger by not stereotyping men. I try not to call them "them" and I work at changing my needs from them. That is, I used to need men to support me financially and I needed their approval to feel that I was worthwhile. Lately, I've been concentrating on being financially independent, and getting my emotional support from myself and from women. I now find that I like a different kind of man, a man much more an equal, because I don't need that daddy-type authority like I used to. Again, it's a process, and each woman interested in being liberated is going through it. Share your journey with your sisters. They understand; and, between us, we have all the answers for doing it successfully.

I Feel Bad that the Only Orgasms I Can Have Are With a Vibrator.
Don't feel bad. Orgasms are orgasms—and there are no right ways or wrong ways. Some women put themselves down for not being able to use their fingers to have orgasms, saying that fingers are more organic, more natural.

Well, sure it's nice to know how to use your fingers. That way if you get stranded in Guatemala with dead batteries in your vibrator (this actually happened to one group member) then you have an instant alternative. In addition, it's just plain fun to have more than one way to reach an orgasm. Variety is the spice of life, you know.

But if you use a vibrator and you're happy with it and you like your orgasms and you can use it easily with your lover, that's great, too. Enjoy!

Are Women's Genitals All Alike?

No, not at all. Our genitals are as different as fingerprints, as unique as snowflakes, as individual as our personalities.

One of the most instructive and liberating experiences women report doing is taking a self-help course at a feminist clinic. There they are taught how to use a speculum and give a pelvic exam. In learning this, they get a chance to look at each other's vulvas. The "oooh's!" and "aaah's" would make an outsider think she was hearing the audience response at a couturier fashion show.

If a group requests it, we will spend the last of the ten meetings using our specula and studying each others' features. It's fun and intimate—I recommend it for every woman's group.

Not only are our vulvas different, but our vaginas are, too. My best friend Stela and I both discovered this when we attended the self-help class. I'm tall and she's short, but our vaginas were the opposite. She needed a large speculum to see her cervix; and since the discovery of her amazing length has referred most proudly to her "tunnel of love." I needed a short speculum for my salmon-pink orifice—and short little Stela has never let me hear the end of it!

One woman in group was curious if genital features run in the family, like chins and eyes and noses. So she, her mother, and her sisters all sat down and compared vulvas. There was no similarity, they were each very different. You might like to do the same with the women in your family.

I Feel Sexually Dead. I'm Not Turned On at All, and I Certainly Can't Have Orgasms. What's Going On?

Because your sexual feelings and your sense of being powerful are inextricably connected, when you're not feeling turned on, most likely you are also not feeling that you are being a powerful person. For instance, if you are not getting what you want from your job, or if your relationship with your partner is keeping you from your goals, or if you are just generally feeling that the world is moving you, rather than you it, then it is not an unusual reaction to shut down your sexual feelings. The first feelings to be sacrificed in times of high stress and struggle for survival are the sexual ones.

Another common reason for these feelings is just being too plain busy. There are other things in this great world to do than work on sex and relationships and so on; and if you are putting your energy into other areas that satisfy you, then you may, quite naturally, have none left over for sex. That is perfectly reasonable. If you have a new job that is taking all your energy to conquer, or if you are learning a new form of art and your entire heart and mind are being given to it, or if you're exercising and want your physicalness to be without sex—these are all perfectly normal reasons why women don't feel sexual for periods of time.

If you are feeling disinterested in sex, determine which of these reasons seems most appropriate. If it is the first reason—that you're feeling powerless—determine where this occurs and get support to change your life. Many women who are in unhappy relationships with their lovers are surprised to discover that their sexual feelings return a few days after they assert themselves and institute changes to make themselves feel happier—even if this means leaving their partner. Some women like to call a moratorium on sex, and just masturbate for a while; they find such release from the stress of partner-sex enables them to feel sexy again.

Asking for what you want and working insistently to get it always makes you feel more powerful. Keep that in mind.

If you aren't feeling sexually turned on now because you're turned on to your job, or some other pursuit, relax and enjoy it. That energy which you normally experience as sexual can inspire you in other ways—and it's good to know that.

Particularly if you are the kind of woman, like so many of us are or have been, who has been scripted to believe that sexuality is your *only* power. You will probably be pleased to realize that you are powerful in other ways and that the energy you've been using exclusively for partners can also be used for you and for your own good feelings.

One thing to watch out for, though, is the feeling that some women have: that they don't have *time* for sex. Busy, busy, busy! like the White Rabbit in *Alice in Wonderland,* they rush around and leave no time for personal pleasure—and sex is personal pleasure. There is always time for relaxing and masturbating. Women have been in groups while in the middle of composing doctoral theses, and yet were able to find time to spend luxuriating in the bathtub and having an orgasm or two. They found it helped their work, because it relaxed them physically; and, like a meditation, cleared their brains for an hour or so. You may not have time for the complications of partners—but don't forget that you always have you.

Orgasms Mean Going Out of Control. I'll Hurt Myself. Or Go Crazy.

Some women get very close to having an orgasm, and then they stop themselves. They fear that last plunge over the edge because they think they'll never come back, or else come back in bad shape.

For women who are concerned about being out of control, let me assure them: you will never be out of control until you *want* to be. A woman's body and mind control her orgasms. Do you know that you can even stop having an orgasm right in the middle? If you follow the masturbation exercises provided earlier in Chapter 10, taking it slow and talking with your women friends, you will have an orgasm that you yourself control. Yes, you might feel out of control for a few seconds. But by the time you reach that point, you will feel comfortable with those few seconds of being suspended in time.

As for hurting yourself. If you are a wriggler and are worried about banging against something, then protect yourself. Pile pillows around you, masturbate on the floor, use your whole bed. In the tub? Don't fill it too deep. We haven't had a drowning yet—but if you're worried, take precautions.

There is also a myth that orgasms mean your body explodes like Chinese firecrackers. So many women expect it. In all probability, your orgasms will not be like that. Some first orgasms are so gentle as to be barely noticeable, and are experienced as a "flip-flop" or "nice feeling."

Some women worry about going crazy because they have found the Path to Orgasm lined with so many emotional awakenings. Some have gotten in touch with sadness, anger, grief, profound longings, great joys. They have burst into tears at some point in their masturbation—and this deep well of emotions has frightened them. They worry that when they actually reach orgasm their emotions will tear them apart.

This will not happen. You are in control of those feelings, and can let them go or stop them at will. After all, you've been controlling them for many years now. Also, these are *good* feelings. It is beneficial to feel and express them; because those very feelings have probably been the ones blocking the Path to Orgasm.

One woman, a law student, had tried to have orgasms for years and never succeeded. She was desperate, and had come to our workshop to learn what she was doing wrong. At one point she was talking about how she masturbated, and suddenly couldn't go on, her body racked by an uncontrollable flood of tears. Immediately she was surrounded by women friends who comforted her and asked her to explain. When she spoke again it was to sob out months' worth of hurt feelings. She felt very relieved, she said, and a huge burden was lifted from her heart. A couple of months later I got a letter from her. She'd learned to give herself orgasms, she wrote happily. Letting all those feelings go had opened the way for her to feel her sexuality.

*When I Have an Orgasm I'll Probably Urinate, or Fart, or Make
Ugly Sounds.*

After seeing women in porno films, or even in standard
X-rated Hollywood movies, a woman gets the idea that she
should come with all the softness and delicacy of a magnolia
blossom. And if she's read D. H. Lawrence she finds that she
ought to come quietly, the maximum sound being a soft moan.
The ideas we get about orgasms from the media and literature
are male ideas. Lately, of course, men have discovered that
women do make noise; and now some women think they have
to "whoop and holler" to convince a man they're climaxing.
So sound is a problem with orgasms.

Erase the "should's" from your mind. And when you
masturbate next time, notice if you are making any noise. If
you're having trouble finding your orgasms, you might like to
add some of your own sounds. Many women say their sex
noises turn them on. But don't perform them. Do the noises
you enjoy—and forget about Choo-Choo Lamour and the
other porno weirdos, or the fancy ladies in novels. Your
sounds will not be ugly. They will be you-sounds, the sounds
of you enjoying your passions. Unfamiliar, yes. But not ugly.
Let them flow. After some experience, you will find they are
beautiful and you enjoy them.

As for urinating. It is not uncommon for women to urinate with orgasm. Some women enjoy this, others don't. If
you enjoy it, make sure you have a towel under you so you
don't stain the sheets.

The reason many women urinate is because their bladder
muscles are weak and the release of orgasm also releases the
bladder. Kegel exercises, given earlier on pages 130 and 131,
strengthen these muscles and will prevent most of the urinating.

It is a very common feeling just prior to orgasm that one is
going to urinate. Some women feel this, and yet don't actually
urinate. Again, if you're concerned, put a towel under you.

The most embarrassing time to pass gas, or "fart"—which
is a perfectly good Middle-English verb—is when your lover is

kissing your genitals. If you feel it coming, you might leap out of bed and get a glass of water. If you're lost in orgasm feelings, he probably won't even notice because he (or she) is so turned on, also. Don't hang on to not having orgasms because you're worried about being indelicate. Bodies are bodies—and next time maybe refrain from eating beans at dinner!

Women in group discovered a funny noise which we named "varts." These are vaginal farts, the sound made when air leaves the vagina. They are non-odiferous and sound funny. You can safely giggle at them.

I'll Get Violent If I Have Orgasms.

Some women explain that they fear having an orgasm with a man because they will get violent. These women are confused about the relationship between power and violence—they think they're the same thing. So when they begin to experience all the strong emotions that come with an orgasm, they are sure that these also signal violence. One woman told us she feared she'd bounce up and down on a man so vigorously that she'd break his penis. We told her not to worry—he'd be taking care of himself and would let her know. In any case, vigorous bouncing up and down is not violence. When the woman understood that, she was able to begin distinguishing between her angry feelings at men, and her sexually powerful ones.

The woman learned to express her anger in healthy ways—by talking, pounding pillows, blowing off steam through jogging. Then she was no longer fearful of her sexual feelings, and let her passions flow.

If you continue to be concerned about violence, share your concerns with other women. Be specific about what you might do. "I'll stab myself with a knife," one woman said, fearfully. The solution here was simple. Once she'd said that, she knew she wouldn't do it—because she didn't want to hurt herself. She also made sure she had no sharp objects around, so she wouldn't even have to worry. When she found her orgasms, she discovered no desire or need to hurt herself.

By expressing your worries, you can, with the feedback of other women, decide how to handle them. You will also find that you aren't weird or crazy. Many other women will have had the same concerns.

I've Had a Traumatic Sexual Experience. Can I Ever Get Over It and Enjoy Sex?

Yes, for sure. One of the beauties of doing the sort of sexual problem-solving discussed in this book is that it is physical, not merely psychological. This physicalness enables women to overcome the psychological blocks that have kept them separated from their sexual feelings. By concentrating on the body first, and the mind second, women who have had a traumatic sexual experience can use the loving they are giving their bodies to deal with the traumas they still feel in their hearts and minds.

Women who have been brainwashed by Catholicism, or have been raped, or have had painful abortions, or who have experienced any sort of sexual violence often come to group convinced they will never overcome their fears. Leona, for example, had been celibate and non-orgasmic for six years. She was twenty-six, and when she was twenty had consented to her first intercourse with a man at college. Like many of us, she had sex with him solely because she didn't want to be a virgin by the age of twenty-one and felt it was time to get the whole thing over and done with. The trouble was, Leona got pregnant on her very first fuck; and because she didn't know anything about her body didn't find out she was pregnant until after she'd missed two periods.

Leona, who was living in Texas at the time, went to see a doctor. He told her she was not pregnant. So did a few other doctors. But Leona knew she was. Finally, when she was already four months pregnant, her condition was confirmed. Leona arranged for an illegal abortion in New Mexico. She still remembers it as one of the most painful, humiliating, and frightening experiences of her life. No wonder she swore off sex and men.

For three years Leona had been in psychoanalysis trying to rediscover her sexuality and overcome her trauma. She was getting nowhere fast. Deciding she had nothing to lose, she joined a pre-orgasmic women's group.

With the loving help of other women Leona spilled out her unhappy past, got all her questions answered, and by the eighth session of group was quite happily having orgasms in her bathtub. Now that she knew how to take care of herself, and also that she was not alone in her traumatic experience, Leona was free to open up to herself and to the possibility of other lovers. "I never thought I'd be able to even consider having a lover," she said at the end of group. "But now I know I can—and, besides, I want to. I'm looking around."

Then there was Kathy. A Catholic, she had been told by nuns at school and by her grandmother that sex was "bad," and that only "tramps" had orgasms. Plunging in—body first, mind second—Kathy was at last able to liquidate the residuals of Grandma and Holy Ma Church by discovering the beauty of her body. She saw that the women she admired most were orgasmic and not "tramps." Kathy was so excited about her success that she gave herself a necklace that she had originally intended for her first true love. "My first true love is me!" she told the group as she placed the gold chain around her own neck. She also decided to join an ongoing women's group in order to receive strength and support for accomplishing successes in other areas.

To overcome traumatic sexual experiences requires good sexual experiences. You can have these with yourself. In doing so, you will not only discover that sex is enjoyable, but you'll also come to value yourself. The more educated you are about your own sexuality the fewer unhappy sexual experiences will you have with others.

If I Come Once, I'll Never Come Again.

The reason I ask you to go one step at a time in learning to have orgasms is so that the above won't happen to you. The purpose of step-by-step exercises is so you can plot how to have your orgasms, making you familiar with every step, every touch, every wiggle along the way. Each woman has her own Path to Orgasm; and if you pay careful attention to your own you will be able to repeat it again and again.

It is common for women to have their first orgasm, get very excited about it, rush home to do it again—and then discover, to their horror, that they can't. That's because they are forcing it, pushing themselves to feel those good feelings again. Relax. Follow your body's pleasurable feelings. Don't force feelings onto your body. Once you relax, orgasms will happen again.

My Shrink Says That When I Get My Head Together My Orgasms Will Occur Naturally and Simply. Is That True?

No.

Some of the craziest women in the world are easily orgasmic, and some of the sanest women in the world are not. Having your head "together" (which, of course, is a relative term) has very little to do with whether or not you are orgasmic.

Orgasms are a physical response accompanied by a mental release which says "Yes, you can come." You must learn how to give them to yourself physically, as you let your mind open up your body to its sensations. Basically, orgasms are a learned response, a skill. They are not an indication of mental health, the way the body temperature is of physical health.

So if your head doctor is telling you this, switch to a woman's group, or a feminist therapist, who know what they're talking about.

There Is an Orgasm Economy: If I Come Too Often I'll Use All My Orgasms Up.

Actually, the opposite of this is true. The more you come, the more orgasms you can have. Like push-ups, the more you do, the more you can do.

Of course, there are physical limits. If you have had two orgasms in one day and then that evening find yourself

172

orgasmic-less with your lover it's probably because you are just plain tired. Or you're just not interested in any more orgasms right now. In any case, you haven't run out. If you wanted to, you could have more.

The more often you have orgasms, the more familiar your body becomes with that response; hence, the easier it is to coax orgasms from it. You have a limitless supply of orgasms. Remember: you can have as many as you want to have.

Men Tell Me I'm the Best Fuck They Ever Had. I Like That. But I've Never Had Orgasms? Why?

Because you are too concerned with being the perfect sexual partner. When a man's praise means more to you than your own personal pleasure, you will not be able to have orgasms. To have orgasms, the priorities must be reversed: You must come first. You will be pleased to know that when you are taking care of what *you* want, your lover will find you just as sexy as ever. Lovers like their partners to be truly turned on and having orgasms.

Another reason you might consider is whether you are involved in some kind of power-play with your lover. Sometimes women who are invested in being in control, in staying one-up on their lovers, have a difficult time letting go and experiencing orgasms. A woman especially feels this if she senses that her lover truly wants her to come, her orgasms meaning more to him than they do to her—but only as a proof that he is such a good lover and she is completely in his power.

If you are competing with each other sexually, you will probably have a difficult time becoming orgasmic. You might even have to fake it in order to convince your lover that you're really a hot, sexy woman. And we all know from experience that, once you've faked orgasms, it's difficult ever to have the real thing with that particular partner.

You also may not be having orgasms because you are adapting to his style of love-making, and not asking for what you want.

Other women are not orgasmic with partners because they

are too passive, waiting like Sleeping Beauty for their lover to push the right button to send them into total orgasm. Only that, they believe, will indicate they have found True Love. Such women are often orgasmically monogamous, though not necessarily sexually monogamous. They have orgasms only with Mr. Right, and offer that as proof of their fidelity—although they still may enjoy having sex with other partners. Personally, I think that's pretty "game-y," but some couples seem to like it.

I've Been Faking Orgasms With My Lover. If I Learn How to Have Them, Won't He Know I Was Faking Earlier and Get Angry? What Do I Do?

Some women like to tell their partners, others don't.

I believe in being totally honest and telling them.

After all, your partner plays a significant part in why you have been faking it. It was for love of him, a desire to not hurt him, or a fear that he might not still want you if you weren't sexually "healthy" that drove you to lie, in the first place. Also, he is going to have to cooperate in making changes in how you both do sex in order for you to become orgasmic. It will be easier for your lover to understand these changes if he knows they are really making you happy.

You will also feel better after telling your lover. Hiding something as significant as pretending to enjoy love-making is a big burden. It may continue to keep you from being orgasmic. After all, you need the freedom of knowing he likes you for who you are, is willing to help you discover your orgasms, and will support your being sexually fulfilled. If you don't have these assurances, you will be trying to have orgasms all by yourself with a partner who thinks everything is A-O.K. Frankly, such contradictions are too much for most women to deal with, especially when trying to have orgasms at the same time.

If you're worried your lover will be angry and leave you, that's a chance you must take. If he's that kind of guy, you're better off without him. If he feels hurt and humiliated, you in turn must be prepared to reassure and comfort him. Being lied to under any circumstances is demeaning, so it is to be expected he'll get upset. But after you apologize and console him, you don't owe him anything further, except continuing to tell the truth. Don't let him get away with revenging himself on you by not being cooperative when you ask for what you want. Make an arrangement to start all over, to wipe the slate clean. No resentments. No past vindictiveness. You were both in error to some degree, and you both deserve another chance.

Are All Orgasms Alike?

No, not at all.

Not only are orgasms very different from woman to woman, but each woman has a variety of orgasms.

If you ask a woman to tell about her orgasms, she will probably describe at least two different kinds. She has strong ones, and weak ones. Some she feels in her vagina, others in her clitoris. There are those, too, she feels all over her body. She has orgasms which are a perfect combination of the physical and the emotional, and others which are either purely physical, or purely emotional. She feels like "a little something turning over in my belly" while others feel like "I'm flying away to the stars." Some women can feel their uterus contract, others cannot.

Depending upon the mood she is in, the time of the month, and her feeling about her lover, a woman will have a different kind of orgasm in almost every situation. Many women have testified that the orgasms they have while masturbating are quite different—often stronger—than the ones they have with partners.

So if you are comparing orgasms with your best friend Sally and hers are different than yours, don't wonder what's wrong. Nothing is. And, above all, don't feel competitive. There are no rights or wrongs in orgasms—all are good and natural.

The only thing in common concerning orgasms, to judge by what women say in group, is that in all of them there is a certain feeling of exciting build-up leading to a kind of satisfying release. Women also report that the more experienced they become in having orgasms, the easier they are to have, and the stronger they feel. Beyond this, orgasms are as unique as kisses.

How Long Does It Take to Have an Orgasm?
Longer than you think.

The average time for women in our groups has been forty-five minutes.

"Forty-five minutes!" I hear you exclaim. "But, but—?"

Yes, it's true. Not five, not ten, not twenty. Forty-five. That is going from cold to hot, from not even thinking about orgasms to having one.

Of course, if a woman has been fantasizing all during the day, then returns home and masturbates to orgasm in twenty minutes, she has not gone from cold to hot. She's gone from warm to hot. Her fantasies had already excited her to some degree.

So take your time. Give yourself all day if necessary. You will have lots of company.

I Thought When I Learned to Have Orgasms, All My Problems Would Be Solved. They're Not. Now What Do I Do?
Orgasms are not a cure-all. You are not going to have orgasms and, because of that, suddenly turn into a liberated, strong, in-control woman. You will have taken a major step toward that goal, though. Learning to have orgasms will prove to you that you *can* succeed—that you can accomplish what you want when you set your mind to it. You can then apply the same technique to your other goals in life. But just as it took you time to learn to have orgasms, so it will take time to accomplish these other desires as well.

Having orgasms will solve some problems in your life, but create others. For instance, many women, prior to being orgasmic, were quite content with the men in their lives. Things weren't great; but they weren't bad, either. After having orgasms, many women see men quite differently, and they are not happy with what they see. They see the effects of sexism— the inequality, the emotional disparity, the male's tendency to value sex more than friendship in his dealings with women. Such orgasmic women seek changes in their relationships with men, and it takes time to make those changes. So having orgasms doesn't mean instantly good relationships with men. But it does mean that the ones you eventually establish will be of a higher quality than those you had before.

Sometimes I Cry During Sex, and Often During or Right After Orgasm. Why?

The deep breathing that accompanies orgasm often brings very deep feelings to the surface. If you have ever done any body therapy, such as bioenergetics, which uses deep breathing as a fundamental technique, you are aware of the enlightening and cleansing effects of taking deep, slow, regular breaths. These feelings which surface can evoke tears, for they may be feelings of great sadness, hurt, anger, or even joy. Don't stop the feelings—let them happen. They will provide answers to many emotional concerns you may have been having lately, and you will feel relieved and psychologically cleansed afterwards.

How Can I Come in New Ways? I Seem Stuck With Just One.

Every time we group leaders of pre-orgasmic women forgot how difficult it is for women to learn to give themselves orgasms, a reminder would be to teach ourselves a new way to have our own orgasms. We would then go through all the frustration and boredom inherent in such a situation, and thus understand once more the tortures pre-orgasmic women were undergoing. Of course, there were rewards, too: the heady rush that accompanied eventual success—and the fun of having an orgasm a new way. It still took time, though, because we, too, were re-learning.

Consequently, whenever you decide you want to learn to come in a new way, remember that it will not happen overnight. Remember you are teaching your body to respond to new sorts of stimulation. Don't give up. Do it a little bit at a time. And when you've tried long enough, give yourself an orgasm by going back to your tried-and-true way. If you work on a new method diligently enough, you will eventually be able to have orgasms in that manner also.

Some hints from women who have made switches in their routines: If you want to learn to enjoy cunnilingus, try teaching yourself to have orgasms under the tub faucet or by using a European shower. If you want to learn to come during intercourse, you might start out by first having orgasms by rubbing your clitoris—and entire vulva—against your lover's thigh. Want to learn to come on your stomach rather than your back? Some women like to put a pillow under their belly to elevate their genitals, for easier stimulation and more abdominal pressure. Many women like to masturbate to orgasm by putting a pillow between their legs. And one woman I know had a broad-backed fuzzy-haired white French poodle, who, being old and sedate, didn't mind in the least being used for her mistress's orgasmic pleasures.

To get the full story on orgasmic inventiveness, talk with other women. You'll learn a lot of new tricks and get permission to be silly and "kinky" and free.

I'm Not in Love with Anyone Right Now. But I Want to Learn to Have Orgasms with a Partner. What Can I Do?

Got a good friend? Good friends often make good people to learn to have orgasms with. That's because you are not entangled in the web of romance. You're not worried about impressing him as the woman of his dreams, and he's not worried that you might want to marry him and chain him down. The interest is good sex, pure and simple. And there's almost nothing nicer or easier than having sex with a pal.

Last Christmas I got a card from a woman who had done exactly this. She thanked me for the group, writing: "I am now having the romantic and sexual affair I always dreamed of!" When Ilene came to group, she was in the process of divorcing her husband. Yet she wanted to learn to have orgasms with him because they still liked each other and she felt secure with him. They made an arrangement to meet twice a week for two hours to be sexy together.

Ilene discovered that she had more sexual drive than he. She also discovered that he came too soon for her satisfaction. She found she had to work hard to have orgasms with him—so hard, in fact, that she finally decided it wasn't worth it. "I guess that's just another instance of why we're getting divorced. He's just too difficult for me." Ilene felt good about her decisions, and confident of her abilities in the future to be orgasmic with whomever she wanted to be. And she was, as her rhapsodic letter at Christmas testified.

I Have Better Orgasms When I Masturbate Than I Do With My Partner. What Can I Do So My Partner-Orgasms Are As Good?

First of all, keep in mind that masturbation-orgasms and partner-orgasms are two completely different kinds of orgasms. Also, as you have probably heard already, many women say the orgasms they have by themselves are stronger than those they have with lovers. This is quite common.

But if there is too great a disparity, perhaps it is because you change too completely your love-making style with a partner. As I suggested earlier, when you are with a partner emulate as closely as you can the situation when you are alone. Try for the same amount of time, the same touches, the same lubrication, the same atmosphere. Doing this may make your partner-orgasms as pleasurable as the ones with you. Oh—and this should go without saying—make sure you like your partner as much as you like your first lover—yourself. That makes quite a difference, too!

I've Heard So Much Talk About It But I'm Still Confused: Is There Such a Thing as a Vaginal Vs. a Clitoral Orgasm?

There are vaginal orgasms. And there are clitoral orgasms. There is no "vs."

There are also lip orgasms, and ear-lobe orgasms, and

big-toe orgasms, and small-of-the-back orgasms, and neck orgasms. There are orgasms for any part of the body. Why am I sounding so silly? Because I want to make the point that no matter where you feel an orgasm on your body, the fact is it's due to your clitoris being stimulated—directly or indirectly.

You may experience the orgasm wherever your body is sensually sensitive enough to feel such strong feelings. But the reason it happened is because your clitoris got excited and your body went through the normal response cycles that come with any orgasm.

You may, then, feel an orgasm in your vagina. But the reason it happened was because your clitoris was stimulated. If your clitoris weren't stimulated, you would not feel a vaginal orgasm.

Why Can't I Be Multiply Orgasmic?

You can, if you want to be. Any woman can. It is a potential each of us carries.

But many women are perfectly happy with one ever-so-satisfying orgasm. That does not mean that they are less sexy, less turned-on, or in any way not sexually up to par. It means that they are happy with *one* orgasm. And that's good.

The emphasis placed on multiple orgasms is due to the male model of what is sexually good. Because men view orgasm as the goal, the whole point, of sex, they figure "the more the better." And, of course, many men feel that the more orgasms a woman has the better lovers they are. By women's standards, however, the point is whether or not you had fun and if you are left feeling satisfied.

Some women say they feel frustrated, even after having had an orgasm. Because the blood dissipates so slowly from the pelvic area, women still have enough potential pressure remaining to experience another orgasm if they desire. So if you feel you would like more, re-stimulate yourself—and enjoy.

Women report that being singly or multiply orgasmic comes in cycles. For instance, when some women first begin to have orgasms they have so many years of sexual energy pent up inside them they find they are multiply orgasmic quite easily. After a few years, though, they may be satisfied with one big one. And then, after a few years more, discover that once again they'd like to be multiply orgasmic.

Other women are multiply orgasmic alone, but singly orgasmic with lovers. Or vice versa. And some women are multiply orgasmic with some lovers, and not with others.

In the end, it seems to be a matter of choice—as well as a question of just how comfortable a woman feels in each particular sexual situation.

Fantasies

CHAPTER 12. "I like to pretend I'm dessert, spread out on a table at some huge banquet. Everyone there—men and women alike—kiss me, lick me, eat me, make me come as their own special dessert treat."

Do everything to indulge fantasies like these. Many women, sadly enough, report not having had such fantasies since they were in their early teens. "I gave them up at puberty in favor of boys," was how one woman put it. Well, now's the time to pick them up again!

Of course, it may take a while for you to find your fantasies once more. Fantasies become weak, like muscles, when they remain unused. Daydreams, sexual thoughts, wild sensual ideas—all these are fantasy material. Some women have bought anthologies of women's sexual fantasies to stimulate their own imagination. Others find what they are seeking in porno magazines. Still others go to X-rated films. "Whatever turns you on," as the current saying goes.

Fantasies play an important part in women's sex lives; yet many are too shy to admit this, much less discuss it. We have discovered in our groups that even women's fantasy worlds have been greatly affected by sexism. Fantasies are often our most tightly guarded secrets; and we are so ashamed of them that only a secure situation, such as a group of loving women, will finally prompt us to reveal them. Women have even quit having them altogether because they were told by various so-called "authorities" to keep their minds exclusively on their lovers—that thinking about anything else constituted a betrayal, and a perverse one at that. When women are at last given permission to share them it often becomes one of the most freeing experiences imaginable—and also one of the most fun!

Our fantasy worlds are as controlled by our social world as are any of the other activities in our lives. Because so much of our society is sexist, it makes sense that some of our fantasies may be that way, too. Take rape fantasies, for example. Women worry about them: "If I say I fantasize about being raped it will prove I'm not a liberated woman." Therefore, it is important for us to know that our fantasies do not reflect what we would enjoy in reality. That's a major highlight of fantasies: they represent a totally imaginary world. Yes, you may fantasize getting raped—but that doesn't mean that, *in reality,* you would enjoy it, much less seek it out.

Rape fantasies are so common because rape has been represented as the major social/sexual fantasy. It is the main one all women know. We have been informed by those "authorities" we discredited earlier that women secretly desire rape. We have also been told that that's what sex is, basically: a man dominating, in all ways, a totally passive woman. We've been given the impression that the only way to sexual pleasure is through total submission. And some of us have been told that pain is part of the pleasure.

Woman have also been taught to hide their sexual feelings, to diminish them. So many feel bad about their sexual needs, and quite frustrated, because etiquette (i.e., social conditioning) does not teach women to pursue and ask for what sexually pleases them. Only in rape fantasies, then, can women enjoy sex—because rape means being *forced* to enjoy it. If a woman is forced to enjoy, then it's permissible to let go and allow sexual feeling to overwhelm her. She has not made the decision: it has been made for her, in the most absolute manner possible.

Some assertive women have explained their rape fantasies as supplying them with the only acceptable way of being taken care of by a man. They say such fantasies allow them to be submissive, to take a back seat, actions completely at odds with their real lives. Even this indicates the influence of sexism. That powerful women fantasize the only way to get taken care of by men is to be raped demonstrates how profoundly we have been led to believe that force, not gentle loving, is the way truly strong men take care of women. (Many of the women characters in Ayn Rand's novels—Dominique in *The Fountainhead,* for example, who falls in love with Howard Roark only after he harshly rapes her—illustrate this fantasy at its most extreme.)

An important note here: Don't let your politics interfere with your fantasy life. By this I mean, if you have fantasies of rape, bondage, male domination—whatever—and you consider yourself a feminist, a liberated woman who is certainly above such sleazy sexist ideas, you may try to stop these fantasies, hoping to program your eroticism into something more wholesome, non-sexist, and politically correct. Don't. It won't work. Fantasies are like emotions: if you try to block them, rather than experiencing them, you never grow through them and evolve into another phase.

If you have fantasies that focus on situations in which you are hurt, either emotionally or physically, don't stop them. (I'm speaking of purely imaginative pain, of course.) Pay attention to what they mean concerning your opinion of yourself, and what you expect from sex—but let them flow. These fantasies also show how difficult it is for us as women to imagine being in control, to feel comfortable with power. Notice that; but don't censor. Start adding, slowly, more assertive power fantasies to those you already have. One woman who spent years suppressing fantasies about being raped by cold men wearing watches finally let her imagination loose. After only a few months she noticed a change. She had grown beyond these rape images; and her latest orgasm creator was a fantasy of herself as a seven-armed, dancing Indian goddess—happy, powerful, all-wise and all-knowing. She attributed the reversal in subject matter to a slow, but ever stronger, change of opinion about herself. "I like myself now, and I didn't used to. It's only natural my fantasies are reflecting that."

So, what to do to feel comfortable with your fantasies? Share them with other women, for starters. If you're in a group, devote one meeting, at least, to discussing your fantasies together. You'll love it. Also, with men you trust, try sharing fantasies instead of sex—or as a "tease" before it. It's silly, but also fun. And enlightening.

Read the current books devoted to women's fantasies. Decide which fantasies you recognize, which surprise you, which offend you. Immerse yourself in your fantasies. Not only have them—enjoy them! Never edit your imagination.

Keep a journal describing your fantasies for a year or more. See how they grow and change. You'll be surprised. It's fun to go back and reread them, too. You'll have written your own erotic novel!

But if you don't have fantasies, don't think there's something wrong with you. Many women don't fantasize. They prefer to excite themselves through reality; of course, one can debate that this, in itself, constitutes still another form of fantasy.

You can use your fantasies to determine what sort of lover and sexual situation you'd enjoy in reality. Fantasize a grassy, flowery meadow with a lover wearing a black eye-patch. You may decide to try the meadow in reality but keep the black eye-patch strictly for fantasy-land. Try out in your head what you'd like to try in reality. For instance, do you want someone to talk kinky to you? Inform your lover and see if it turns you on when it's done for real. Want to try some bondage? Tell your lover—but do this sort of thing only with a lover you trust to take good care of you physically and emotionally. Be careful whom you share your fantasies with. Make sure they care for you and the most fragile parts of your psyche.

Drawings

If you are artistically inclined, you might find it very stimulating to illustrate your fantasies. In one of my groups a woman confessed she had a secret yen for Oriental men. At the final group, with much embarrassment, she revealed a sheaf of drawings of David Carradine, star of the *Kung Fu* television show. "I feel like a silly teenager," she said, "but he does turn me on."

"Like a teenager." Since that's where most of us stopped having fantasies, that's probably where we'll pick up again. Don't kick yourself—enjoy.

Other women have drawn their genitals, etched themselves masturbating, done nude studies of women in sensual poses, or portraits of men who excite them.

Write Your Own

If you can't find the right kind of pornography to warm you up, try writing your own. For example, I recently wrote a story about the delights of being served as dessert at a businessmen's luncheon. (You've already read the opening paragraph. I started this chapter with it!)

My friend Louise, who kept a running story in her head that she edited each time she fantasized, has one word of caution, though. "I got so wrapped up in editing and sentence structure I forgot all about getting turned on. Stick to the story. You're not out to create a work of art!"

SOME COMMON QUESTIONS ABOUT FANTASIES

Thanks to the *Hite Report*[1] and other books about women's sexuality, we have learned that fantasies are a perfectly normal part of women's sex-lives. But just hearing about them isn't enough. Women still have qualms about what's normal and what isn't. What follows are some of the most common questions about fantasies that come up again and again in group.

Do I Have to Have Sexual Fantasies to Be Sexually Normal?

No. Many women don't have any particular sexual fantasies. They prefer the fantasy of reality. They like the here and now.

Other women have fantasies but don't recognize them as such. For example, one woman said she didn't have fantasies; yet she admitted she daydreamed while walking down the street about having sex with various men she saw. That's fantasizing, the group told her.

If you don't have fantasies, don't worry about not being normal. Remember that everyone is sexually unique and fantasies are just one of the many ways women use to express themselves sexually. It is no comment on your creativity or your sexuality if you are not excited by sexual fantasy.

Sexual Fantasies Play a Big Part in My Masturbation. But What About With My Partner?

Many women believe it is wrong to fantasize while having sex with a lover. They believe it constitutes some sort of intimate betrayal, because we have all been told we must keep our minds and hearts on our lovers only.

---

[1] Shere Hite, *The Hite Report* (New York: The Macmillan Company, 1976).

I disagree; and so do many other women. Fantasy is a very important part of many sex lives and there's no reason why we should ignore our fantasies when we are with our lovers.

"But doesn't that mean my lover doesn't turn me on enough? After all, if I have to use fantasy to have an orgasm, isn't something wrong?" many women wonder. Not necessarily. If you are using your fantasies to escape the sexual situation you are in, then, yes, something *is* wrong. But if you are enjoying sex with your lover and like to use your fantasies to enhance it, there is nothing wrong with doing so. Having your fantasies is like using any fun prop—like a vibrator, or a special location, or music, or "naughty" talk, or candlelight.

"But shouldn't I tell my lover about my fantasies? What if he's insulted?" Your fantasies are your own private world. You don't have to tell your lover about them unless you want to. I wouldn't tell my lover any of my fantasies unless I thought he would enjoy them. As a matter of fact, it can be a very erotic thing to tell each other your sexual fantasies. But because they are so intimate and so profound a part of you, make sure you share them only with someone who will appreciate them.

Another thing to remember about fantasy is that it is just that—fantasy, air, "all in the mind." Just because you have a fantasy doesn't mean you want it to come true. You may tell your lover you have rape fantasies, but that doesn't mean you'd like him to rape you. If you feel safe with him, you might want to act out some of your fantasies merely to see if you enjoy them. If you don't—feel free to stop them at any time. Many women have found their fantasies are much more erotic as fantasies than as realities, so they prefer to keep them just for themselves.

I Shouldn't Need to Fantasize. It's a Crutch.

Baloney. Fantasy is an enhancement of reality, and there's nothing wrong with that.

The only time to be concerned that fantasy is indeed a crutch is if in reality you feel that your lover is Elmer Fudd, while in fantasy you have him imagined as Paul Newman. If fantasy is propping up an otherwise collapsed relationship, then, yes, fantasy is doing you a disservice.

Under any other circumstances, enjoy it.

I Stopped Having My Fantasies Because They Seemed Very Neurotic. I Found Myself Getting Off When I Imagined Myself in Pain or Humiliation or Something Equally Messy. But What Do I Do Without My Fantasies?

Resume them and watch them change. Fantasies develop along with the rest of our psychology and mentality. However, because most of us quit having fantasies when we hit puberty and switch to boys, our fantasies quit growing and changing with us. As we resume them, now that we have discovered they are perfectly normal, we may find they are out-of-step with the rest of our development.

Often our fantasies are as media-influenced as the rest of our sexuality. We imagine what we have been told should turn us on. Slave girls, rape, pain—all those submission scenes we have seen in porno movies or read in men's magazines. Things men have told us are exciting. Now, as we talk with other women and discover what it is we, as women, find sexually exciting and satisfying, our fantasies will change.

Don't stop your fantasies. Rather, let new things turn you on. Let your womanliness turn you on. Be excited about the beautiful, sexy, strong you. Take care of yourself in your fantasies the same way you are learning to do in your real life. Many women discover their first orgasm by letting their fantasies nurture them to the utmost. Don't push them to grow and change. Just watch how naturally it happens as *you* grow and change.

My Fantasies Are Too Kinky.

No fantasy is too kinky. Because fantasy is purely imagination—anything goes! Remember, just because you imagine it doesn't mean you want to live it in reality. Don't censor your fantasies. You can be as naughty and bad and silly and wild as you want in them.

I Want to Try Everything and Act Out Everything My Imagination Thinks Up. Is This O.K.?

It's O.K. as long as you take care of yourself. Act out any and all fantasies you want, but make sure you do it with people who care about you and won't let you get hurt—either emotionally or physically.

If you want to do all this with men, don't forget your women friends. Too often women plunge into a world of sex with men, counting on getting all their strokes and goodies from them, and only seek out their women friends after they have run into trouble with the men. Don't make this mistake. Not only is it sexist, but you'll also feel very lonely living in such an unbalanced world.

How to Have Orgasms With Your Lover

CHAPTER 13. The exercises suggested in this chapter can help you to become orgasmic with your partner—or partners. I suggest you do this work with just one person however; and, preferably, make it a steady partner. If you don't have a reliable partner to share these exercises with, read over them and adapt them as well as you can to your situation. Primarily, you will be responsible for asking for what you want and making sure your partner gives it to you.

The most difficult thing in sex is to ask for what we want. So these exercises are designed to help women define and discover what it *is* they want, and then to help them ask for it.

The focus is communication. You will be asked to share, explain, argue, and ask for what you never thought you could before. It will require some daring on your part; so I suggest you undertake this work with the support of at least one other woman. That way you can share your defeats, difficulties, and victories.

Talking sex is touchy. In doing groups and discussing this with women, one learns that women fear discussing sexuality with their lovers. "I don't know what I want, so I don't know what to ask for," they say. "I'm afraid to tell him what I want because he may not want to do it," is another common complaint.

And yet, in this period in our history, marked by so many changing relationships between the sexes, women are suddenly talking about their sexuality and solving their sexual problems far more openly than are men. It is, perhaps, the first time this has ever happened in any culture. We have cultivated the concept of getting support from women in groups, a system which men have still to adopt. I know many women's sexuality groups being conducted—but men's groups? Well, maybe a couple.

When a woman joins a group to work on her problems with a man, she immediately has a support base. She has guidelines and helpers to aid her in determining what she wants sexually, and to cheer her on as she pursues her goals. When she and her lover experience difficulties, this woman has a place to turn to for advice and confidence. Her lover, however, does not. He is going through similar changes, too, making new decisions, trying to figure out what she wants—but alone. This is not comfortable for any person, let alone a man who has been scripted to "run the show." Often such men become hostile and defensive, refusing to cooperate.

Up until now, males have believed they had no sexual problems, or certainly none as complex as their partners'. When they come to the single session we hold in our groups for the partners to ask questions and meet with the leaders, we ask them why they think their lover is attending the group. Invariably, the response is: "She has a lot of psychological hang-ups about sex. I hope this group can do something about them." They are surprised when it turns out they play an important part in these difficulties, and sometimes resent it greatly.

Often partners have been totally unaware that what they have been doing sexually hasn't been good, right, or enjoyable. No one ever told them it wasn't fine—or they didn't really believe it when they did. Consequently, some resist working on the problems. It threatens their ego, which now gets reflected in their penis. Men have been taught to devise a sexual "performance" which will work for them—that is, guarantee an erection. In a society which pokes fun at untrustworthy erections, a performance that guarantees getting it up is as reassuring as money in the bank. When a woman asks her partner to do something different that breaks up his routine, he may have much more difficulty getting an erection than he did using the routine. Whenever this happens, both people often panic. She doesn't know what to do, never having experienced her lover this insecure or anxious before. She doesn't know whether to assume he's turned off to her, or just plain nervous—and, for that matter, how can she handle either? He, in turn, notices his lack of instant "up," and may assume it's gone for life. Impotency has set in; and anxiety about it only makes it get worse. In other cases, the male may respond in an opposite manner—and find his ejaculations almost impossible to control now. Again, this causes his partner to become upset. She may believe it will never be controllable, and throw up her hands in frustration.

The rule to follow here is: Don't anybody panic. This work creates changes. And changes take time. Be kind and reassuring and patient with each other. You are teaching each other what you enjoy. You are both learning to take care of yourselves first so you can enjoy being together. Sexual difficulties are the result of each partner worrying about the other to the point that they give up their own pleasure, and neither enjoys themselves.

I like men. I also believe in their basic willingness and desire to be "good guys." But changing sexually does mean confronting the power situation in any relationship and breaking up established habits. If a man has a large traditional investment in being the sexual expert (i.e., being the aggressor and always in command), he's going to have a difficult time seeing the value to being cooperative. In his heart of hearts, or even right out front, he may not want to have an equal relationship. His expectations may be quite different from yours; and this may show itself when you start working towards sexual equality. When you ask a man who is used to being dominant to cooperate sexually, you ask him to give up some of his power. People are always unwilling to give up power unless they see they are getting something better in return. Keep the rule of equal rights in mind, put your best food forward, watch those power plays, and stand firm for what you want. Most men come to realize that equal relationships, and equal sexual expressiveness and satisfaction, means more pleasure for them. It takes the burden of performance off, it relieves the anxiety of having to be responsible for a woman's orgasms. For this sort of pleasure, the power of being sexually in command is worth losing.

However, no matter how depressing it is to admit, there are some men who cannot make such a change. They always need to be in command. The pleasure resulting from controlling the situation and enforcing stereotypical sex roles is one form of power they feel they must retain. If you're working with such a man, consider what you're up against and make your decisions accordingly. You can struggle to change him—or switch partners. Be assured that there are a lot of good men out there; and more and more of them are coming to understand the benefits of equal relationships, and the power that comes with giving up the *macho*.

Because the focus of this work is asking for what you want—both of you—what either of you accepted as immutable before now becomes open to discussion and compromise.

Times have changed, fortunately, and women can be much more assertive in getting what they want—not only in the world at large, but also personally, at home with their lovers. Still, it is hard to overcome old habits of conformity and assumptions that someone else will take care of us. We are not accustomed to making decisions. It will take us time to learn to make decisions for ourselves sexually. It's a long process. There are no short-cuts. Give yourself time to learn.

Keeping this in mind, you and your partner can launch into the project together. Note where each of you is passive or active. Some role reversals will be happening. Watch for them: you can recognize them because you'll suddenly feel scared, out of control, and very awkward. By all means, when this happens, keep talking to each other—and to everyone else! The success or failure of this work depends on your communication skills. So keep no secrets, say what you mean—even if it is to confess, "I'm absolutely confused." *And when you decide what you want, ask for it.*

Remember, too, that what you decide you want today may be completely different by next week. Sexuality is not set in concrete, and your decisions may be as whimsical as you wish.

A NOTE TO PARTNERS: WHAT TO EXPECT

It's difficult to know exactly how you feel about doing this work with a woman. Most partners are interested, but insecure about where it will all lead. Sexual problems, as you've read earlier, don't happen alone; so you may be a little worried about just what will happen to you in all of this. All you can anticipate now is that things will change between you and your lover. Whether or not you'll like the changes you cannot predict—nor how they will affect your relationship. For the better, one hopes.

What you are now engaged in is: untying a communication knot. It takes two people to communicate, but it also takes two *not* to communicate. You haven't been understanding each other sexually—and probably in other ways, also. What this work is about is not only having a good time sexually, but also learning to communicate so you can appreciate and enjoy each other in every sense.

Some couples have found this work stirs up hidden dynamics in the relationship that affects their stability as a couple. Usually such dynamics have been sexist, so more changes than just the position for intercourse must be made. Sexism shows up as soon as women express the fear that getting what they want sexually will be impossible. Used to feeling powerless, most women have little faith in being able to change their environment—and you are part of that, remember. They assume ahead of time that you, their partner, won't want to give it to them. Therefore, no matter how they ask, they won't get. And if they don't get, then they'll feel so bad that the relationship will have to end. In a situation like that, insecurities can run wild between the two of you.

Therefore, keeping this in mind, be as reassuring as possible with her about the security of your commitment. Some women have asked that their partners make an additional contract with them guaranteeing the relationship will last a certain amount of time, from three months to a year, regardless of what happens sexually. If such a contract would make either of you feel more secure, arrange it. But only guarantee what you can honestly offer. No Rescues.

Whatever you do, talk straight. This work is as valuable for you as it is for your partner. You will be relieved of a lot of responsibilities regarding sex. One of the benefits of equalizing the sexual part of your relationship is that you get to enjoy sex for yourself more than ever. You won't have to be worrying about whether or not you're doing it right for her.

In addition, you will be able to ask her for what you want. This is no one-sided unilateral contract. You both get to figure out what you like, and then cooperate to make it possible.

Whatever problems you think you may have, or discover that you do, can be resolved. The major physical ones for men—premature ejaculation and impotency—are anxiety reactions, for the most part. (If there is a physical reason, your doctor can tell you about that.) Anxiety arises from performance pressure. By equalizing your sexual responsibilities, so much anxiety is eliminated. And with that anxiety go these problems. This work will not necessarily turn your lover into your sexual fantasy dream woman. At best she will be a companion, a friend, a sexy, sensual woman who also has needs to be filled. She'll be more assertive than you've ever known her, she'll be more talkative, and she'll express more of herself sexually. You may like this or you may not. For some couples, this opens up vistas and experiences they had always been seeking, and they relish the experience. Others may find their sexual lives and needs quite different, and compromises will have to be reached. Still others will find they are sexually incompatible and their entire relationship must change accordingly.

Whatever you do in this work, talk straight, be honest. It may prove painful, or take you places you didn't really want to go. But the key to a fulfilling sex-life is having the freedom to be expressive, to be understood, to be appreciated. Usually this work brings couples closer together, heightening the intimacy between them. At the very least, it clarifies the relationship. It reveals precisely what the two of you have between you. That alone makes all the work worth it. Be gentle, be generous with each other.

Equalizing sexual relationships requires that you, too, take on responsibilities for making yourself sexually independent. As your lover is learning to take responsibility for her sexual happiness by learning to love herself and understand herself through masturbation, and by asking for what she wants from you, you also must respond in kind.

Just as women have been dependent on men for all their sexual O.K.-ness, partners have been dependent on women for sexual satisfaction. Now that she is discovering her two sex lives—her own with herself, and the one with you—her new confidence in her sexuality will cause old dependencies to disintegrate. She can satisfy herself sexually. It is important for you to feel as good, as self-loving about masturbating as she does. There's no reason why men and women both cannot do the exercises in this book.

For men, these exercises can open up new sexual feelings, by introducing the concepts of sensuality and cooperation. And for men, too, *loving* masturbation liberates you from restrictive stereotyping.

MASTURBATION FOR MEN

Most men strongly resist the idea that masturbating can be done for pure, sensual, personal pleasure—as a way of expressing love for yourself and for feeling good about yourself. Like women, men are dependent on the opposite sex for their sexual pleasure. What sexuality happens to them alone does not count as pleasure, merely as relief.

Women have discovered that explaining to their male partners how much they enjoy making love to themselves, and suggesting that their partners begin to value masturbation as an enjoyable and loving alternative to partner sex, is a real boon to their relationships. Not only does a man's orgasmic independence remove the pressure that the demand for intercourse creates, but it also helps men realize there is more to sex than intercourse. One woman said, "He thought I was crazy at first. Masturbation always meant a lonely, guilty experience. But when I hugged him while he masturbated in bed, he agreed it was very nice. Very loving, too. We liked it, and it's part of our regular sex life now."

Masturbation also provides a rich fantasy world. So rich for some people that a woman in group actually found herself feeling competitive with her lover's masturbatory images. Her lover enjoyed masturbating in front of the afternoon soap operas. "Whatever turns you on, I'd always said," explained Jan. "But now I'm jealous. I think he likes those soap operas more than me!" She finally demanded to know, "Who do you like best, me or those television actresses?" He explained the two were different experiences, not to be compared. Reassured, she herself experimented before the set and found herself excited by a baseball star. He excited her so much she spent afternoons trading bubble-gum card photos of him with kids on the block.

MAKING A CONTRACT

Before embarking on these partner exercises, make plans to ensure your journey will be a successful one. In group we call such plans "a contract."

A contract is an agreement, like a legal commitment, that you and your partner make to solve mutual sexual problems. If you are not having orgasms with him, you must both agree to share the responsibility and put in equal effort to finding the solution.

In our groups we have discovered that the success of these specific exercises depends on three things:

1. The woman's ability to ask for her sexual needs and desires.
2. The partner's willingness to cooperate (and that includes talking straight and sharing feelings.)
3. Both persons putting in enough time.

Therefore, before starting these exercises, make sure you both want to do them. By making a contract with each other to do this work you make your commitment clear. The basic contract we ask women to make with their partners is:

"1. We agree to spend at least two hours a week of prime time with each other to do the exercises.

"2. We agree to follow the rules of cooperation; to give strokes; to not Rescue; to be nurturing.

"3. We agree to refrain from having intercourse until the exercises give us the go-ahead and the woman agrees."

DID YOU SAY "NO INTERCOURSE"!?!

I know, I know—"No intercourse!?!" I can hear you

shouting. Don't panic. This does not mean no affection, no hugging/kissing/smooching, no getting turned on, no orgasms. It simply means no fucking, no penis in vagina. You can hug, smooch, cuddle, kiss, frolic, swing from chandeliers—do anything else you want. But, please, no intercourse for a couple of weeks.

Why not? The reason that sex is unsuccessful for you right now is that you and your partner have some old sexual patterns you've developed which aren't working for you. Many of these patterns focus on intercourse. In talking with hundreds of women, we've found that women feeling pressure to please their partners agree to have sex (that is, intercourse) when they don't really want to. This results in painful intercourse, guilty feelings, instant sexual turn-offs. The women blame themselves for all the resultant unhappiness. This is so common that many women don't know what it's like to feel truly turned on, to really want to have intercourse, to decide for themselves that they wish it. A pattern develops, and it goes from bad to worse. I call it "fucking-phobia" because many women come to dread intercourse, and do anything to avoid it or get it over quickly. (That's another cause of premature ejaculation: men learning to get in and out fast.)

So the reason for stopping intercourse for a while—just a couple of weeks—is to take pressure off you. A woman will be free to decide what it is that turns her on, to discover that sex and intercourse are not one and the same, and that there's a lot more to sex than "penis-in-vagina." In turn, this gives men a chance to discover they can take care of their sexual needs without being totally dependent on women. (See "Masturbation for Men," pp. 198.)

In such a contract, men—who are often non-monogamous—agree to suspend all other sexual relationships and give their energies totally to this one. Focusing on solving sexual problems with one person while maintaining other sexual relationships puts too much of a strain on most people. Also, as many couples realize, non-monogamy is often a way to avoid intimacy—which is the crux of many sexual difficulties. Keep in mind that most sexual problems are relationship problems.

SHARING ORGASMS WITH YOUR LOVER

What follows is 15 hours, and a minimum of 3 weeks, of doing sensual work with your lover. It is divided into three parts:

1) Self-Loving (masturbation)
2) Love Play
3) Orgasms

Theoretically, each section takes a week. But, even in a problem-solving group which furnishes not only support but also helpful leaders, these exercises may require a month or more for some couples. So don't push yourself. Proceed as you feel comfortable. On the other hand, don't go so slowly and procrastinate so much that you lose interest.

This is, of course, not intended to be an absolutely fool-proof system; but, rather, a guide to help you communicate and discover your own sexual needs. What follows are the basics. Call upon your creativity to personalize them to suit your own needs. Remember: spontaneity is a requisite for good sex—so be as experimental as you like with these exercises.

PART 1: SELF-LOVING

Before you can be orgasmic with a lover, you must be orgasmic with yourself. Although many of us have masturbated for years, as a rule we've never paid much attention to how we do it. Nor have we usually done it with the attitude of making love to ourselves. The purpose of masturbating now becomes three-fold:

First, this work can be frustrating; and it's important you be able to satisfy yourself, when you want to come.

Second, when you hit low points and believe you can't have orgasms, your masturbation reminds you that they're in you all the time. All it takes is the right combination of touches to release them.

Third, you know best how to reach orgasm. By studying your technique, and the ambience or mood that opens up your body to orgasms, you can then create the same situation with a partner. For example, if it takes you twenty minutes of constant clitoral-stimulating, then it will take you at least that long to reach orgasm with a partner.

If you haven't masturbated in a long time, or use a vibrator and now wish to have orgasms with your partner sans machine, it might be wise here to turn back to Chapter 10 and the section, "Three Steps to Orgasms." Review the exercises given there (they are divided into hours) that explain how to make love to yourself with your fingers.

If you've masturbated recently, you may skip through the exercises. But make sure you're certain of your masturbation techniques. Before working with your lover, do the masturbation exercises set forth below. Even when you finally decide to go on with your partner work, don't stop your masturbation. At this stage you will be with your lover only two hours a week, according to contract—so that leaves time for you to enjoy *you!*

Some Suggestions to Help You Along

Atmosphere and Assertiveness: Be very aware of your atmosphere. Set it up to be as cozy, warm, and sensual as possible. In your bedroom, lower the lights, use candles, burn incense, catch a ray of sun in the morning or afternoon, play music. Make your room secure, even if it means putting a lock on the door. (This security is difficult for many women. We have an ingrained feminine notion we must be available at all times. That is why some women find it almost impossible to stake a claim of even one hour alone a day.)

Atmosphere is important because many women become accustomed to accepting the atmosphere around them rather than changing it to suit themselves. Just as we've adapted to accepting whatever sexuality has come our way, so we have accepted the environment surrounding it. Assert yourself by establishing the environment around you that makes you feel most sexy and sensual.

Genital Liberation

Those long lips got you worried?

In Africa some tribal women stretch their lips out very long, the way we do ringlets in our hair, because "the longer the lovelier" is their code of sexual beauty. To do their daily chores, they tuck their lips up inside their vagina so that they won't get in the way.

In other societies, women decorate and perfume their genitals with scented oils and shiny ribbons. Recently some women friends and I celebrated this ancient custom, on top of a mountain at a nude spring picnic. We frolicked in the grass, picked spring bouquets that we arranged aesthetically to frame our vulvas. We then took photos of each other's gaily decorated genitals. Later, we framed these pictures and gave them to our special friends or hung them in a special place in our homes.

As for your fragrance . . . A woman in Illinois discovered a great way to dissolve any doubts she had about her genital odor being unpleasant. One morning, after she masturbated, she let the genital smell remain on her fingers the entire day. She went to her job, shook hands with friends, changed none of her routine. "Every now and then I'd take a whiff of my perfume, and I found it really stimulated me," she said. By the end of the day she had a much friendlier attitude toward her furry friend. Needless to say, none of the office crowd even noticed.

I'm sure that "in days of olde when knights were bolde," the reason they carried their lady's handkerchief around inside their armor was because she had personally perfumed it with her own musk. Before Madison Avenue took over and insisted we smell like everything but ourselves, the most common cologne that the sexually aware woman knew worked every time was a dab of genital perfume behind the ears.

Hour #1: *Making It Last—A Bit of a Tease*

This time when you masturbate, do it slowly. Purposefully draw it out to last at least twenty minutes. Watch yourself carefully—the object being that you will be able to describe specifically the various touches, positions, amount of time, techniques, fantasies, and rhythms it takes for you to have an orgasm. You might also find it a good idea to explain to yourself out loud, after your orgasm, just what it was you did to have it. Pretend you are telling a lover, giving them instructions.

The point of noting the specifics is not to take the romance or abandonment out of orgasms. Rather, it's to enable you to begin noticing what truly does excite you so that you can re-create this excitement with a lover. The next hour, repeat this exercise; but this time stretch yourself out to twenty minutes, drive yourself crazy with excitement, feel you must come or you'll die—and suddenly stop. Get up and move around for five minutes.

In that five-minute break, pay attention to other parts of your body—caress your thighs, kiss your own breasts, tickle your abdomen, rub your feet. Your whole body is sexually responsive, remember—not just your genitals.

After this pause, you can have your orgasm. Most women find it to be a particularly intense and pleasurable one.

Hour #2: *Movement Masturbation*

Sexual energy is part of every movement. Women are

frequently unaccustomed to being active in sex. "Erotic wiggling," as one woman put it, is the crucial difference between frustration and orgasm for many women.

Masturbating Against a Stationary Object

This hour, after your bath and oil, experiment with changing your style of reaching orgasm. Try to have an orgasm by masturbating against a stationary object. There are a number of ways to do this. You can hold your hand still and move your pelvis against it, instead of the other way around which you may be normally accustomed to doing. Try using a pillow held between your legs, or move under a direct stream of water. One woman enlisted the help of her miniature poodle and found her firm curly back quite accommodating.

You may not be successful with this new way the first few times. It's not easy to change your masturbation style, so try it until you get bored or very frustrated, and then return to your old masturbating method and satisfy yourself with an orgasm. Try again another time. Eventually you'll find that it works, and you can come by moving against an object.

The reason for learning to move your body against an object to reach orgasm is to help you get used to wiggling, in order for you to do this later with your lover. You can then adapt this to moving around on his thighs, or against his pelvic bone.

A Further Suggestion: Sports

More than one woman has said that some favorite sport also leads to orgasm. One friend of mine jogs a mile a day because she considers the fourth lap around the track—the one that makes it a mile—as her "orgasm lap." Her lips rub together steadily and rhythmically throughout the first three laps, pressure builds with the exertion . . . and by lap number four she's literally "coming" into the home-stretch! Any sport can be sexually exciting. A woman who jogs eight miles a day through woods told me, "Never do I feel sexier than at the end of those eight miles."

Of course, horseback riding is an all-time orgasm favorite. A modern alternative is the motorcycle. I've found that on my motorcycle I can get the rpm's just right, and after an hour of doing between 40 and 60 mph, I roll off the bike with a very satisfying orgasm. (Make sure you're at a stop for this one!)

An Orgasm a Day

For a period of 3–4 days, make sure you have an orgasm a day. Often we think our sexual energy is with us only on certain days, under special conditions, as illusive and fragile as desert wildflowers. Actually, our sexual energy is always with us. It just needs being permitted to be expressed. It is a type of energy and we can use it at will.

By having an orgasm at least once a day for a continuous period of time (3–4 days) you will appreciate your sexual energy.

To keep yourself interested and excited over your masturbation, pull out all the stops on your imagination. Be creative. Do "IT" any old way you can think of: watch an old Paul Newman movie on TV, and fantasize as you masturbate. Dress in costume as your favorite sexy lady. Find a friendly knoll hidden away in a park and masturbate before God and everybody.

There is a delightful poem about a woman who goes to a dinner party and finds herself bored to tears. She decides to entertain herself by slipping away to the hostess's bathroom to masturbate. When she returns to the dinner table, flushed with her "secret" (as she calls it), she hardly notices the dullness of those around her, so filled is she with her own contentment and daring.

The purpose here is for you to gain confidence in your

ability to create and keep your orgasms and aroused feelings. With a partner we can't be as exact in stimulating ourselves as we are used to being when we are masturbating alone. Sometimes our partners do something not quite right, our minds wander for a moment, and we suddenly realize, "I lost it." You have more control than you realize, as this exercise will help prove.

FOR THE TWO OF YOU WHILE YOU'RE MASTURBATING:

Use the two hours of homework time you have together to do something that you, the woman, want to do. This is practice in being assertive, in beginning to give yourself permission to think for yourself and then make it happen. Spend your two hours with your partner doing something YOU enjoy. Go for a hike, sit in bed and watch television, cuddle and make out, cook a delicious meal together—anything! (Anything but intercourse, that is).

If you don't want to spend two hours with your lover, you have that choice also. But do use those two hours for your pleasure—either alone, or with friends.

Whatever you do, this week is your personal sensuality and sexuality week. The focus is on you and your pleasures. Be "selfish"—take care of yourself. Do what *you* want. See how strong *you* feel.

CONSIDERATIONS BEFORE MOVING ON . . .

The next part will be devoted to sensual love play, which means you and your partner will start working together. Don't move on quite yet if you are experiencing any of the six difficulties listed below. You'll defeat your purpose if you proceed without making sure you're settled comfortably with your own orgasms first. You might find it beneficial to take another week to continue to masturbate, repeating the exercises you especially liked. Don't be afraid you're going too slow. You're not. It's natural and healthy for women to want to establish their own sexual confidence before braving it with a lover.

Six Difficulties

1. You can't have orgasms with your fingers or with water and you don't want to introduce your vibrator (if that's your technique) to your partner.

2. You haven't been able to have orgasms with yourself at all; or, anyway, not on a regular basis. They still seem too illusive and magical.

3. You've decided you don't particularly like your partner. Your lover may not be acting cooperatively as far as you're concerned, and you have some ambivalent feelings you both need to discuss; or you have discovered that the problems are relationship ones, not just sexual, and you need to talk before working on sex.

4. You're doing this work more to please your partner than to please yourself. Actually, you don't care that much right now if you have orgasms with this lover or not.

5. You can't explain in specific terms how you stimulate yourself to orgasm, and can only say, "They just happen, that's all."

6. You're not enjoying your masturbation because you've been having trouble letting yourself go and putting your imagination into your self-loving times.

If you've decided this partner isn't the one for you, stop right there. Remember: Your sexuality can be absolutely O.K. and your relationship still un-O.K.

PART 2: LOVE PLAY

Sensuality in love-making is the most important part of all; and yet being sensual remains virtually ignored in the average sexual relationship. Here is an area both partners should concentrate on raising to a fine art. Being sensual is the part of sex that most often gets forgotten. Many men deem it unimportant, "just foreplay"—to be done quickly, and rather begrudgingly.

Women in groups often complain of this lack of sensuality in their partner's love-making; but generally feel that their need for it is some indication of their own not being sexually O.K. They are quite at fault to blame themselves. Sensuality is a right of sex—and playfulness a necessity for enjoying. Realizing this, the women in one of our groups renamed foreplay "love play." After all, the term "foreplay" implies that sensuality and touching happens *before* the real thing. As these women found, that sort of play *is* the real thing.

Love play delights both men and women for it keeps sex from becoming dull and routine. But many men, due to performance expectations and genital focus, have a harder time appreciating it. These can discover love play by letting the ticklish parts of their bodies relax. When they relax, by breathing slowly into the ticklish area while they are being caressed, they will notice how good it feels. Ticklish spots are sensual ones; and being ticklish can be a first-line body reaction for letting erotic, pleasurable physical sensations through.

The following exercises are *not to be done with orgasms* as a goal. They are to be done simply for pleasure. For the next week, or as long as it takes you to complete and enjoy these exercises, do not have orgasms with each other unless you wish to masturbate together. The purpose here is to keep the pleasure of orgasm out of the sensual situation. It is difficult for a woman to relax and enjoy a massage, for example, if she's concerned that she'll have to "pay" for her massage by giving her lover an orgasm at its completion.

So, as you do these exercises, relax and let good feelings sweep over you. Get to know each other in sensually new ways, while you learn the benefits of taking lots of time with each other.

Don't stop your own masturbation as you move into this next work. Masturbation is not simply a means to an orgasm with partners. It's continually important throughout our lives, as a means of loving ourselves, centering ourselves, and discovering ourselves. While you are integrating your sexuality with your partner's, don't stop loving yourself, both spiritually and physically. Use your masturbation to inspire your work with your partner, to remind yourself that you are sexually fine during those times when the partner work isn't going as smoothly as you wished.

It's a mistake to give up your love-making with you just because you are spending sensual time with a lover. You'll miss yourself. Besides, it's too typical of women to give up our own pleasures and replace them with pleasures someone else gives us. Keep your two sexual lives separate: that with yourself alone and that with your lover. The two complement each other.

Sometimes these partner exercises don't work as well as you want the first time you do them. They can bring up a point of conflict, a surprising difference or two, and some questions the two of you hadn't anticipated. If you are in a typical women's position of depending on your lover to make you sexually O.K., you don't have too much flexibility when a problem arises unless you know that you are, indeed, sexually fine. Many women get scared when they discover that their partner is having doubts and sexual difficulties too—especially after having believed until now his sexuality was as solid as the Rock of Gibraltar. It comes as a shock to them to learn their lover is human. They find trouble being patient and nurturing, when it appears that two sexualities are at stake, not just one.

The meditation of masturbation—and the quiet luxurious hour alone—can help you feel assured, an independent woman, confident of her sexuality. It will afford you time to consider how to handle problems with your lover, and keep up your confidence as you and your lover learn to have orgasms together.

Scheduling Your Time

These exercises will require at least four hours out of your week. For two hours each week do the following exercises with your lover. The other two hours, do masturbation exercises with you.

Hour #3: *Exchanging a Massage*

You begin by sharing massages, which is a wonderful way to get to know each other, not only physically but psychically.

Learn how you each enjoy being touched, and how much you can communicate through each other's fingers.

I suggest you do each of these massages twice.

Exchanging a Non-Sexual Massage: A good idea with this first massage is to exchange it with another woman, rather than with your male partner. There are two advantages to this. First of all, this will prove that women can give each other touching strokes without worrying about it being sexual. Too long have we been kept from touching each other out of fear of being accused of being lesbians—or, worse yet, feeling within ourselves that we *are* lesbians if we enjoy it. This is ridiculously sexist and restrictive, and keeps us from being affectionate with one another. It means we must give and get all our physical strokes from men, other than light kisses or brief hugs. Women are good for each other. Feeling free to touch each other gives us 50% more population from whom to get strokes and loving attention.

The second good thing about massaging with a woman is that it's usually easier to learn to say "no" and "I prefer this" to another woman than to a man, especially a lover. As many women point out, "It's easier to tell a woman I'm afraid of hurting her feelings if I say I don't like what she's doing than it is to tell a man." By learning with a woman who is honest with you, you can discover that when you ask for what you want, and say what you'd prefer not to have, you don't hurt feelings or offend. You'll discover your directness is appreciated. Since the object of this exercise is to begin to feel confident in your ability to ask for and to take "you" pleasures, start by doing it with a person you feel most comfortable asking; for many women, that's another woman.

How To Do It: To get into the mood, think of yourself as a cat. You've noticed how decadent and sensual cats are. That's you during a massage.

Reserve an hour convenient to both of you, and not a time when you are both so exhausted that you can barely stay awake. Make sure that you give this prime time, like before dinner, or in the morning, or on a weekend afternoon.

Each of you is to give and receive a half-hour massage for the pure pleasure of it. During the massage neither of you is to speak except to say "no" to what you aren't enjoying. Don't say "thank you" or punctuate silences by filling in with an "ooooh, that's wonderful." Don't make any noises that don't involuntarily escape, other than "no."

The point of not speaking except to indicate what you don't like is to accustom you to soaking up pleasure without feeling obligated to return it or reward it. Body pleasure with a lover is a right, not a privilege. You don't need to feel grateful for every touch. You deserve it!

Give only what you want to give during this massage, just as you are taking only what you want to take. Don't massage genitals or erogenous zones; remember, this exercise is meant to be sensual, not sexual.

If you or your partner is sexually aroused after this massage, you are not under any obligation to "reward" your partner with an orgasm. You can masturbate together, or separately; or, if you sincerely want to, you can give your lover an orgasm. But only if it turns you on, too!

Massage Tips: A warm room, a warm blanket. You can leave your underwear on if you wish. As for oiling the body: any oil but mineral-based oil products will stain sheets and blankets. Because vegetable and nut oils don't wash out, sheets eventually become rancid if you massage too often on them.

However, mineral oil isn't as good for your skin as natural oils. So you might take an old sheet and set it aside as The Massage Sheet, because you will probably want to massage each other often after you discover how good it feels. Some couples don't like oil at all. They use cornstarch, finding its silky, satiny texture extremely sensual.

Hour #4: *Initiating the Massage*

Do the same type of massage this hour as you did in the previous hour, except this time you will be the initiator. You determine whether you want to be the first to give or the first to receive the massage.

This is to give you some practice in assertively obtaining your pleasures. Most of us have been educated to defer to partners, to fulfill their sexual needs first, and ours last. This is a simple exercise to help you confront whatever tendency you have to defer. Notice which position you choose first—the giver or the receiver? Usually women choose to give first, and explain that they do so because they find it easier to accept a massage when they have "earned" it by giving first. (Of course, you can also choose to be first because of the "save-the-best-for-last" theory.)

You may talk during this massage. Order your pleasure. Ask for what you like—"More right there, honey"—and stop what you don't like—"Ouch, that pinches!" Again, don't feel required to say thank you. Soak up the goodies.

POSSIBLE PROBLEMS

As simple as massaging sounds, it can create some difficulties. Differences between partners, between men and women particularly, can glare even here. Here are some typical complaints women have brought to group, and how they dealt with them.

"My partner can't massage very well." Many times partners, particularly men, have never done a massage in their lives.

Sexism prevents many men from touching; therefore they've never learned how. Now they must—and you're the teacher. If your masseur feels like Attila the Hun pawing his way across you, the European continent, teach Attila to be gentle. A frequent massage problem is not understanding the rhythm and continuity required, so that your lover may massage you like a kid learning to play the piano—sort of here and there but never really making the melody clear. Teach him your tune.

Say what you want. Be specific. Try to put your requests positively: "It would feel better if you used a lighter touch" gets you further than "Cut it out, buster, you're killing me."

A good technique for learning how you both like a massage is by exchanging them. Agree beforehand that you will each massage the other the same way you yourself want to be massaged.

Massage is a learned skill, not an inborn talent. You can always buy a good massage book or enroll in a massage course to increase your skills and sensitivity.

"My lover keeps missing our dates. The last time he arrived so late I was furious and we couldn't do the work." Halt! This, take note, is a power play and indicates sabotage. It is not unusual for a partner to feel threatened by sexual problem-solving, and to react with hostility to working on it. "We could do it better by ourselves" or "It will work out on its own accord" are two such rationalizations. In addition to *macho* defensiveness, fear can cause such a reaction. What's more, many males panic at the thought you are discussing their penises and their inadequacies with other women. They worry they are being put down behind their backs.

Out of a plethora of confusions concerning sexuality, partners can feel resentful doing any work to make changes. "Dumb, stupid exercises don't make any difference!" they insist, failing to see the importance of massaging as well as failing to feel the sensuality.

If things keep cropping up between you that interfere with completing this work, talk about it together. Figure out what's going on. Unless one of you has a one-hundred-hour-a-week job, there are few valid reasons for this lack of interest. Be cooperative. Discover what reassurances are needed, give the ones you can. Don't Rescue. But do talk straight.

Be forewarned that unless this situation becomes a cooperative one on both sides, you might as well stop the work. You can't succeed alone.

"My lover wants to know when we're going to get to the Real Thing." You *are* doing the Real Thing. Love play is sex, too. Unfortunately, many partners think intercourse is sex and sex is intercourse. If your lover can't understand the value of love play, that explains a major reason why you're not having orgasms with him.

Granted, it's not easy to suddenly adjust to not having intercourse for a couple of weeks; but, as time will prove, there's more to sexual pleasure than intercourse. Don't let the hankering for intercourse prevent you and your partner from getting maximum pleasure out of these exercises.

Hour #5: *Show and Tell*

Remember the good old days when you were four years old and played "Doctor" out behind the shed? How you used to peek and poke, discovering each others' bodies and what made them feel good? And you sure hoped that nobody would catch you!

Now you can do the same thing, without worrying about getting caught. This time it's for science, and you're the object of the experiment.

This hour, take a bath or shower together. Soap up, really rub each other all over. Play in the tub, relax with each other. Be kids together. After you get out, dry each other off. Make sure the atmosphere is sensual.

Then, sitting on the bed or any other comfortable place, show each other your genitals. You go first, pointing out the parts, and explaining how they work. Tell your partner which places are particularly sensitive. One woman used a dental mirror to show her boyfriend some of her finer features.

Then let your lover do the same for you.

Following Show and Tell, exchange a massage, as you've been doing. But, this time, include your genitals and erogenous zones. This is still not to be an orgasmic situation. Massage each other's genitals in order to get friendly with them. We have been taught to respond to genital touching only in a sexual manner, and that limits us. This exercise enables you to get acquainted with each other's genitals, and learn to appreciate them the same way you do the face, or hands, or any other favorite part of your lover's body.

Do this massage twice.

The second time, make it non-verbal. That is, only say "no." Soak up the good feelings, like a cat does the sun.

Hour #6: *Show How You Masturbate*

Many women surprise themselves and have an orgasm doing this exercise. So—if you feel it, let it happen!

Take a bath together. Afterwards, sit folded in your lover's arms, your back against their chest. Take your partner's hand and show them how you like to be touched all over. Guide their hand over your breasts, lips, thighs—wherever you like to be touched. Then, guide their touches to show them how you masturbate. Teach them how to touch your genitals.

Showing how you like to be touched will enable your partner to caress you the way you want when the time comes to have orgasms together.

After you have shown your lover how to touch you, reverse positions. Let your partner guide your hand over their body and erogenous zones as they like to be touched.

Some couples really love this position. Women find it free-ing and cozy immediately—freeing, because facial expressions can occur without the partner seeing; cozy, because they are wrapped in their lover's arms.

If you find this position uncomfortable, though, adjust it

to suit you. Sometimes a woman sitting behind a hefty male partner finds she can't reach her arms quite around, which makes her feel foolish. By moving to the side a bit, the position can be made more comfortable. Other couples, particularly two women, prefer to look at each other, so they change positions to see each other's faces.

After doing this, share a massage. Use the massage to spread any feelings aroused throughout your body. That way you can begin to understand how sexual feelings are in every bit of your tissue.

Hour #7: *Making Out*

Remember how hot you used to get kissing and smooching and petting when you were a teenager? Swoon city! Well, it's nostalgia time now. Over the next 3–4 days, devote at least one hour—and that's a minimum—to a make-out session or two—or three. Go necking at a favorite place. Get really turned on. Kiss, and hug, and pet like romantic fools.

Most couples can't stop at one hour. (Pant. Pant. Pant.) Women in one group decided to have three make-out sessions, each at a different locale.

Libby and Jane smooched in the movies; then while waltzing dreamily at a woman's dance; and finally at an intimate dinner for two at Jane's apartment.

Simone and Bill drove themselves mad in a cove at their favorite nudist beach. The next day they picnicked on wine and *pâté* and French bread in the countryside and spent the afternoon hiking, smooching, and being loving in the secluded hills.

Kay and Sam spent an hour in a city park, another at the end of the pier under a full moon, and still another at the local drive-in. "In the back seat, of course!" Kay happily noted.

This exercise, as many satisfied women will testify, is designed to make you hot!

Energetic Sensuality

Often I get calls from physically active women expressing the need for movement to turn them on. All the same, incorporating mountain climbing, jogging, swimming, biking—whatever physical exercise you enjoy—into your sex-life is not always easy. Let's face it—you can't white water raft in your bathtub!

Besides the fact that physical exertion is good for the body and the mind, the feelings it generates in the body are like those worked up through orgasm. The body fills with tension, blood flows to the most excited areas, breathing comes hard and fast, and the pulse quickens. Exercise and orgasms match right up.

Here are ways some women found to incorporate their physical activities into their sexual ones:

First of all, find a physically fit partner. If you're an energetic, sporting woman, it makes sense that an equally vigorous lover will excite your fancy. Good health is a turn-on, just as knowing that your lover takes the best possible care of himself. It's not big muscles that excite, it's the vitality and odor of a body that is beautiful because it is cared for.

Wrestling. Wrestling is sexy. Until you learn all the holds guys learned back in junior high, to make this an equal proposition he might agree to fight with one arm behind his back.

Rolling around on the living-room floor, the bed, or the back yard, huffing and puffing and laughing and challenging—a real arouser.

Jogging, Hiking—Moving Together. Exercise is a communion with your body, and a peaceful meditation. To share it with a lover can be special. Some couples say they love to make love after exercising together. They like each other's smell, they like the faint salty taste, and they like to complete with sex the excitement generated by exercise. A hike in the hills, a bike-ride through the country, followed by some sweet sex, is a fantasy fulfilled for many women.

Dancing. Going out dancing, bumping and grinding together on the dance floor, is very seductive. You can tell a lot about a person by watching them dance, too. Flirtatious, intoxicating—bebopping and boogying with someone who's as much of a dancer as you are is very sensual.

COMMUNICATION TURN-ONS:

Strokes For Your Strengths: When a lover recognizes what you're doing to win, to be strong, to dare and take chances—that's exciting. Especially since they probably have to overcome some competitive feelings before being able to tell you, "You're great!" Getting strokes exclusively for being pretty and sweet keeps us that way—pretty and sweet. When was the last time you got a sexy, sincere compliment for doing something strong—like having a brilliant idea, running a mile, sticking up for yourself?

When our lovers don't give us support for our strengths, they are by omission supporting our weaknesses. A very sensual thing is to have your strengths whispered in your ear. Strokes like "I love how you think" and "I'm crazy about the muscles in your arms" are more exciting to many women than candy, flowers, and other traditional enticements.

Questions About Sexy Me: As you become more confident about your sexuality you will want to know if your partner appreciates you as much as you're learning to. To find out, you'll have to ask. Scary, huh? With the help of friends, make up a list of questions you want your lover to answer. Your partner may not be able to be precise at first, so keep asking.

Here is a list of typical questions women in groups find they want answered:

Do you like my smell?

How do you feel about my genitals?

What turns you on most about me?

Do you think I'm weird? Explain.

What's your favorite part of my body?

What's your most erotic fantasy?

Discussing the answers often provides verbal eroticism.

Try such a discussion over dinner. Much more interesting than "Seen any good movies lately?"

BEFORE MOVING ON . . .

By now you know three things about your body that will make having orgasms with your partner much easier: (1) you know precisely how you reach orgasm through your own masturbation, and you have showed your partner how it is done; (2) you and your partner have been talking with each other and are familiar with the wholeness of sensuality, realizing that all of you is sexual, not just the genitals; (3) you and your partner know much more about each other's sexuality, and you now feel more comfortable to ask for what you need.

If you feel secure in these things, you are ready to proceed to sharing your orgasms.

Don't abandon what you learned about your sensual preferences. Make sure you include it in the new exercises you will be sharing. Keep having fun with your sexuality and don't omit what you've already discovered turns you on.

Don't be pressured to move on to orgasms. If you still feel unsure, scared, or unwilling, don't go on. Pay attention to your feelings. Figure out why you're feeling hesitant. Is it because you fear the same old thing: failure? Or is it because you truly don't want to work on having orgasms with this particular lover? If it's the latter, stop and don't proceed. If fear of failure is your obstacle, ask for support from women friends and your lover—but keep on trying.

Reassure yourself by keeping in mind that you know more now than you did when you tried to have orgasms before. You know how to have orgasms when you masturbate. You've showed your partner how you like to be touched. You have a cooperative working agreement. And you've spent at least two weeks going slow together, being accepted, and getting to know each other in ways you never did before.

There are some standard problems that arise at this point. If you are experiencing any of the four listed below, don't go on to orgasms yet. Instead, determine what you need to make sex appealing to you. Renegotiate contracts, if necessary. Or stay with doing sensual work together until you truly feel the urge to make genital love.

FOUR POSSIBLE PROBLEMS

1. You are unable to give yourself orgasms regularly with masturbation.

2. You find you are absolutely not interested in orgasmic sex with your partner right now. Other feelings are more immediate and need to be resolved.

3. Your partner seems to be sabotaging your work, has been uncooperative, and you're too angry and upset to want to have orgasms with them.

4. You are enjoying your masturbation now, want to explore it further, and would prefer to have a private sex-life for a while.

DO go on if you are so excited about having orgasms with your lover that you can barely restrain yourself.

PART 3: ORGASMS

This is the part where you learn to have orgasms with your partner. You've had a minimum two-week break in intercourse, or even longer if you've felt like it.

By now you are sure of your masturbation. You've had pleasant and exciting times massaging each other, introducing each other to your sexuality, playing together, wrestling, making out—in short, having fun. You've also been talking a lot and sharing your experiences as you've gone along. You know each other much better now; the parameters of your relationship are clearer. You have begun a new kind of intimacy based more on reality than on romance.

With all of this going for you, all you need to make orgasms work for you is to ASK for what you want. SHOW IT,

SPEAK IT, DEMAND IT, GET IT! There's no magic, no mystic chants, no bolts of lightning—no other instrument for success than you and your ability to assert your needs. You might think of yourself as a gourmet at favorite restaurant. The menu is complete, the foods of the world are on it. The waiter is at your command to bring you whatever you order. If you ask, you get. (Although sometimes the waiter may be a little hard of hearing, or a little slow to react.) So order up, be a gourmet. Be a gourmand! Request your erotic menu.

There are many, many ways to have orgasms, and each way is equally viable. An orgasm is an orgasm, physiologically speaking. Every time you go through the bodily cycles of orgasm, the same reflexes occur. Whether it's your earlobe or your clitoris being stimulated, the same things happen: your genitals react, your vagina expands and tents, your clitoris swells, your skin turns a mottled pink, your breathing and heart-rate increase—all the same physiological changes occur each time you come.

There are many ways to reach orgasm. And there are many ways to feel orgasms. For instance, here are some of the ways various women have achieved orgasms without having their clitoris directly stimulated: hanging from a gym bar by the arms, body fully extended for maximum tension; having the base of the spine rhythmically rubbed; having erotic dreams and waking up to an orgasm; being kissed by an expert kisser, nothing touched but the lips; doing specific yoga positions; letting water run on the neck; getting kissed and licked on the ear.

Women and men have been brainwashed into believing that the only true orgasm results from the use of the penis during intercourse, without the help of hands, tongues, fingers, vibrators—whatever you want to include. Due to this male interpretation of true sexuality, the vaginal orgasm has become a center of controversy. Does it exist, or does it not? The vaginal orgasm does not exist if the vagina is considered to be an erotic organ which can be stimulated to make orgasms. The vagina does not do that—the clitoris is the organ for that sort of stimulation. The vagina does not have the nerve endings or the sensual capacity to be the main focus or creator of orgasms. In this sense, if vaginal orgasm refers to the vagina as being the center of stimulation then there is no such thing as a vaginal orgasm.

However, if by vaginal orgasm one means that the vagina is where the orgasm is primary felt, then there is, indeed, a vaginal orgasm. There are also clitoral orgasms, abdominal orgasms, genital orgasms, breast orgasms—an orgasm can be felt in any erotic part of the body. Because the vagina contracts during orgasm, and because with a penis in the vagina the contractions can be felt strongly all around it by some women, there is a sensation of having a vaginal orgasm. The whole body reacts to orgasm; but women report they feel it more strongly in specific places. Of course, this depends on the woman. No orgasm is ever the same among women, or within the woman herself. Some women report feeling very strong vaginal contractions and they particularly enjoy having something inserted in their vagina, finding the filled vagina to offer a stimulating sensation. Women who feel this term their orgasms "vaginal," because they experience them most strongly in their vaginas.

However, this is not the only way to have or feel orgasms. This is but one of many; and even a "vaginal" orgasm is rarely achieved without the use of hands, tongues, fingers, and such to stimulate the clitoris. Actually, as we discovered after talking with over two hundred women, 70% of them agreed that intercourse with no stimulation except a thrusting penis is a guaranteed no-orgasm position. Most women preferred cunnilingus and digital stimulation *along with penis stimulation,* or vibrators to enhance. What surprised us most was the number of women who preferred cunnilingus over any other form of orgasmic stimulation. Intercourse, when women are speaking frankly, isn't all that universal a desire. Women are much more diversified in their pleasure needs than most men realize.

So keep it in mind that *any* way to orgasm is the *right* way. And don't let old myths, prejudices, or "should's" prevent you from discovering your particular way—or for asking for what you need to enjoy your way.

Exercises

Because you're embarking on a new phase in your sexuality with your lover, make sure the situation is as conducive to it as possible.

Of course, you may be a little worried and may not want to go on because it's been so easy and you've felt so nice being sensual. Don't give up the sensuality. Take this all slow and easy. Keep talking with each other—ask every question that comes into your head or heart. You *can* do it!

Hour #8: *Masturbating Together*

I suggested masturbating together to a woman friend once and she announced, "I'd die before I'd do that!" A few months later I received a note from her:

"Well, I did it! I never thought I could share how I masturbate with my lover. Oh God! In front of someone else? How embarrassing, how difficult, how utterly impossible!

"When I finally screwed up my courage and did it, it proved wonderful. It was difficult, don't get me wrong, but not nearly as scary as I thought. It took me longer than usual, but I did it. My lover told me I looked absolutely beautiful, which of course made it all worthwhile. A very freeing experience. I feel like shouting it to the world that I'm so *free!* Thanks for suggesting something so perfectly outrageous."

Contemplating this exercise, most women get scared because they feel the performance pressure on them once again. As one woman said, "I figured all this would do was prove to my lover, once again, that I cannot have orgasms—even with myself!" Take the pressure off yourself by realizing that you don't have to come, and that an orgasm is not a necessary part of this exercise. Just showing your lover how you masturbate is the point—not whether you have an orgasm.

In this exercise you and your partner masturbate in front of each other. The positive purpose of this is that you show each other how you masturbate and thus get to see what each of you finds arousing. This exercise is guaranteed to kick the jams out of any sexual shyness you may have.

For that reason, masturbating with your partner is optional. Some of us consider our masturbation too private to share. Don't feel terribly pressured to do this exercise. If you feel the performance is too demanding and that your masturbation is something you'd prefer to keep private—fine! Perhaps some time in the future when you feel more assured you may want to add this exercise to your sex-life.

Your partner may not be as reticent as you, so why not ask if he or she wouldn't mind masturbating in front of you? See if you enjoy watching, and note what feelings it arouses in you.

I urge you to give this exercise a try. Most women discover it's a lot easier than it sounds. Also, the assertiveness that it requires is very stimulating to the psyche as well as the physique!

Hour #9: *The Inspection Fuck*

At last, you can do IT!

This first time, though, it's for getting acquainted, and not for orgasms. This is exploratory, so don't worry about coming. The purpose is to notice what you enjoy, and what you would prefer.

This is the first step where you physically start determining how to have orgasms with your partner via intercourse, which is the way many women want to learn. Others opt for cunnilingus. Some say digital stimulation is their preference. Whichever way is yours, you must give your partner instructions. Here's how to handle intercourse:

Begin with exchanging a massage and a lot of touching

and smooching. Make sure that you get at least *a half-hour* of love play.

There are only two rules to be observed:

a) Your partner must keep his erection for at least five minutes.

b) He must not come inside you this time.

Now. After you are turned on, so your vagina is open and ready to receive visitors, get on top of him and insert his penis. Just sit there, wiggle a bit, and feel it. Put your hand down there and feel the connection. Feel where your clitoris is in relation to his penis. Explore. Does anything hurt? Move around, find the most comfortable position.

Squeeze your vagina gently, as you do in the Kegels. How does that feel? Try numerous positions and notice which ones seem to turn you on the most. Stay on top so you can avoid getting pinned under a heavy body where you can't erotically wiggle.

Talk to your lover while you are doing this. Get used to talking about what's happening, and what you're experiencing. Embarrassed silence and good sex don't mix.

If you feel like having an orgasm, by all means go ahead. If you don't feel like having one with your partner, but are feeling turned on, leave your partner and go masturbate. Don't come out of this hour frustrated.

After your hour, contemplate what happened. Consider:

—I felt most comfortable when _____.

—The position which turned me on the most was when we _____.

—I wish he wouldn't _____.

—I wish he would _____.

—The next time I'm going to ask for _____.

You may want to do the Inspection Fuck more than once. It's a good idea if it will make you feel more at ease.

The Inspection Fuck is also a good technique for any first-time sex with a new lover. With a new partner, there's so much going on you may not be able to work up the concentration or desire for orgasm. Don't worry. See if you like your partner enough to have orgasms with them. Many women have a personal rule of "no orgasms on first fucks" because they prefer to explore their lover first.

Hour #10: *Intercourse For Orgasm*

After your Inspection Fuck, you have a pretty good idea of the materials you have to work with now. If you're asking for what you want, your partner is being cooperative, and you're single-mindedly persevering in wanting to have an orgasm with your lover, you *will* have them.

This hour make sure you get at least a half-hour of love play before you have intercourse. If a half-hour doesn't turn you on, ask for more. Don't have intercourse until you are truly ready. Don't do it because he wants to and seems ready before you. He can wait for you—it's worth it. The longer he waits, the more intense his orgasm will be, too. So don't get flustered due to pressure. Remember, this is for *you*.

When you feel ready for intercourse, make sure you are on top. Wiggle around to keep your clitoris stimulated at all times. You might press against your lover's abdomen, making sure you have lots of lubrication; or you can use your fingers or your hands while your lover also uses his fingers or hands. Do not rely totally on the penis: the odds are against your having an orgasm that way.

Don't rush. Don't push yourself. Make an agreement with your partner that *you will have your orgasm first*. He has to hang on until you are satisfied. This is one of the purest forms of equality in sex!

Do the same for oral or digital stimulation. That is, get all that love play and teasing—and then you come first.

Don't be discouraged if this doesn't work the first time. Try it again. Give yourself lots of time, think "selfish," and don't do anything you don't want to do—just do everything you want!

Make sure you *say* what you want. Give directions. "I like that!" "Suck here." "Diddle there." "Put your finger in my vagina." "I need more lubrication." "Harder." "Lighter." "Faster and to the left." You may feel like a traffic cop the first time you do this, but after your partner knows what you enjoy, you won't have to be as verbal. Follow the feelings of pleasure. Don't get distracted by "should's."

Hour #11: *More Orgasms* . . .

Do it again. Don't leave out any of the sensualities. Take a bath together. Massage each other. Tease. Flirt. Give yourself lots of time.

Again, make sure you're on top in a wiggling position, and that you ask for what you want—even if that means saying "Lie still and I'll wiggle on you." You come first, again.

Having Orgasms With Cunnilingus

A great many women—more than most men realize—consider cunnilingus the *crème de la crème* of sexual stimulation. A few years ago a Berkeley woman, Kathie Kelly, wrote an inspiring paper highly recommending oral stimulation because: "(1) it is direct and therefore not a 'hit-and-miss' method of producing female orgasms; (2) it provides constant lubrication so as not to irritate the sensitive area over the clitoris and around the urethra; (3) it leaves the hands free for stimulating other areas: breasts, the vagina, thighs, etc.; and (4) it feels good."[1] Also, it doesn't require birth control.

Because cunnilingus has not been given the status and recognition it deserves, how to do it well remains a mystery. Yet this is most important, since so many women consider cunnilingus one of the most intimate and truly erotic expressions of sexual passion.

Cunnilingus has been an appreciated form of sexual artistry

---

[1] Kathie Kelly. *A Radical Sex Manual for Women and Men* (unpublished paper), 1972.

from the earliest of times. A certain queen in ancient China was noted for her insistence that courtiers and ambassadors greet her by kissing her genitals. He who kissed her best rose fastest politically.

If you want to have orgasms this way, remember that, as with any other orgasm, it takes specific directions, time, experimentation, and patience.

First of all, begin by bathing. A fresh and clean cunt is a pleasure to kiss. It not only smells good and tastes good, but you also have the confidence of knowing it does.

Although one woman I talked to bragged her lover licked her no matter what condition her cunt was in—including yeast infections and days without bathing—this kind of funkiness is not necessarily a proof of genital liberation or love. Your cunt—and his cock—should be as clean as the rest of your body. And there's no reason you should hesitate to ask each other for that courtesy.

The most comfortable position for oral sex is on your back with your lover lying or kneeling between your thighs. This way he or she can hold your thighs in their hands and cup their face with them, while you feel their hair, breath, and body moving against you. Women sometimes complain they feel lonely with cunnilingus: their partner seems so far away. But this position enables you to grab onto hair, and even swing around to the side a bit to touch a back or an ass for reassuring contact. Your lover's hands are free, too, to touch your breasts, your stomach—any other part of your body. The touch should be continuous and rhythmical so as not to break the mood.

Begin by using hands. "Muff-diving"—zeroing in on the clitoris with your mouth like a dive bomber—is too sudden. So, before you direct your attention exclusively to the clitoris, put some general pressure on the entire vulva. Wrap your legs around a thigh, hold a hand firmly over the vulva, press against the bed. Accompany this with over-all love play—kissing, fondling, gentle whispering.

Next, wet the clitoris and manually stimulate the hood above it. Don't touch the clitoris itself—that's painful, like touching a raw nerve-ending. While stimulating the hood and mons area, your partner or you can use his/her fingers to take some moisture from your vagina to keep your clitoris and the inside of the inner lips wet. The pearly smooth skin there is delicately sensitive, as you may have discovered with your masturbation.

When you are feeling sufficiently aroused, indicate to your partner you are ready for oral stimulation. The clitoris responds happily when the labia are sucked on, and the hood and inside the lips are excited by long, broad strokes with the tongue. Some women say that it also feels good to have the clitoris and hood gently sucked on at this point. Your partner's tongue should not be restricted to the genitals. A great tongue-teaser is to begin at the breasts and nipples and then work wetly down over the belly to the clitoris.

When your partner begins to focus on your genitals, communication is important. Let them know what you like, what you need more of, and when and where not to stop.

Your lover may begin by parting the labia and continuing to run the tongue over the clitoral shaft. As you've noticed in your masturbation, you have a reliable rhythm you respond to. Mix this rhythm with variety—variety here being whatever you desire. You might like a finger inserted into your anus (and not put back into the vagina until washed!). Others find Kegel exercises stimulating. Some devise various other ways to excite themselves. Don't be shy—let yourself go! The perineum (that sensitive skin between vagina and anus), when licked in alternation with clitoral stimulation, drives some women wild. Others like their vaginal opening to be titillated by the tongue with a circular motion.

Remain with whatever maintains your excitement. When it's not exciting any more, try something different. Give yourself time and latitude to be experimental. It may not work the first time, but if you pay attention to what's enjoyable, soon you'll have a path made to a cunnilingus orgasm.

When breathing increases in speed, some women feel contractions, and notice slight sweating. When such signs of high excitement are obvious, or stated—"Wow! Am I turned on!"—you're ready to have an orgasm. Have your lover slightly increase the speed and pressure, insert their fingers into your vagina, and expand them with a scissor-like motion; the pressure on the vaginal walls is extremely stimulating. A real thrill for some women is having their uterus "flipped"—this is when a partner puts their fingers in far enough to jiggle the cervix, causing the uterus to move. The tongue in this case should keep moving rhythmically, rapidly on the clitoris. If stimulation stops now, the frustration of losing it can be maddening.

At this point women are highly individual in what they like to put them over the top and into orgasm. Show or tell your lover precisely what it is you need. "Faster!" "Lighter!" "Harder!" "Slower!" "Wetter!" "Kiss!" Cunnilingus is not a passive way of having orgasms. You must participate actively. By moving your pelvis you can guide your lover's tongue and fingers to the most sensitive spots. Your hands are free—use them to rub your breasts and your belly.

During an orgasm, women react differently. Some can't take another touch on the clitoris—it's suddenly too sensitive. They want to be held, but not genitally stimulated, while they come. Other women prefer continued oral stimulation because it creates rapid multiple orgasms. Others like a hand firmly placed over the entire genital area to prolong the sensation. After the orgasm, relax . . . slowly . . . gradually. Sudden, sharp moves, such as your lover pulling his or her fingers out of your vagina suddenly, or brutally sticking his penis in, can be very disrupting and violating of your space. Wait until you're ready to go on; then indicate to your lover what you want next.

Possible Orgasm Problems

"I get excited, and then I lose it." Your clitoris retracts at high arousal. It's there. You or your partner must seek it out.

If this isn't the problem, think back on how you masturbate and figure out what you're omitting or short-cutting. Copy your masturbation technique as closely as possible—particularly as to the amount of time needed.

"I'm holding myself back." Why? Sometimes women just don't want to have orgasms with their partner. They don't like sharing those feelings, they don't trust their lover, or feel insecure in some other way. If you have such hesitations, talk to your partner. Women can't let go to come unless they feel secure. Ask for what you need to feel secure.

Take care of yourself by confiding your concerns to your lover. Ask what you need to know: Are you bored? Do you think I'm odd? Are you enjoying this?

If you're like most women, you've been giving and giving to your partner for a long time. You enjoyed giving; now let yourself be indulged.

Another reason for holding back is because you have unsettled feelings towards your lover. At those times when I feel angry, unhappy, confused, or just plain tired of the same old sweetheart, my own orgasms remain illusive. Take it in stages: Clear up those feelings. Get some resolution behind them, and some verification as to their origins. Then see if you're turned on. If so, proceed. If not, cuddle and be sensual—and see where that takes you. Don't ever feel responsible for having to invent sexy feelings when they're not there.

"I'm afraid to ask my partner for what I want." If you don't ask, you don't get. Without asking, you settle for the least. And you should get the best—nothing less will satisfy you.

"I'll go out of control and never come back." Worrying about being out of control is a quite common fear. Many women report having such intense orgasms that they forget their lover is even present. "After I come I open my eyes and say to Charlie, 'You still there?' All the same, you can go very far away emotionally, and snap right back when you want. You really are in control," reported one group member.

"Frankly, my partner doesn't turn me on." If you have decided that your partner, pure and simple, does not arouse you

sexually, don't feel you have to be sexy just because "they're so nice." You can't create chemistry if it isn't there.

"My partner doesn't seem interested." Obviously, you have to ask them about this. But some possible problems could be:

—You and your partner have different sex drives. One woman in group arrived looking like a prim New England schoolmarm, and by the end of the sessions had let her hair down and turned into what she herself called "a real tigress." Her male partner, who had always considered her sexually timid, found this sudden energy of hers intimidating. Quite overwhelmed, he took off. Although it hurt her to lose him—he left her for a less energetic woman—she was nevertheless relieved to discover that their sexually inhibited relationship hadn't been totally her fault. A few weeks later she phoned another group member to report she'd found a man who liked the tigress in her, growled, giggled, and hung up.

This is an extreme case, of course. Usually you and your partner can make compromises about disparities in sexual energy. Ask. Don't assume big differences until you've discussed them in specifics.

—Your partner may be "a lazy lover." Men, in particular, have become very used to having women do things for them. They lie there and just enjoy . . . while a woman massages them, arouses them, and gives them an orgasm. Because it takes a shorter time for most men to reach orgasm (which is their sexual goal), such love-making is over almost before it's begun: he's satisfied, and she isn't. When she decides she wants to be satisfied, the tables are turned. He's got to put in more time and attention than he thought and, since he's been spoiled, he's a little slow to get his energy up. Talk about it (but not in bed!). Be specific in stating your needs, insist without getting angry or insulting, and he'll probably do as we wish. Most partners are eager to be cooperative.

"Intercourse hurts." First of all: Are you lubricated enough? If your natural juices aren't enough, use jelly, saliva or a cream with a non-petroleum base to help you out. If you are making sure you don't take in a penis until you are really turned on, and

it *still* hurts, see a gynecologist who thinks that women, sex, and fun all go together. You can find a pro-sex doctor by calling the local feminist counseling or health center for a referral. Or take a friend with you to your doctor, if you're concerned about getting sexist treatment.

A number of things could be wrong. You could have a yeast infection, or some other vaginal irritation. Endometriosis makes intercourse painful, and so can an ovarian cyst. Get it checked.

If your doctor finds nothing wrong, change the angle of intercourse. A penis in the wrong way can bump a tender ovary. Your cervix may be sensitive; and, when you're not stimulated enough, it's not elevated and out of the way of whatever you put in your vagina.

When the time comes to begin learning to have orgasms with a partner, some women get over-anxious. They often state, "It won't work. It just won't work. I'm afraid!" Those worries make absolute sense. After all the years of negative conditioning women have undergone regarding sex, like Pavlov's infamous hound, many have gotten well-trained to expect the worst.

In a group we discuss such fears openly and gently. Sometimes just exposing them to the light dispels them. For example, Simone was extremely pessimistic concerning her chances for orgasmic success. The group reassured her: In the past few weeks hadn't she become very certain about her masturbating? She knew she could have an orgasm whenever she wanted to, and also how to create one. Hadn't she told them she felt very comfortable with herself as her own lover? Besides, hadn't she and her lover, Bill, had fine times together massaging each other and being sensual without intercourse? The group reminded Simone how she had felt so excited once she'd even "cheated" and let Bill have an orgasm in her. She'd been disappointed by not having her own, of course, but happy, nevertheless, to realize she had felt aroused enough to actually desire intercourse.

That one failure lay heavy on Simone's mind, however.

"If I felt so turned on, why didn't I come?" she pleaded. "It's the same old thing."

"That's exactly why you *didn't* have an orgasm!" Libby explained. "It *is* the same old thing. You used your old way which is *his* way and you know it doesn't work for you."

"You're right—Bill did it the way he likes it. If I'd had my way we would've taken fifteen minutes longer, been in a warmer room, and I'd have been on top. Also, I'd like to have an orgasm with cunnilingus before we have intercourse. I'll tell Bill all that over dinner tonight. I feel much more hopeful now about the possibilities for a sexy evening!"

In Kay's case, she was not at all scared—just not too eager for orgasms to begin. "I'm not sure I'm sexually turned on to Sam. I like him. He's an old friend. We've been together for a long time. I've enjoyed making out with him and playing around—but I don't know if I want to have intercourse with him. I think I'd rather do it with someone new."

When a woman feels this way, the group proceeds carefully with their advice. Kay could be truly feeling this way—or she could be running away from her fears by believing that sex will happen easier with someone new. If a woman's lover has been cooperative and she's been enjoying sensual times with him, we urge her to also try having orgasms with him. We point out that no lover will magically give one orgasms. In addition, she will have to overcome the same fears with a new person. Besides, if there is no one immediately available to take the place of her old lover, then she is procrastinating.

Although this may sound cold and like reverse sexism, we urge her to "experiment with him." We phrase it in such a way to help her separate romance from sexuality. If Kay can approach sex as an experiment, an adventure, rather than as a pass/fail, love/leave situation, she'll feel in control. And if she feels in control, she can shape the situation to her advantage.

"A friend of mine had a good way, I think, of approaching sex," Kay suddenly remembered. "She said there were three ways to have sex: Intercourse, Playing Around, and Making Love. She defined the first as having just plain physical sex, with anybody, because you feel hot. Playing Around she described as having sex with a friend—fun, comfy, and passionate for the moment, but no big thing. The last, Making Love, was what people in love do with each other; here sex is not only sex, but an expression of something much deeper. My friend felt the main problem between men and women is that women want to Make Love and men want to have Intercourse. She felt that if more people could get into Playing Around, it would be healthier all around. For one thing, it'd take the mystique out of sex, and help more folks have more fun. I always thought of her as extremely liberated because she felt so sure of herself sexually. Now that I'm more sure of myself, I find her way of thinking even more to my liking. I may not be in love with Sam—but he is a good friend. And we could learn a lot from each other just by Playing Around."

As for Jane and Libby, both had been having a rough time because of Jane's desire to have other lovers, and Libby's great fear of what that might do to her. Jane was Libby's first true love, and she saw heartbreak just around the corner. Libby feared the minute she herself had an orgasm, Jane would leave her for another lover. Finally, the two of them made a contract that Jane would not drop Libby once Libby had an orgasm. "If I sacrifice my pleasure because having it means Jane will leave me, what kind of a relationship is that? No good—that's what!" With the reassurance of a contract Libby felt secure enough with Jane to begin sharing her orgasms with her.

Besides these problems experienced by group members, there are two others many women face that can equally create obstacles for having orgasms with lovers.

The Affair with the Married Man. Many women are all involved in what "should" be a romantic tryst, and yet they can't understand why they are not orgasmic. When they describe the situation, it becomes immediately clear. Their lover is married, or at least is part of another couple. This prior relationship is the one he still feels primarily obligated to. That means his time is limited and his activities restricted in his affair with the new lover. She, on the other hand, has no other lover; and therefore counts on him for all her loving and sexual pleasure. There is too much of an imbalance here. Keep in mind that the best sex is *equal* sex.

Their time together amounts to a few odd hours during the week. She sees him once a week, between 10 P.M. and midnight. She gets up for work at 8 A.M., and he has to be home shortly after midnight. She's tired, he's anxious. No wonder the pressure is so terrific during those two brief hours.

Such power imbalances, coupled with the short amount of time, make orgasm impossible—unless, of course, a woman finds this type of affair truly a turn-on, a playing-out of some fantasy, and thus all she expects from a lover. Otherwise, no matter how kind the lover, how complete his knowledge of sexual techniques, this situation remains a set-up for giving him what he wants, while ignoring hers. He controls it, because his time is most limited. If she asked for what she wanted, she probably couldn't get it. "I want more time with you," she could request; but she's at the mercy of his primary relationship. After a while she will begin to feel angry, hurt, and used. Having an orgasm in such a situation where she cannot get her own needs fulfilled is not possible.

One woman came to group totally strung out after an affair of this sort. She felt her sexuality had been destroyed. With prompting, she reviewed the affair: at its start she'd been sexually happy with herself, easily orgasmic through masturbation; yet, by its end, she could not be orgasmic in any manner whatsoever. "The last thing he said to me as we ended the relationship was, 'It's too bad you don't have your sexuality together.' And I thought he was right!" She shook her head angrily. "I really thought I had to put up with that situation!"

Listen to your body. When you can be orgasmic through masturbation, but seem to clamp down with a partner, your body is sending you a message: "You're not getting what you want." The next step? Figure out what it is—no matter how silly or impossible it sounds—and ask for it.

The Same Old Lover. After a woman has been with a lover for a long time, and gone through various arguments and reconciliations, the physical chemistry may be gone. You may have created a solid friendship, have a great many things in common, but, still, you're turned off sexually. You feel burnt out.

All those exhausting efforts to make the relationship work have destroyed the sparkle and the mystery. You may feel, "We've gone as far as we can with each other. The relationship is as it is." If what it is isn't what you want, making love can be a dead-end street.

If you feel this way, fine. Don't blame yourself, think that you're "frigid," or "maybe a bit weird." Many women feel like this. If they are wise, they take a break. Quit having sex with your lover (they may object vigorously, but do what you need to feel good), and concentrate on being friends, appreciating each other in this way. Later on, you may find yourself coming around to a new cycle of feeling turned on again—or you may not.

In any case, you can regain your confidence by being celibate or by finding a new lover to inject some needed spirit into your drab sex-life. With such a break, you can take the time to decide what you want sexually from your former lover—if anything. You can also find out exactly how you feel about him now.

Some Questions About Men Plus a Few About Intercourse

CHAPTER 14. Women who have participated in the women's movement in any way usually find that their relationship expectations of men have changed. The old roles no longer feel comfortable. Their awareness of sexism and their consequent desire for equality between the sexes have created a new style of relationship: one where romance still excites, but where the foundation is based on friendship and equal power.

Many women are having a difficult time finding men who are interested in the same things. Every day women ask me, "Where ARE the men?" They become impatient and frustrated: "*We've* made changes," they complain. "Now when are the men going to do the same?"

Even those women who are presently in relationships with men continue to ask, "How can we change things so we're equals?" The double standard persists, role changes create confusion, and women want to know how to be themselves, pursue independence, and still keep their loving relationships with men.

There are no quick and easy answers to social problems. Each relationship is a microcosm of the cultural upheaval that has been going on ever since women said: Liberation, Now! Basically, there are two things women can do about men right now:

1. Be patient, keep looking, rest assured there are some "good ones" out there even if it will take time to find them.

2. Keep up contact with other women to discuss your feelings and desires concerning men. Many of us are going through the same things, and we can get advice and much help from each other.

What follows are some of the basic questions women ask about men. The answers are a summation of many groups' worth of advice.

Where Are All the Men?

The men are learning. But, as one frustrated English major noted: "I wish they'd quit reading and studying about women and feminism and get down to the practical application!" They're getting there. They're just slow. After all, feminism is more beneficial to women than to most men. Men are being asked to give up power so that women may share it with them. Needless to say, this is something not many men are willing to do. All the same, there is a vanguard of men who are happy about their changes—and in time they will be a big and strong enough group to be able to teach their brothers how to change also. (At least that's what I hope will happen. Am I a dreamer?)

Part of what men are learning is about emotions. Women have always been the experts there. Just as men have always been the experts on business. Now women are going into business, and men are learning how to express emotions. In the meantime, we endure the time gap.

Another problem with men is that they have, in many current situations with women, lost their privileged positions as Head Counselor, Number-One Friend, Sweet Baby Boy, and The Final Word. Where they used to rely totally on men for advice, support, strokes, meaning in life, women are now valuing their women friends as they never did before for precisely these life-needs. Women tell me they want their men friends to be as good to them as their women friends are. They want the same ease of communication, the same availability of nurturing, the same exchange of emotions, the same potential for playing and having fun. Some men are having a hard time accepting and understanding this.

Men are threatened by how women are changing. They were quite comfortable in their standard roles, and the changes demanded of them by these suddenly "angry" and "uppity" women don't look like fun. Men seem to have lost their understanding of how to relate to women: it used to be so clear and simple, and now it is all up for grabs. For men who basically fear women, or dislike them, new relationship expectations demand they do some changing, or remain alone, or else become as extinct as dinosaurs. For men who basically like, and admire women, the changes can be creative and challenging as well as rewarding. The men I've spoken with say they like the feeling of things becoming equal: as she learns to take care of herself, so does he learn to take care of himself and not be so dependent on her.

We women are adding our own complications to Where the Men Are, of course. Most of us are in the middle of deciding who we are, changing our lives to incorporate all the new women we can be. We are often confused, trying to keep a balance between being independent liberated women and still having loving relationships with men. Our indecision does not always make us easy to get along with; and men expecting consistency from us can be driven crazy by our vacillations. We're no more sure how to relate to men in the new ways we want than they are how to relate to us. This does not make for easy times between the sexes.

There *are* good men out there; men who make good friends and good lovers. But they are, as yet, quite rare. So, be patient and persistent. Don't give up. You'll find them—usually in the most unlikely of places.

What Should We Do With Penises?

Penises are to play with—to have fun with. Discussing this in groups, women say penises often make them feel awestruck, fearful, or pressured to do something they really don't want to do.

241

The questions that immediately follow, then, concern common penis problems and what to do about them.

I Don't Like It in My Vagina.

Many women don't enjoy intercourse. Psychiatrists can make up any number of Freudian reasons why, and make it sound like not liking intercourse means you're an emotional disaster area. But that's leaning toward sexist analysis again. In fact, it's possible to just not like intercourse because you just aren't interested in it. You can dislike it, too, because it's not done well, not the way you would like it. You may not enjoy penis in vagina because that's all your partner enjoys in sex, and you're feeling tired of this goal-oriented, penis-focused sex.

A possible compromise which many women will find enjoyable is this. You get what you want—you have your orgasm, or orgasms, how you like to have them. Then, after you're satisfied and your vagina is relaxed and lubricated, intercourse may feel good. As one woman put it, "After I've come, it's comforting to have him come in me. His penis in me feels sort of cozy, like hugging a teddy bear."

If you don't like intercourse, take a break for a month. Ask your partner to masturbate while you hug him, or help him have an orgasm with your mouth. Without the pressure to do "it" you can explore your feelings about intercourse, decide what you want to do about it, and tell your lover what will please you.

I Don't Enjoy All That Thrusting.

Not many women do. If you have the kind of partner who requires what seems like hours of banging against you to reach orgasm, to the point you're getting chapped lips and chaffed vaginal walls, tell him to stop. Ask him why this technique? If he truly enjoys this style and it's the only way he can come, you are not compatible lovers.

However, if he's under the impression that this is how sex happens but he's willing to try new approaches, then tell him what you'd enjoy. Tell him about the pleasures of going slow and easy.

How Does One Stimulate a Penis, Anyway?

Just like women, each man has his own particular preference of stimulation. But, basically, what I've been told is this: the base of the penis is where to stimulate for a slow sensual turn-on, and the tip is what to stimulate for orgasm. Obviously, there are many variations on this theme, and the best way to find out is to ask a man.

I Don't Like to Eat Him.

Many women feel that in order to get the cunnilingus they desire, they must perform the fellatio they don't enjoy. Most of us have taken it for granted that this is the necessary barter. But women are revealing to each other in the security of groups that some of us don't like to take a man's penis in our mouths. "My jaw gets tired." "I gag." "It's difficult." "It's just not fun." These are among the reasons given. Some women have taken a bold step, told their lovers they don't enjoy fellatio, and have stopped doing it. The women are very relieved by this, and not many have heard any recriminations from lovers. They note that cunnilingus hasn't stopped. "My partner really likes to do it," they are pleased to discover.

I Don't Like "Come." Is That Odd?

Women seem evenly divided on liking and disliking it. The one thing they do agree on is they don't like being forced by male expectations to swallow sperm when they don't want to. There are many other pleasurable things to do with it:

—Ask your lover to ejaculate on the tensest part of your body—back, chest, shoulders—and then use his come for a slippery, warm, sensual massage. You can leave it on like any massage lotion because it doesn't smell and it doesn't irritate your skin.

—Some women have confided that they and their lovers

find it ever so sexy to ejaculate in their beautiful hair. It's not a bad creme rinse, and it feels good on your sensitive scalp.

—Let him come in your hand, and then massage his belly and chest with his sperm. This is a startling experience for men at first, but a great way to turn them on and at the same time help them get closer to their own sexuality.

—If you do take it in the mouth, share some of it with him in a kiss.

Whatever you do, don't feel you have to do anything. A lot of what we think we ought to do with penises is because men told us we should. But, in fact, many women confess they aren't really that turned on by male genitalia—that *whole* bodies turn them on, and genitals are only a small part of that. Enjoy penises yourself. Put chocolate on them, or plastic flowers, or whipped cream, cookies, or silk scarfs tied in big bows. My favorite penis trick is performed by a close friend's best lover: He unzips his pants so his penis hangs out, then turns his pockets inside out—*voilà!*—he makes an elephant face. The penis is the trunk and the pockets are the ears. (I tried to get a photo for you, but he's too shy to go public with his funny invention.)

Is Contraception All My Responsibility?

"What do I do now that I'm off the Pill? Every time I get up the nerve to ask my lover to use a condom he makes me feel guilty." Barbara is not the only woman concerned with the problems of equal responsibility for birth control. For many years it has been assumed that birth control is the woman's responsibility, and a pregnancy her own fault. Men have been reluctant to participate in sacrificing even the smallest bit of pleasure to do their share.

Men fail to understand how worrying about the possibility of getting pregnant interferes with a woman's sexual enjoyment. Women say, "I start worrying about getting pregnant every time I think about sex. In situations where I'm turned on and would like to have sex, I'll stop myself because I'm so worried. It's so difficult to ask a guy to wear a condom or pull out." Other women notice, "Some men won't have sex with you unless you're using birth control. They ask if you're on the pill or got an IUD and when you say no, they lose interest."

Women cannot relax and enjoy sex, much less experience orgasms, when minds are preoccupied with anxieties about pregnancy and bodies are irritated with certain means of birth control available to women. "So you can have an abortion," some men reason, and they even offer to pay for it. But the fact remains that no matter how blasé we are about abortions, they cost more than money—they are physically exhausting and emotionally draining, and we can't have one a month. For many of us, abortion is morally out of the question, so accidental pregnancy means motherhood. And that's a pretty big complication.

"I can count on the fingers of one hand the men who have initiated discussion of birth control prior to having intercourse," say many women. The usual technique is to get started, and then as the situation grows to fever pitch, the man may inquire at the moment of highest passion: "By the way, what are you doing about birth control?" Discussing such a thing at this point is like throwing a wet washrag on a roaring fire. Many women are so excited by then that they lose their heads and blithely advise their lover, "Nothing—but come inside me anyway." That's the answer he was hoping to get, of course.

When she gets pregnant, it's her fault. Or: another common approach to contraception is for him to ignore it, come in her, and then ask afterwards, "Oh—were you using any birth control?" He's already had his fun, so it's safe to express concern now. Most men don't ask at all. They just assume she's taking care of it herself.

A man can use any number of power plays to make a woman feel totally responsible for birth control. He can suggest she's not liberated. He can lecture her on the need to protect herself. He can refuse to have sex with her unless she uses birth control. He can ignore it, never mention contraception, and hope it isn't a problem. He can assure her he'll pull out before ejaculating, forget himself in his pleasure, come in her anyway, and then try to appease her with apologies. You can bet if it were men who got pregnant, the American Medical Association would have financed a male birth control pill and distributed it universally by now.

In equal sexual relationships, both partners are responsible for birth control. It is not fair for a man to assume his lover has taken care of it and all he has to do is freely enjoy. With more women abandoning the Pill and having IUDs removed for reasons of health, not to mention finding diaphragms uncomfortable and the acidic jelly distasteful, the time has come for men to assume their share in keeping sex and pregnancy two different subjects. It takes an emotionally mature and sexually comfortable man, one who really appreciates and respects women, to negotiate graciously on this problem. And it takes a confident and equally self-respecting woman to ask her lover to do so.

I Am Scared Anticipating Sex With My Lover, Although Once We Get Into It I Enjoy It. What Can I Do About These Fears?

Talk over with your lover what scares you. Women who have these worries usually have a specific reason: they are concerned that their partner expects something of them they cannot or do not want to do; they don't trust their lover; or they assume they cannot get what they want from the situation.

Often these worries peel off our psyche like the skin of an onion. That is, we feel one concern, expose it, feel relieved, and then notice another one beneath. Just talking about our fears and getting nurturing responses from our lovers helps get rid of them. We are fearful when we believe we are not in control. Therefore, it is not only important to expose our fears, but also to ask for what we need to feel safe.

Should I Be Turned On by Everything He Does?

Women often think this when they are unsure of themselves sexually and worry that they aren't sexy enough. They assume that their lover knows what's right and that they should, therefore, be enjoying whatever it is he does.

Women have been culturally trained to want to please men. When we incorporate this sexually it means that what *he* enjoys is more important than what *we* enjoy. His ego is at stake, our reputation as a good lover is on the line, and it would just make things simpler all around to be turned on by whatever he does.

This becomes especially difficult to handle when we have gotten up the nerve to ask a lover for what we want and he has been cooperative and done it. However, he has also added a few things we don't like. Then we have to ask for more, or settle for what we're getting. Women say, "But he's such a nice guy and he's trying so hard. Why don't I enjoy it?"

It is mathematically impossible to be turned on by 100% by everything one's lover does. There is such a wide range of what people enjoy in sex that we must each take responsibility for letting our uniqueness be known. It's not fair to a "nice guy" to pretend to enjoy what you aren't enjoying, and it certainly isn't fair to you. As many women will tell you, good men are eager to hear what women enjoy and are happy to be cooperative.

I'm Never Sure I'm Touching My Lover the Way He Wants to Be Touched. What Are Some Good Touches for a Man?

Every man is different, so you'll have to ask each one how he likes it.

You will find they usually reply, "Oh, I like everything." This may give you confidence, but it still doesn't answer your question. Press for specifics—you can have a lot of fun "pressing" in the right places to see what touches feel best!

You can also ask the same question with your women friends. They can give you specifics, too: "Men like to have their balls gently kissed," "Men like their nipples to be licked with a tongue." "My lover likes me to bite his ear gently and pull his hair." "Robert loves me to get on top of him and wiggle all over him." Every pair of lovers has special things they like. You can pick up some creative and fun ideas by having a cozy chat with other women over a cup of tea.

How Come Sex Is the Only Good Part of Our Relationship? The Rest of the Time We Fight Like Crazy.

It is possible for people to have sexual chemistry for each other and nothing else in common. It is also possible to be sexually turned on to someone, feel threatened by that sort of passion, and do battle to keep yourself from going under, from losing your power, to such passions. Arguing prevents intimacy, for sure. And, finally, it is also possible to be turned on to someone solely because you are afraid to live without them. In such a case, because you are still basically dissatisfied, when you aren't fucking, you're fighting.

For whatever reason, relationships in which sex is the only good part fade after a while. The end can come after one week or seven years: some people have a higher threshold of pain than others. The only thing to do in such a situation is to tell yourself you'll stay with it for as long as you're getting more good out of it than bad. Don't get scared and think that this is the only choice you have. There are many other people—a big glorious world out there.

Passion and fighting are not the same thing. An occasional argument helps clear the air and ensure trust. But constant fighting is wear and tear on emotions that could be used for equally strong loving.

I Really Love My Partner, but Whenever We Have Sex, I Get Bored. How Can I Feel More Excited?

Once again, by asking for and doing what satisfies your fantasies.

Usually women who ask this question consider themselves sexually unimaginative. They worry the reason they are not excited is because they are basically unsexy. Not true. They have just not found out what is sexually exciting to them yet.

Begin by thinking of all the things that excite you in life. Make a list of them: dancing, singing, running, eating, dreamy afternoons, a wrestling match—whatever. After you've made your list, look over it and imagine how you can work sex in with what excites you. Dancing, for example. Maybe you would like to plan a day ahead to go dancing some evening to get turned on. Then you could dash home, or out to your van, to be sexy. That's what one woman decided suited her. Another wanted a picnic in the sun in a remote spot where she felt safe enough to make love after lunch.

The point is: don't isolate sex from whatever else makes you happy in your life. Sex should be a natural part. Much of the male stereotyping of sex proceeds from separating it from all the other good and natural things that flow between people. Men tend to see sex as an end in itself, and thus have a hard time understanding that for women it is an organic outcome of so many other feelings and events. You might have to teach your lover this; but rest assured he'll like it much better than the old way.

Every Time I'm the Aggressive One, My Partner Finds a Way to Delay or Avoid Sex. If We Do Have Sex, He Will Then Criticize My Style in the Middle of Love-making. What's Going On?

Sounds like power plays. Some very *macho* men don't like to give up even one ounce of power, especially not sexually. If a man is *macho* he has a lot riding on his reputation for being sexually active and in charge. When you come along with what you want and asking to be in the lead for a change, he can't help but feel threatened. When he feels threatened he will try and turn the tables so he can be in the lead again. That's why he delays, avoids, and criticizes.

If you think this is happening, you must talk with your lover before you can ever hope to enjoy sex with him. But don't talk to him about this in the hay. Chose a time and place when he will be the least defensive. Maybe over the phone, or in a crowded restaurant. Tell him what you're worried about, but don't sound accusing.

If he admits to feeling threatened in any way, you have a fairly good chance of resolving the situation. If he defends himself and pleads innocent, then you know what you're up against. All I can say is, "Good luck! it's not going to be easy!"

How Can I Become More Aggressive and Less Passive in Sex?

First of all, let's examine that "passive." I ask women not to use such a word to describe themselves unless they mean they do not want to be active with a partner in sex and have no desire whatsoever to be initiating. I do this because most woman are not passive at all. What they really are is uneducated and shy. They just don't know what to do.

There are two basic things you can do to become more initiating in sex. First, you can find out what your lover likes, so you have an idea of where and how to begin. One excellent way to do this is to interview them over a good dinner. If you are sexually interested in someone, this makes for great dinner-table conversation!

The second thing to do is to ask your lover to tell you what he likes and what he doesn't like. If you are assured that he will give you honest answers you won't have that strange feeling of tickling a frozen body or diddling with a strange object ever again. Couples have worked out various means to communicate their sensations: One woman said she and her husband rated each other on a scale of 1 to 5. They did this by holding up one finger when something felt "not-so-great" and five fingers when it was "mind-blowing." Other couples make certain noises. Some like to speak: "That's great" or "I'd like it better over here." But make sure you get response. Otherwise, you'll never feel confident being aggressive.

I Found Myself Using Sex in Order to Get Nurturing From Men. I Don't Like That Sort of Barter. What Can I Do to Stop It?

One woman solved this problem by resolving not to have sex with men she went out with until they had dated at least five times. That gave her enough time to determine whether they were nurturing men in ways other than sex.

Unfortunately, some men are able to express gentleness and tenderness only through sex. (Women, luckily, are not so restricted.) This is the reason why many women who are desperate for sweetness from men will sometimes have sex they don't really want merely in order to receive that nurturing as well. This is not fair to women—and certainly not fair to men, either. Once again, we adapt to sex; and men don't learn any other ways to express tenderness and care.

How can you tell if a man is tender and caring physically besides what he can do sexually? Notice how he touches you. Is it always sexual—or is it friendly, too? Does he like to make out, do a lot of sweet kissing? Is he into cuddling, touching for warmth and closeness, and not exclusively for sex? Can he give you a massage just for the pleasure of it, and not merely as a prelude to intercourse? Does he say sweet things to you—or are all his references sexual? Does he have any women friends? Are all his women companions exclusively sexual ones?

Don't compromise your sexual feelings for male nurturing. Tell a man how you like it and find out if he enjoys that, too. If you barter for what you don't really want, you're the one who'll end up unhappy and not-O.K. in the end. Take good care of yourself. You deserve the best!

I Have More Sexual Drive Than My Lover. What Do I Do?

Women who have this problem have solved it in one of three ways:

Compromising.

Finding another lover (becoming non-monogamous).

Ending the relationship because of fundamental differences.

More than once a woman has come to group believing she was not sexually O.K., and it turned out what was actually going on was that she had been closing herself off sexually in order to match her lover's low level of sexual interest. No wonder she felt unhappy. Cutting off good healthy energy is like stifling a belly laugh, or walking when you want to run, or starving yourself when you're at a banquet.

I particularly remember a woman named Rose. When she first walked into group her hair was pulled back into a knotted bun, she wore unflattering glasses, her heavy woolen skirt dragged the ground (it was 80 degrees outside!), and as she sat down she placed both feet together ever so primly. Rose told us her problem was she couldn't have orgasms and her lover wanted her to figure out why.

Within three weeks, with the help of the loving women in group, Rose was giving herself satisfactory orgasms. She admitted she was enjoying her sexuality for the first time in her entire life. Her silky black hair now fell softly down around her shoulders, her skirts were still long but quite sheer, and she had bought new glasses that accentuated the deep blue of her eyes. Despite all this, and much to Rose's surprise, her lover refused to share in her excitement. He found another woman, one not so aggressive and confident. Rose was only momentarily depressed. She had already met another man who appreciated her confident sexuality.

All the same, this is a difficult situation to handle if you still want to keep a lover who is lacking in sexual drive. Each couple must decide what satisfies them. Take it step by step . . . and talk about it as you proceed.

Keep in mind that sexual energy is basic life energy. How a person expresses himself sexually also says a lot about who he is.

I Want My Partner to Be More Playful, More Touching, Less Intercourse-Oriented. How Can I Change Him?

Make a deal with him to refrain from intercourse for a month—or however long you think it will take for you to be interested again. Ask him to spend that month doing what you like sexually. Show him the kind of play you prefer, the touching you enjoy. Teach him what sex means to you. As for intercourse, have it only if you truly feel like it. Don't do it to appease or reward him for being so nice to go along with your requests. Remember: this is your month!

By the end of the month you will both have a pretty good idea of what you like sexually. Are you compatible? Has he learned to enjoy a lot of what you like?

Some men are happy to change, pleased to discover there is more to sex than intercourse. Others aren't. See which kind of guy you're with, and make relationship decisions accordingly.

He's Impotent Lately. When We First Got Together, There Was No Problem. What's Happened?

Here's a typical example to illustrate what could be the problem:

Dan and Cecilia had been together for six months. They were very much in love and planned to stay together. Dan was an artist and spent much time working alone. Cecilia was a therapist, quite the extrovert, an active feminist, and a member of a woman's group. She had a child from her former marriage. Dan had accepted this child as a daughter, and the five-year-old called him "Dad." Dan had also been married once before, but his wife had left him for another man.

When Dan and Cecilia first moved in together they had no sexual problems. It was only after four months that Dan began having difficulty getting an erection and Cecilia had trouble not feeling hurt about it. So they came to talk with my co-leader and me.

It turned out to be a matter of power. Dan believed with all his heart in Cecilia's feminism, and wanted her to be a strong woman. He did not feel threatened by her power. On the contrary, he enjoyed it. But he also felt guilty about being a strong man; and because he didn't want to dominate Cecilia, he went too far the other direction and gave in to her. Because Cecilia was a therapist, she had the skills to convince Dan she was right, even when he felt in his guts that she was power-playing him. The most obvious example of this concerned Cecilia's daughter. "She's a little brat sometimes," Dan said, "but Cecilia won't let me discipline her. She says anger is too frightening an emotion and she doesn't want me to express it. Well, I'm furious!"

Cecilia explained that anger scared her. Yes, she knew that the child was a brat and needed discipline; but she was too scared to let it be done. Consequently, she let the child literally run their lives, interfering with meals, work, and even the times they wanted to be sexy together.

Dan was not sure his wanting power to solve the situation was justified. We told him it was. If he was "Dad," he also had to be given the power to be that person—and that included disciplining as well as nurturing.

Cecilia was scared, but realized the necessity of this. She saw that Dan was not in an equal position with her unless he had the same rights in the household as she. Together they worked out a way for Dan to discipline the child. Dan's fury dissipated, and Cecilia was able to see how she had power-played out of fear.

Dan went on to say he feared Cecilia's leaving him. His former wife had done that to him, and now he lived constantly with the worry that Cecilia might also. He agreed to believe Cecilia's assurances that she wouldn't, and to work out his rage at his former wife with someone other than Cecilia. He would no longer hold Cecilia responsible for his unhappy past.

Thanks to this exchange of confidence, Cecilia and Dan were able to end a painful two-hour discussion with a big hug, many words of love, and a clean slate. In the course of talking they had compared what they enjoyed sexually and found themselves absolutely compatible. Dan's impotency stemmed from not having power in his relationship and from being afraid of being deserted. By sharing his feelings and getting reassurances, his sexual problems were resolved.

The point is: unless a man has a physical problem (which is rare), impotency is a result of emotional dissatisfaction. An impotent man is the equivalent of a woman who isn't turned on. Just as such a woman needs to say what's on her mind in order to free her sexual feelings, the impotent man needs to express his feelings to get his erection back.

What Do We Do With the Children When We're Making Love?

Mothers often feel guilty about any time they spend on themselves that doesn't also include their children. Having time for sex is very important to a woman's well-being, and she can reasonably expect her children to be cooperative.

Many woman tell their children that they want time alone for an hour or so, that Mommy and Daddy will be "playing together" just like they themselves play with their friends. They explain that they are having fun, so that the children understand that love-making noises are good ones. They also tell them they can come into the room when they have finished playing. That way children know that all the funny sounds resulted in two nice, happy people and the time away wasn't an excuse to shut them out.

Some couples make dates to spend a full day and night together for sexy fun. They arrange for a baby-sitter to take the child to his or her home. Or, they ask the baby-sitter to stay at the house while they themselves go to a motel, or to some other place that suits their fantasies.

Women in group report children aren't happy at first about being left out. Babies cry, older children try to interrupt. But if mother is kind and firm about wanting her space, the children learn to take care of themselves and soon are playing happily alone or with a friend. Mothers are pleased to learn how resourceful their children are; and children learn that love-making is a perfectly natural part of life.

There are many books which illustrate sex for children. You can choose the one you think is best. What is basically important is for children to understand that sex is gentle and fun and loving, even if they go "Ugh!" at the physical description of it.

He's Nice, But He Doesn't Turn Me On Sexually. How Can I Tell Him?

Just tell him that: "I like you but I'm not turned on to you sexually."

Don't feel that just because a man is sweet and kind you must feel sexually turned on to him. You may wish you were—because you can see what a good person he is. But if you're not, you're not.

255

Give yourself permission to have men friends, and not just men lovers. That's another good thing to tell a man: "I need men friends, not lovers."

If you want to keep from feeling constantly pressured about it, take care of that part right at the start. Many women complain that when they tell a man they think he's nice but they're not sexually into him, the man usually replies, "Well, I can always try to change your mind." After that, the woman feels the constant pressure of the unspoken question, "Have you changed your mind yet—huh?" Avoid this right at the beginning by saying, "If and when I ever feel sexually excited about you I will let you know." You must take the responsibility yourself for changing such things if they are going to change.

I'm Afraid to Ask my Partner for Cunnilingus Because I Think He Doesn't Like My Smell. What Do I Do?

Ask him if he likes cunnilingus. Then ask him if he would like to do it to you. And then ask him if he likes your genitals, including your odor.

A word of warning: Don't expect him to be excited by genitals that aren't clean. I'm not saying to use Lysol and a petunia douche. I'm merely saying: Wash your genitals like you do your armpits. Keep yourself naturally fresh and sweet.

Taste and smell yourself, too. You'll discover that your fragrance is lighter and sweeter than you had probably imagined, and the same goes for your flavor, too.

I'm Very Olfactory. Smells Turn Me Off or On. Is That Normal?

Sense of smell is one of the most primitive and basic of sexual turn-ons. It is reasonable to be turned on or off by someone's body odor, no matter how clean or how dirty they are. There is a famous letter Napoleon wrote to Josephine, telling her not to bathe because he would be home shortly. . . .

Body odor is part of the chemistry that exists between certain people. Women report in group that they have had very good lovers, but weren't turned on to them passionately because they weren't excited by their body smell. It is really a matter of personal choice.

For example, I can't stand so much as kissing someone who smokes cigarettes. I find the smell revolting, and it doesn't help even if the man brushes his teeth and washes his hair first. The smell still permeates everything and turns me off. Yet I know women who find the smell of nicotine sexually exciting.

On the other hand, it is as important for me that a lover be turned on to my smell as he is to my mind and my looks. It is a fundamental part of me that I don't want to mask with any cologne or herbal shampoo. As my friend Peggy put it, "A lover who can bury his nose in my armpit at the end of a hot day is a real hot lover!"

He Comes Too Quickly? What Do I Do?

Sit down with him, tell him what you're experiencing, ask him why it happens, and talk about what you can both do to improve the situation.

Keep in mind that premature ejaculation—as it's called in the sex therapy biz—reflects an emotional rather than physical problem. The problem can be as simple as his ignorance of the fact he's coming too soon for you. After all, he's comfortable with his pace—no woman has ever told him otherwise—and so he's just doing what he enjoys. If you ask him to slow down, he will have a bit of a problem changing his style at first, but after a couple of times with your nurturing cooperation, he'll be able to last longer.

The problem may be that he's entirely focused on his penis for sexual pleasure. He can avoid this by learning to notice touches on other parts of his body—his thighs, nipples, neck, and lips, for instance.

The problem may be that he really doesn't want to have sex and is just going through a performance because he doesn't know how to say no, or how to say what it is he really wants.

The problem could be he's angry at you for some reason and doesn't know how to talk about it.

The problem could be he's just been conditioned to come

too quickly by years of masturbating alone in the bathroom and having sex with women who didn't ask him to slow down.

As for the Master and Johnson "Squeeze Technique" which is supposed to be the cure-all for premature ejaculators: perhaps the most valuable thing is that it makes people talk to each other about the problem. It's not the squeezing that works, it's the opportunity to communicate that solves the problem. So, sure, use it if you'd like to try it. It seems to be helpful, too, in convincing a man that he can control his penis if he wants, rather than his penis controlling him. But if you use it, don't do so in silence. Talk, talk, talk—and have fun! Use your sense of humor when you're discussing sexual problems. Otherwise, everything gets so serious that the pressure to do it right only makes you even more nervous than before. A good dose of inspired playfulness solves sexual problems far more successfully than does reliance on any so-called scientific "method."

I Don't Like Intercourse At All. What Do I Tell My Partner?

Tell him you don't like it. Tell him what you *do* like.

And then work out a compromise that does not involve intercourse for at least a month.

If he says anything like, "It's too bad you're so frigid!" or "Gee, it's terrible how sexually uptight you are!" you might want to consider changing partners. Someone who believes that women who don't like intercourse have a sexual problem is going to have a hard time enjoying and accepting what it is they do like.

You may find after a month without intercourse that your feelings about it are much clearer. Maybe you just plain don't like it. Maybe you don't like your partner, or his particular style. Maybe you only like it under certain conditions.

In any case, if you don't like intercourse, that's perfectly normal. You can be sexually healthy and happy without it—so don't pressure yourself into enjoying what you think you *ought* to enjoy. Instead, put your energy into doing what it is you *do* enjoy sexually.

It Takes My Partner Too Long to Come. All That Thrusting Begins to Hurt. What Can I Do?

When it gets uncomfortable, ask him to stop and withdraw.

Then talk about what's happening. Ask him if he enjoys that kind of intercourse. If he does, then you may not be compatible lovers.

Some men have only one way they can come: thrusting intercourse. Some women enjoy this, but others complain they feel like they're at the mercy of a pile-driver. If you don't enjoy it, find out if he has an alternative method. Can he withdraw and masturbate? Can he come more quickly? Can you do anything to help?

One woman said her partner agreed to withdraw and not have his orgasm. This was perfectly O.K. with him, he said, but she didn't like it. It felt bad to her that he didn't come after he had given her such a good orgasm. "It doesn't feel fair," she complained. He was unable to change, she refused to accept his solution, and eventually they quit being lovers.

As with any other sexual problem, it's important to talk about the "why's." Why does it take him so long to come? Is that the only way he enjoys it? Or has he learned to take a long time because he thought that that's what women wanted—and so now he's over-controlled at the expense of his own pleasure? Does he perhaps not want to be fucking, actually, because he's tired or turned-off or distracted?

I Should Come. Look At All the Time and Effort He Put Into Me.

Talk about feeling pressured! As soon as you feel this way, you can be pretty sure you're not going to come—and you may even feel tempted to fake an orgasm or two just to satisfy him. Don't do it. Remember that there's more to sex than orgasms. Relax.

You deserve hours and hours of time. Even days. You deserve as much as you want, so long as you are doing your fifty percent by asking for what you want. You are teaching yourself a new skill: having orgasms with a partner. It takes time and patience to learn something new, so be gentle with yourself and expect the same of your lover.

It may take you several long lazy sessions with your lover before you have orgasms with him. That's quite normal. Expect it, even.

If you're worried that he's getting bored, or resenting the touches he's giving you, ask him about it. Make an agreement with him that he tell you honestly when he is bored or tired. Then you don't need to worry about it. You can relax, knowing he will take care of himself. Men need to learn to say "yes" and "no" as much as women. Your orgasms are not his responsibility. When you want to have them, you will. Tell him to relax and not work so hard. You know how to take care of yourself.

With the both of you, the key word is:
ENJOY!

The Future of Sex

CHAPTER 15. For centuries, in western culture, what is enjoyable and good regarding sex has been based entirely on male standards. Hence, the great focus on penises and intercourse. Rarely has the double standard been questioned . . . until now.

As women unite (the current women's movement is ten years old) they are discovering that sex for them turns out to be quite different from what they were conned by society over the past hundreds of years into believing. Comparing notes and discussing honestly, without any false modesty or shame, what they themselves have experienced, they are concluding that woman-sex and man-sex are two different things.

Looking towards the future, then, I see the emergence of a sexuality based on an androgynous blend of the best of both sexes. Of course, for all those men out there who consider penis-pumping intercourse the summit of sexual expression, this new sexuality will probably seem like "the broads are taking over." The rules and standards are changing already, as what we women want in sex becomes as important as what men have wanted. For a time, on the path to this androgynous future, civilization will enjoy a woman-oriented phase of sexuality. It is to be hoped that this phase will serve as a teaching era to educate both men and women to the subtleties of women's sexual world.

Woman-sex will be sensually focused. In general, women do not like the "slam-bam-thank-you-ma'am" style of male love-making. Women want sex and orgasms to be the culmination of sensual seduction, not its entirety. They want to be touched and teased and tickled. Women want the men they have sex with to care about them. Not care about them as in "Marry them" (don't panic, guys!) . . . but care about them as women, as fellow human beings who deserve honesty and respect.

Out of this desire for respect and care, women are becoming more selective about whom they share their sexuality with. They are opting for quality, not quantity. Being able to give ourselves orgasms has freed us from depending upon men for sexual strokes and loving. We can do it ourselves—so we know what's good and what isn't. In the future we women will not tolerate the sexist treatment we accepted out of ignorance or desperation all these past centuries. Nor will we continue to make excuses for men, rationalizing their inadequacies out of fear of having to do without them, or because, until now, we've considered the situation as hopeless. Women want men who are *whole* people. Such men must be capable not only of thinking out complex logical problems but also of feeling and expressing complex emotions.

Sex once meant giving one's heart to a male as well as one's body, culminating in a desire to live together—in short, to being owned by the male. With our release from having to marry for security, or having a man around to give us social status, we will be free to choose our lovers more capriciously. Many men are going to be quite shocked to discover that the woman who seduced them the night before and asked for their telephone number the next morning is not interested in staking a claim. She's simply out to have fun—and looking for still another good lover to have it with.

If a woman wants more than a brief romantic episode, her

increasing ability to talk honestly and her confidence in asking for exactly what she wants will enable her to say what she's thinking without subterfuge. No longer will women resort to being coy and manipulative. Their straight-arrow talk will be stunning in its forthrightness. And men, in turn, will be forced into being equally honest—or they will find themselves left out in the cold.

As for sex itself, it also will change in style. For one thing, there'll be less emphasis put on intercourse. As study after study has proved, the majority of women do not experience orgasms through intercourse. Intercourse is for men. Men who are now blaming the women's movement for making them impotent should be glad to hear this. So what if they can't get it up? They can use their tongues . . . or their hands! Intercourse will become merely one aspect of love-making: it will no longer be the be-all and end-all.

With less emphasis on intercourse will come more concentration on kissing and cuddling, and more time taken for orgasms. "Making out" and "petting"—those staples of the Fifties—will stage a comeback. Sex will be more friendly, no longer alienated, as women choose lovers whom they feel equal with rather than just for protection.

Romance will return also. But not as old-style courtship with all its taboos and cultural voodoo. Romance this time will be happy, spontaneous, fun-filled—a poetic expression of friendship between two people who admire each other's strengths and view one another as equally powerful. Romance will celebrate the androgyne in us all . . . the man in woman and the woman in man. She'll give him flowers to stir his heart, and he'll give her a buck-knife to celebrate her strength.

As women become more independent they will also feel less pressure over sex. Many women rage now in remembering how they once agreed to have sex with a man solely because they feared being labeled "frigid." As we discover that we are sexually O.K. and emotionally "just fine," we won't feel we have to prove ourselves by using sex. If we're criticized by power-playing men for our supposed sexual deficiencies ("You're boring in bed." "You don't come enough.") we'll have the courage to know in our guts that we're fine, and no longer be cowed by such empty male bullying.

With women wanting to enjoy sex only with those they consider to be friends, it will logically follow that more among us will opt for bisexuality. Sex between two women is often easier, slower, sweeter. Women know what they enjoy; thus there's less talking out to be done, fewer communication gaps, and a more natural understanding between both partners over what is physically enjoyable. As women feel closer to each other spiritually, many will rightly decide there is no reason not to get closer sexually as well.

Ageism will disappear. Joyful women in their sixties and seventies and eighties will put the lie to that cultural epitaph presently placed on every woman's fortieth birthday-cake: "Sexually Out to Pasture." As women take better care of themselves not only physically but psychically, their sexuality will not fade with the passing of the years; forming an intrinsic part of their being, it should continue to flourish, remaining "alive and well" until they are a hundred years old! In the future, the only standards governing active sexuality will be health and chemistry and energy. Young men will love older women, and young women older women. Older women will love old men, young women, and other older women. Each woman, no matter her social condition or age, can look forward to a lifetime of loving. (As for the men, I haven't any idea what will be happening between them in the future. They haven't made enough moves yet for such predictions.)

Concerning children, women will have more options there also. They will expect men to take equal responsiblity for birth control. They will also have babies only when they want; and thus won't be undergoing debilitating abortions. With the economic freedom many of us are winning, we will be able to raise a child without having to depend upon a man for economic support. Therefore, fathers—as well as children—

will be a matter of choice. A group of women may decide to raise all their children together, and leave men out of the picture entirely, except as loving uncles.

With the emergence of androgyny, men will feel no qualms about participating in all the joys of raising babies right from the cradle. They will feel free to openly embrace both sons and daughters without any stigma of effeminacy or sentimentality put upon their affections. Relieved of being sole breadwinner and "Big Daddy," a man will no longer have only a few minutes each night after work to be with his family. Gone, too, will be those dreary weekends when "Pop" is too exhausted from earning money all during the week to make only the feeblest of gestures towards getting reacquainted with the rest of his family. Equal relationships between women and men will enable both sexes to enjoy children—and not necessarily within the confines of the standard nuclear family.

As women gain more political power, more day-care centers will be financed. Women and men both will be taking their children to work with them. Women, receiving the support of various women's groups, will by this time be experienced enough to consider raising their children in an extended family situation, one where friends exchange children and where children learn to take care of themselves.

There's no turning back. As we women feel our power— "this ol' world is gonna change!" No doubt about that. Some of these changes will be frightening, admittedly, at first. And there will be, for women and men both, great periods of loneliness and confusion. After all, our emotions will be used and stretched to their limits. But, once these changes are made, men and women, *as equals,* will discover a world of loving they never thought possible. The potential for richness and goodness in life is limitless when we feel safe and secure, and strong enough to love as we want to love. Our sexuality is one of the best ways we can express our love of life and of others: We can love ourselves; and we can share that love with those we care for.

When you feel a little unsure of yourself, remember these three things:

1) Give yourself permission to feel your sexuality.
2) Take time to decide what you want sexually.
3) Ask for it, ask for it—and ask for it!

Keep in mind that our sexuality ebbs and flows throughout our lives with the same predictability as the ocean. A new current, a strong wave, a wind from far away will sweep us to new, and sometimes confusing, unfamiliar places. Our sexuality is always with us, but it doesn't necessarily look or act as we imagine it should or would like it to do. Let your sexuality accompany you, like a good friend, through your life. Treat it with gentle concern and respect; and, when you've got questions, ask a woman friend for help. Your sexuality is an integral part of your womanhood. Enjoy!

In the future—which means: beginning right now!—let us celebrate and love our own sexuality. Love it as a way to care for ourselves, to keep ourselves healthy, to celebrate our strength, to enjoy our energy. Let us treat it as a precious part of us, and expect all our lovers to do the same. We are beautiful, and full of powers we've hardly yet explored. May our sexuality be used to remind us of all the goodness we are—and can be.

suggested further readings

Barbach, Lonnie Garfield. *For Yourself: The Fulfillment of Female Sexuality*. New York: Doubleday and Co., Inc., 1975.

Blank, Joani. *My Playbook for Women About Sex*. Down There Press, P.O. Box 2086, Burlingame, California, 94010. 1975.

Boston Women's Health Collective. *Our Bodies Ourselves: A Book by and for Women*. New York: Simon and Schuster, 1973.

Chesler, Phyllis. *Women and Madness*. New York: Doubleday and Co., Inc., 1972.

Dodson, Betty. *Liberating Masturbation: A Meditation on Self-Love*. Bodysex Designs, 121 Madison Avenue, New York, New York, 10016. 1974.

Friday, Nancy. *My Secret Garden and Forbidden Flowers: Women's Sexual Fantasies*. New York: Pocket Books, 1974.

Hite, Shere. *The Hite Report*. New York: The Macmillan Company, 1976.

Marcuse, Herbert. *The One Dimensional Man*. Boston: Beacon Press, 1964.

Steiner, Claude M. *Scripts People Live: Transactional Analysis of Life Scripts*. New York: Grove Press, 1974.

Wyckoff, Hogie. *Solving Women's Problems Through Awareness, Action and Contact*. New York: Grove Press, 1977.

Selected Grove Press Paperbacks

E237   ALLEN, DONALD M. (Ed.) / The New American Poetry: 1945-1960 / $3.95

B181   ANONYMOUS / A Man With A Maid / $1.95

B334   ANONYMOUS / My Secret Life / $2.45

B155   ANONYMOUS / The Pearl / $1.95

B383   ARSAN, EMMANUELLE / Emmanuelle II / $1.95

E425   BARAKA, IMAMU AMIRI (LeRoi Jones) / The Baptism and The Toilet / $2.45

E96   BECKETT, SAMUEL / Endgame / $1.95

B78   BECKETT, SAMUEL / Three Novels (Molloy, Malone Dies, The Unnamable) / $1.95

E33   BECKETT, SAMUEL / Waiting For Godot / $1.95

B79   BEHAN, BRENDAN / The Quare Fellow and The Hostage: Two Plays / $2.45

B186   BERNE, ERIC / Games People Play / $1.95

B386   BERNE, ERIC / Transactional Analysis in Psychotherapy / $1.95

E417   BIRCH, CYRIL WITH KEENE, DONALD (Eds.) / Anthology of Chinese Literature, Volume 1: From Early Times to the Fourteenth Century / $4.95

E584   BIRCH, CYRIL (Ed.) / Anthology of Chinese Literature, Volume 2: From the 14th Century to the Present Day / $4.95

E368   BORGES, JORGE LUIS / Ficciones / $2.95

B283   BRAUTIGAN, RICHARD / A Confederate General From Big Sur / $1.50 (also available as E478 / $1.95)

B120   BRECHT, BERTOLT / Galileo / $1.95

B108   BRECHT, BERTOLT / Mother Courage and Her Children / $1.50

B333   BRECHT, BERTOLT / The Threepenny Opera / $1.75

B115   BURROUGHS, WILLIAM S. / Naked Lunch / $1.95

GT422   CLURMAN, HAROLD (Ed.) / Seven Plays of the Modern Theater / $4.95 (Waiting For Godot by Samuel Beckett, The Quare Fellow by Brendan Behan, A Taste of Honey by Shelagh Delaney, The Connection by Jack Gelber, The Balcony by Jean Genet, Rhinoceros by Eugene Ionesco and The Birthday Party by Harold Pinter)

E190   CUMMINGS, E. E. / Selected Poems / $1.95

E344   DURRENRICH, FRIEDRICH / The Visit / $2.95

B342   FANON, FRANTZ / The Wretched of the Earth / $1.95

E130   GENET, JEAN / The Balcony / $2.95

E208	GENET, JEAN / The Blacks: A Clown Show / $2.95
B382	GENET, JEAN / Querelle / $1.95
B306	HERNTON, CALVIN C. / Sex and Racism in America / $1.95
E101	IONESCO, EUGENE / Four Plays (The Bald Soprano, The Lesson, The Chairs, and Jack, or The Submission) / $1.95
E259	IONESCO, EUGENE / Rhinoceros and Other Plays / $1.95
E216	KEENE, DONALD (Ed.) / Anthology of Japanese Literature: From the Earliest Era to the Mid-Nineteenth Century / $4.95
E573	KEENE, DONALD (Ed.) / Modern Japanese Literature / $4.95
B300	KEROUAC, JACK / The Subterraneans / $1.50
B9	LAWRENCE, D. H. / Lady Chatterley's Lover / $1.95
B373	LUCAS, GEORGE / American Graffiti / $1.50
B146	MALCOLM X / The Autobiography of Malcolm X / $1.95
B326	MILLER, HENRY / Nexus / $1.95
B100	MILLER, HENRY / Plexus / $2.95
B325	MILLER, HENRY / Sexus / $2.95
B10	MILLER, HENRY / Tropic of Cancer / $1.95
B59	MILLER, HENRY / Tropic of Capricorn / $1.95
E636	NERUDA, PABLO / Five Decades: Poems 1925-1970 / $5.95
E359	PAZ, OCTAVIO / The Labyrinth of Solitude: Life and Thought in Mexico / $3.95
E315	PINTER, HAROLD / The Birthday Party and The Room / $1.95
E411	PINTER, HAROLD / The Homecoming / $1.95
B202	REAGE, PAULINE / The Story of O / $1.95
B323	SCHUTZ, WILLIAM C. / Joy / $1.95
B313	SELBY, HUBERT JR. / Last Exit to Brooklyn / $1.95
E618	SNOW, EDGAR / Red Star Over China / $3.95
B319	STOPPARD, TOM / Rosencrantz and Guildenstern Are Dead / $1.95
E219	WATTS, ALAN W. / The Spirit of Zen: A Way of Life, Work, and Art in the Far East / $2.45

GROVE PRESS, INC., 196 West Houston St., New York, N.Y. 10014